Baedeker

Amsterdam

Hints for using the Guide

Following the tradition established by Karl Baedeker in 1844, buildings and works of art, places of natural beauty and sights of particular interest are distinguished by one ★ or two ★★ stars.

To make it easier to locate the various places listed in the "A to Z" section of the Guide, their co-ordinates are shown in red at the head of each entry: e.g., ★Anne Frank Huis H 5.

Coloured lines down the right-hand side of the page are an aid to finding the main heading in the Guide: blue stands for the Introduction (Nature, Culture, History, etc.), red for the "A to Z" section, and yellow indicates Practical Information.

Only a selection of hotels and restaurants can be given; no reflection is implied therefore on establishments not included.

In a time of rapid change it is difficult to ensure that all the information given is entirely accurate and up-to-date, and the possibility of error can never be entirely eliminated.

Although the publishers can accept no responsibility for inaccuracies and omissions, they are constantly endeavouring to improve the quality of their Guides and are therefore always grateful for criticisms, corrections and suggestions for improvement.

Preface

This guide to Amsterdam is one of the new generation of
Baedeker guides.

These guides, illustrated throughout in colour, are designed
to meet the needs of the modern traveller. They are quick and
easy to consult, with the principal places of interest described
in alphabetical order, and the information is presented in a
format that is both attractive and easy to follow.

The guide is in three main parts. The first part gives a general
account of Amsterdam, its land reclamation, people, religion,
communications, economy, diamonds, culture, famous people, history, architecture and quotations. The second part, in
which the principal sights are described; and the third part

*The Singel,
originally a moat
around the city,
is now a delightful
area to walk
beside*

contains a variety of practical information designed to help
visitors to find their way about the city and make the most of
their stay. Both the sights and the practical information are
listed in alphabetical order.

The new Baedeker guides are noted for their concentration on
essentials and their convenience of use. They contain numerous specially drawn plans and colour illustrations; and at the
end of the book is a large map making it easy to locate the
various places described in the "A to Z" section of the guide
with the help of the co-ordinates given at the head of each
entry.

Contents

Baedeker Specials

Canals and

The "Venice of the North" is how the Italian Ludovico Guicciardini once described the city of Amsterdam. That was in 1567. Even today this comparison is still commonly heard when people talk about Amsterdam. It is foremost a city on the water – with more canals than Venice and more bridges than Paris. But Amsterdam is much more than that. A city which gives the visitor a real feeling of history. A city where art and culture have pride of place. An exotic city. A city of contrasts, a tolerant city.

The canals reflect in the water the magnificently decorated façades of the old patrician houses and the elms and lime trees along their banks. Here visitors can absorb their first and unforgettable impressions of Amsterdam – without any of the noise

Cyclists:
there are more than half a million in this city of canals

and bustle – while enjoying a quiet drink or cup of coffee on one of the many café terraces against a backcloth of typical canal houses, or by taking a quiet stroll through the world's largest district of houses built on piles (the best way to get to know the city is on foot), or by a boat trip along the historic network of canals, past imposing cultural centres and the hundreds of houseboats which are home to many of its citizens. At night, especially, when the canals, bridges and patrician houses are lit by thousands of lamps, trips of this kind will evoke memories of the past, and the visitor will instinctively feel transported back to the 17th century, the "Golden Age" of Amsterdam. The streets

Dam –
the very heart the city

Idyll
on the Keizersgracht

Houseboats:
living space for individualists

more . . .

away from the canals bustle with activity – at times can even be said to be chaotic. On the squares street musicians, jugglers and performers of mime – as well as drug-dealers, beggars and pick-pockets, unfortunately – mingle with the locals and tourists. In the shopping quarter, on the markets and in the little hidden shops known as "winkels" compulsive shoppers will be in their element; in the countless museums and galleries art lovers can walk in the footsteps of Rembrandt, Van Gogh and many others; and in over 850 cafés, pubs, discothèques, bars and restaurants, which offer specialities from all over the world, almost everyone can find something to their taste.

Wherever visitors may stop there is one thing that they will not fail to notice: the contrasts and problems of a modern albeit small metropolis on the one hand, and the motley variety of its inhabitants on the other. The Netherlands is a tolerant country, but Amsterdam, the "cosmopolitan village" as it is often affectionately called by the local people, is even more so. Here one will meet people of every colour, religion and culture. The Amsterdamers may appear somewhat independent and unconventional from time to time, but generally speaking they are friendly, good-natured and sociable and hospitable to strangers.

Tulips
from
Amsterdam

Don't just look at Amsterdam, really get to know the city – and enjoy yourself!

Gabled houses
about 7000 are classified as historic monuments

Facts and Figures

Arms of
Amsterdam

General Information

Amsterdam is the capital of the Kingdom of the Netherlands, but it is not the seat of government and only some of the time the residence of the Dutch Queen. Her permanent place of residence and the centre of government are to be found in The Hague.

Importance

From the cultural point of view Amsterdam is indisputably the focal point of activity in the Netherlands, with a large number of artistic treasures which on no account should be overlooked. Most fascinating of all are the architectural beauties to be found among the criss-cross of canals within the old heart of the city. They give Amsterdam its unique appeal and make the city such a special place to visit.

For the close on two million people who come here every year, Amsterdam ranks as a cosmopolitan city of world stature (and this despite only 713,493 inhabitants), though the reason for this lies not merely in the outstanding sights and monuments which it has to offer the visitor, but most of all because of the openness and tolerance which has always been shown here towards people of different beliefs and lifestyles.

Amsterdam is situated in the north-west of the Netherlands, in the province of North Holland, above the deltas of the Rhine (or Waal in Dutch) and the Meuse (Maas) at a latitude of approximately 52°50′N and a longitude of 4°53′E. The Amstel, which flows through the city from south to north, here joins the IJ, which is in effect an inlet, separated from the IJsselmeer by a series of floodgates.

In common with most of the Netherlands, Amsterdam lies for the most part below sea-level.

Geographical position

Since Amsterdam is situated in a temperate maritime climatic zone, the visitor is likely to experience relatively cool summer temperatures (average in July/August only 17°C/63°F) and mild winters. The rainfall is distributed almost evenly throughout the year (see climate table p. 173).

Climate

Amsterdam covers an area of 207 sq.km/80 sq.miles, of which 20 sq.km/8 sq.miles is water, and, with about 713,493 inhabitants, is one of the main centres of the "Randstad Holland" (see p. 11). Population numbers declined in the 70s and early 80s but in the last ten years this trend seems to have been reversed. As a conurbation Amsterdam, with its associated townships of Amstelveen, Diemen, Haarlemmermeer, Haarlemmerliede and Spaarnwoude, Landsmeer, Oostzaan, Ouder-Amstel, Uithoorn, Weesp and Zaandam, has a population of about one million.

Surface Area
and Population

◀ *Montelbaanstoren: once part of the city's fortifications*

9

General Information

The ancient nucleus of Amsterdam was Amstelredam, a 13th c. settlement built on dykes on both banks of the Amstel. A grand project for expansion was formulated in 1612, part of which was the famous "Three Canal Plan". This semicircular belt of three canals ("gracht" means canal) – the Herengracht, Keizersgracht and Prinsengracht – was constructed in the 17th c., with the Singelgracht as the outer ring. The concentrically laid-out canals are traversed by a number of radial canals and streets ending in squares, thus dividing the city into about 90 islands joined together by a thousand bridges and viaducts. The only exception to this arrangement is the Jordaan district in the north-west of the city.

Around 1800 there were approximately 21,000 people (today about 35,000) living within the encircling canals in an area of about 800ha (about 1975 acres). Between 1870 and 1900 the population doubled from about 255,000 to some 510,000 and the area of the city increased to 1700ha/4200 acres, spreading beyond the historic ring of canals and giving rise to the "Volksbuurten" or workers' districts of De Pijp, Kinkerbuurt and Dapperbuurt.

A general reconstruction plan (lasting until the year 2000) was embarked upon after the Second World War. In 1951 a start was made on building garden cities. The overall plan envisages the built-up zones taking shape like outspread fingers interspersed with greenbelt areas. The garden cities were, in the west (around Sloterplas, a 90ha/222 acres man-made lake), Slotermeer, Geuzenveld, Slotervaart, Osdorp and Overtoomse Veld; in the south Buitenveldert; in the north Nieuwendam, Noord, Buikslotermeer and Buiksloterbanne (today districts of Amsterdam).

Although these new residential districts considerably alleviated the catastrophic housing conditions in the overpopulated inner city, the housing shortage is still acute. There are currently 53,000 priority applications on the official housing waiting lists. A small section of

View of the city centre from the Oude Kerk

Houseboats offer much in the way of comfort

Amsterdam residents have made a virtue of necessity and taken to the water, where they live in some 2500 houseboats, moored along the canals. Most of these are provided with gas, electricity and telephones, many even being linked to cable.

Randstad Holland, where Amsterdamers have gone to live during the last few decades, is a conurbation comprising 94 towns and municipalities and embracing the provinces of North Holland, South Holland and Utrecht. In the north it covers the area between the North Sea Canal zone and the southern shore of the IJsselmeer, and in the south between the Brielschen Meer, Alter Maas and Merwede. East to west it covers some 70km/44 miles and north to south it extends for 60km/38 miles. Over 4 million people live within its 3800 sq.km/1467 sq.miles.

Randstad Holland can be regarded as having a northern branch (covering Amsterdam, Haarlem, Haarlemmermeer, Zandwoort, Wormermeer, Zaandam, Aalsmeer, Amstelveen, Weesp, Naarden, Busum, Laren, Hilversum, Amersfoort, Soest, Zeist, Maarssen, Vleuten–De–Meern and Utrecht) and a southern branch (including The Hague, Katwijk, Wassenaar, Leiderdorp, Leiden, Leidschendam, Voorschoten, Voorburg, Rijswijk, Delft, Rozenburg, Vlaardingen, Schiedam, Krimpen aan den IJssel, Ridderkerk, Papendrecht, Dordrecht and Gorinchem).

Because of the concentration in this part of the country of industry, ports, commerce, administration and culture, as well as intensive forms of agriculture, Randstad Holland constitutes the economic heart of the Netherlands.

The city, which is divided up into 30 districts (Wijken), is administered by a City Council consisting of 36 Councillors and nine Aldermen, chaired by the Burgomaster (or Lord Mayor). The Councillors, who elect the Aldermen from among their own number, are elected by the people for a term of four years. The Burgomaster is appointed by the

Randstad Holland

Administration

11

"Crown" (the Queen and the Council of Ministers) for a term of six years. The Stadhuis, or City Hall, is situated at Oudezijds Voorburgwal.

Land Reclamation

In earlier times large areas of water, often 5m/16ft or more deep, resisted man's attempts to dominate them. Then, in the 17th and 18th c., with the assistance of windmills, four large North Holland lakes, Schermer, Beemster, Wormer and Purmer, were successfully drained. It was not until the advent of steam power, however, that anyone dared to attempt the draining of the Haarlemmer Meer (183 sq.km/70 sq.miles) and the vast expanses of the IJ near Amsterdam.

Land Drainage

Land drainage ("droogmakerijen") is basically a simple procedure: a dyke is erected around an area of water, then a "ring canal" is laid (partly with movable "mussel weirs") which channels away the water as it is pumped out. The seabeds which are thus exposed are made up

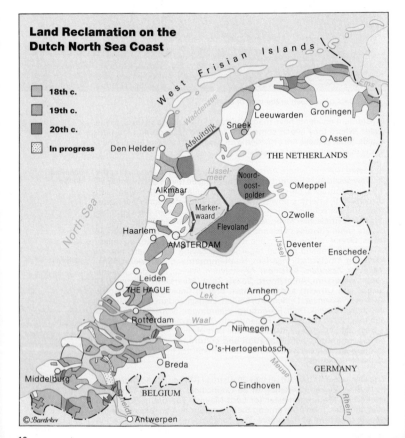

Land Reclamation on the Dutch North Sea Coast

18th c.
19th c.
20th c.
In progress

West Frisian Islands
Waddenzee
Leeuwarden   Groningen
Sneek
Den Helder   Assen
THE NETHERLANDS
IJssel-meer
Noord-oost-polder   Meppel
Alkmaar
Marker-waard   Zwolle
Flevoland
Haarlem
AMSTERDAM   Deventer
Enschede
North Sea
Leiden
THE HAGUE   Utrecht   Arnhem
Lek
Rotterdam   Waal
Nijmegen
's-Hertogenbosch
Breda   GERMANY
Middelburg   Eindhoven
BELGIUM
© Baedeker   Antwerpen

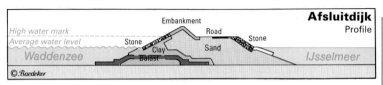

of extremely fertile clay deposits and in consequence the drained lakes are highly prized as agricultural land, equalled only by the most recent of the Frisian polders. Reclaimed marshland, on the other hand, can only be used for grazing.

The greatest land reclamation project, made possible only by 20th c. technology, has been the poldering of the Zuiderzee, the vast inland sea formed by incursions of the North Sea during the Middle Ages. The narrow channel between North Holland and the island of Wieringen was closed off in 1924, and 1932 saw the completion of the "Afsluit-dijk", the great dam which runs for 30km/19 miles between Wieringen and Friesland. Technically speaking, this was a gigantic undertaking because of the twice daily impact of the tides causing the waters of the Zuiderzee to exert a progressively greater force within the narrowing confines of the dam advancing from both the north-east and the south-west. With the completion of the Afsluitdijk, literally the "closing-off dyke", the Zuiderzee no longer remained a sea, and all that is left is the freshwater IJseelmeer. It is now relatively easy to create individual polders where the sea used to be, although this entails a massive programme of all kinds of investment. Initially the section between North Holland and the island of Wieringen (20,000ha/49,420 acres) was drained. The year 1942 saw the completion of the Noordostpolder, the north-east polder (47,600ha/117,600 acres), adjoining the provinces of Friesland and Overijssel, and the first polder to be created in the Zuiderzee itself. The western part of the island fishing village of Urk was incorporated into the dyke. On the southern shore two polders have meanwhile been created. East Flevoland (54,000ha/133,400 acres) and South Flevoland (44,000ha/108,700 acres). A strip of open water has been left between the polders and the shore so that old coastal towns such as Elburg and Harderwijk still have access to the sea and the water table on the mainland can be maintained at an acceptable level. The last of the polders was to have been Markerwaard (40,000ha/99,000 acres) off the coast of North Holland and due for completion in 1980, but because of opposition by environmental groups the government has withdrawn the plan for re-examination. This will leave the IJsselmeer with a surface area of 110,000ha/271,800 acres.

Zuiderzee Polders

Draining the Zuiderzee is, to date, the world's largest coastal land reclamation project. The Deltaplan, approved in 1957, was another such project and brought a merger of the islands of South Holland and Zeeland by closing off the open waters of the estuaries of the Rhine, Meuse and Scheldt. The construction of this dyke was completed in October 1986.

Deltaplan

People and Religion

With its 713,493 inhabitants Amsterdam reflects the population struc-ture of the Netherlands as a whole. Many of those who were forced to flee their own countries for political or religious reasons and took refuge in the Netherlands, came to live in Amsterdam. The Nether-lands, and with it Amsterdam, continues to attract many foreign work-ers as well as citizens of the former Dutch colonies who share the general belief that better living and working conditions are to be found

People

in the mother country. In all there are people of 140 nationalities living in Amsterdam. Particularly noticeable is the high proportion of young people, with 40% of the population being under 30.

Religion

After the Reformation in the 18th c. there evolved in Amsterdam, alongside the Roman Catholic Church, many Protestant sects such as the Evangelical Lutheran or Amsterdam Reformed Church. The many refugees and other foreigners who settled in Amsterdam each brought their own faiths with them so that one finds a great many "imported" religions: for instance, an English episcopalian church, several synagogues, as well as places of worship for Buddhists, Hindus and Muslims.

Communications

Port

Amsterdam's port and commerce are of considerable importance. The port, on the south bank of the North Sea Canal, has expanded in recent decades with new port installations and industrial estates to cover an area of 2725ha/6730 acres. It is in fact easily surpassed by Rotterdam in terms of tonnage. Nevertheless, because of its location between the North Sea and the highly industrialised European hinterland, its significance in terms of the transshipment of freight grew after the Second World War, once the opening of the Amsterdam–Rhine Canal in 1952 brought it within easy reach of the European markets. Earlier in 1876 the opening of the North Sea Canal (270m/886ft wide, 15m/50ft deep and 15km/9 miles long) had provided a passage to the sea and was navigable irrespective of the state of the tide, thanks to the sluices at IJmuiden, part of the the world's largest complex of sluices.

From the 17th c. onwards the port of Amsterdam looked after the country's traffic with its colonies overseas, and the decades following the Second World War have seen it grow into an industrial bulk-handling port. It has a container terminal and up-to-date storage facilities, with a petro-chemical tank complex capable of taking over a million tonnes. Every year several thousand ships are handled; the manufactured goods are destined for internal European markets, the raw materials for national and local industry.

There are ferry services from Amsterdam harbour to Great Britain via Hook of Holland and to Gothenburg in Sweden.

Airport

Amsterdam's airport, Schiphol (13km/8 miles south of the city), is one of Europe's leading airports. In terms of passenger transport – over 21 million passengers are processed each year – it is the fifth largest in Europe. Its role in freight traffic is even more significant, the airport acting as an important distribution centre for high-value consumer goods, such as electronic equipment and optical and medical instruments. Its annual freight turnover amounts to some 720,000 tonnes and Schiphol ranks third, behind Frankfurt and London (Heathrow).

Rail

Through the international railway network Amsterdam is linked to all the important cities of Europe. Some fifty international trains arrive at Amsterdam's main station each day and the volume of freight traffic matches the number of passengers.

Public Transport

Public transport within the city is provided by buses and trams. In addition an underground network with two lines and 20 stations came into operation in 1977.

Road network

Amsterdam can be reached easily from all directions by the country's well developed network of motorways and major roads. The central area of the city, however, tends to be severely congested with frequent traffic jams. By means of stringent parking restrictions and high

Bicycles – the Amsterdammer's favourite mode of transport

charges, an attempt is being made to keep private cars out of the city centre.

The most important means of transport is the bicycle (575,000 cycles for 713,493 inhabitants), although ownership of the many bicycles on the streets is not always clearly defined.

Cycles

Economy

As capital of the Netherlands and possessor of the country's second largest harbour, Amsterdam has always had an important role as port and trading centre; indeed in the 17th c. it was the largest trading centre in the world. Today it is the headquarters of some 16,000 businesses, and about 8% of the Netherlands' international trade passes through Amsterdam. It is also the centre of the country's motor trade and most of the well-known makes of car have franchises here.

Trade

In addition Amsterdam has a concentration of major banks and insurance companies. The stock exchange, one of the oldest in the world, is of international repute. Besides the Netherlands Bank, a further 32 foreign banks and 18 private banks have offices here.

Amsterdam, once the fourth largest tourist centre in Europe, now ranks only eighth. Every year some 1.7 million people, mainly from Great Britain and Germany, visit the city. There are 280 hotels with about 25,000 beds.

Tourism

In addition to shipping and commerce, Amsterdam owes its economic importance to the industry concentrated around it. The city is the focal point of an industrial zone stretching from IJmuiden on the North Sea coast to Hilversum.

Industry

The port of Amsterdam: important to the economy of the city

The industrial development of the port after the Second World War brought about a shift in emphasis from the traditional shipbuilding and ship repairs with the advent, in the western part of the port, of a giant chemical and petro-chemical complex which was established on completion of the pipeline to Rotterdam. With as many as 15,000 industrial companies in all, located on the new industrial estates to the west, south-west and south of the city, Amsterdam is the largest Dutch industrial city.

The major fields of production, besides the fast-growing chemical industry, are motor and aircraft manufacturing, mechanical engineering, and electrotechnical and precision engineering firms.

Amsterdam's diamond industry, established here when diamond-cutters fled the sacking of Antwerp in 1586, enjoys worldwide renown (see below). The city is also the centre for the manufacture of wooden and leather goods, soap-making (one of its oldest trades) and the film industry.

Amsterdam has also long been the centre of the Dutch textile industry, leading the way in fashion and ready-to-wear clothing, and it is also an important producer of foodstuffs, confectionery and similar luxury products, with chocolate and cigarette factories, breweries, etc.

The large number of printing works points to the city's importance as the focus for the Dutch press, publishing and the book trade.

Diamonds

In many people's eyes Amsterdam is not only a jewel of a city, but also a city of jewels, where for centuries diamonds have been processed and sold.

The diamond industry dates back to as early as the 16th c.; the exact date has been fixed as 1586, with the result that in 1986 Amsterdam was able to celebrate its quatercentenary as a diamond city.

The development of the diamond industry was decisively influenced by the arrival of refugees – many of them diamond-cutters – who were forced to leave present-day Belgium in the middle of the 16th c. as a result of their religious beliefs and who settled in the Netherlands. The succeeding years brought both growth and setbacks. Around 1750 there were still only about 600 workers involved in the industry, but with the discovery of vast stocks of diamonds in South America, notably Brazil, it experienced an unprecedented boom. With the further discovery in 1867 of diamonds in South Africa, most of which were cut in Amsterdam, the city developed into one of the foremost diamond centres in the world. It is therefore no surprise that the city should have played host to the first world exhibition of diamonds in 1936. The diamond industry underwent a downturn during the Second World War: tens of thousands of Amsterdam Jews, including 2000 diamond-cutters, were deported and met their deaths in concentration camps.

Today there are more than a dozen diamond-cutting centres in Amsterdam (see Practical Information, Diamond Cutting) and over 60 firms involved in the diamond industry. One of the world's 19 diamond exchanges is situated in Amsterdam (there are also four in Antwerp).

The work of Amsterdam's diamond-cutters has always had an inbuilt guarantee of excellent craftsmanship and quality.

Diamonds are among the most valuable of precious stones. Three characteristics mark them out: their hardness, their crystalline brilliance and their scarcity.

These valuable stones were formed millions of years ago and consist of pure carbon pressed together to form crystals by the massive impact of petrifying volcanic rocks. This impact was so enormous that the diamonds thus formed became the hardest mineral of all, with the highest degree of hardness, 10. This means that diamonds can be used to scratch or make incisions in any other material and equally that it is impossible for them to be scratched by any other mineral (hence the origin of the word "diamond" from the Greek "adamas" = invincible). The fact that diamonds are so sought after, their renown and their preciousness, is to be explained more by their dazzling brilliance, caused by the powerful refraction which occurs because they consist of a material which is completely colourless and as clear as water. Equally their scarcity value enhances their prestige, particularly in the case of the larger diamonds.

Diamonds occur in basic and ultrabasic rocks (Kimberlite; workings down to 2000m/6600ft below the ground) and in alluvial deposits. The world's main sources of diamonds are in Africa (Zaire, South Africa, Ghana, Sierra Leone, Namibia, Botswana, Tanzania, Liberia, Central African Republic, Ivory Coast, Angola), in the former Soviet Union (Urals), Australia, South America (Venezuela, Brazil, Guyana) and in Indonesia and the East Indies.

Only about a fifth of the rough diamonds which are hewn are suitable for converting into jewellery. The rest are used for industrial purposes (drilling, stone saws, glass cutting; for drilling, sharpening, lapping and polishing metals and artificial fibres, and in precision instruments). Since 1955 it has been possible to manufacture synthetic diamonds for industrial purposes by using ultra-high pressure and temperatures.

The four factors determining the value of a gem diamond, also known as "the four Cs", are its colour, clarity, cut and carat (weight).

Diamonds

Amsterdam is famous for its diamond cutting

Weight

The weight of a diamond is measured in carats (1ct = 0.2gm). The word "carat" comes originally from Arabic and referred to the dried red-currant seed used in earlier times for weighing diamonds in India and gold in Africa. The word carat came, via its Dutch use, to enter the language of international trade as a jeweller's measure. However, it is worth remembering that a stone of 1.0ct does not cost twice as much as one of 0.5ct, but possibly as much as three times, given that larger diamonds tend to be much scarcer.

Colour

The second criterion for valuing a diamond is its colour. The scale goes from "River" (pure-white or blue-white) to "Cape" (yellowish) in eight steps which include "Top Wesselton" (clear white), "Wesselton" (white) and "Crystal" (tinted white). Colourless diamonds are considered the most valuable, but there are also stones of every conceivable hue. Depending on the coloration they can often command a high collector's value – as, for instance, the perfect black gem known as "De Amsterdam". Quite by chance this stone turned up in a consignment of industrial diamonds which came into the possession of Max Drukker, an Amsterdam dealer in precision diamond-cutting equipment. From the 55.85 carat rough gem Drukker was able to have a superb precious stone cut – a 33.47 carat diamond with 147 facets. It was ready just in time for the city of Amsterdam's 700th anniversary celebrations (1975). Max Drukker presented some of the diamond dust to the burgomaster's wife, who promptly gave the diamond a name: from henceforth it has been known as "De Amsterdam".

Clarity

The third criterion for valuing a diamond is its clarity. There are seven internationally recognised grades. The highest of these is "of the first water"; this means that even under a tenfold magnification there are no inclusions to be found. Such diamonds are extremely rare. The grading system moves through such criteria as "small inclusions" to

Glittering Marvels

Two of the best known diamonds in the world were given their final cut in Amsterdam, including the historically important "Kohinoor" or "Kohinur" (from the Persian: "koh-i-nur" = "mountain of light"). This diamond has had several changes of ownership during its existence. The first time that it is mentioned was in 1304, when it was in the possession of an Indian prince. In the early 16th c. Babur (1483–1530), the founder of the Mogul dynasty which ruled India until 1858, declared the stone to be his, after his adversary the Sultan Ibrahim had fallen in battle. In 1739 Delhi was conquered and plundered by Nadir Shah, the King of Persia. The booty which he carried off included the Kohinoor. In 1851 – in the meantime it had come into the possession of Queen Victoria of England – it was put on display at the Great Exhibition at Crystal Palace in London. Queen Victoria had the 186 carat diamond recut in Amsterdam; as a result the stone, which on its discovery had laid claim to a phenomenal weight of 800 carats, now only weighed 108.93 carat. Today the Kohinoor decorates the crown of the Queen Mother.

The largest rough diamond to have been discovered to date, the "Cullinan" (3106 carats; this is the equivalent of more than a pound weight), was also entrusted to Amsterdam diamond-cutters. It was given to King Edward VII of England on his 66th birthday and the Amsterdam firm Asscher was charged with the cutting of the stone. In 1908, after months of preliminary study, Joseph Asscher split the diamond into 105 pieces (9 larger ones and 96 smaller ones); the largest is now to be found in the sceptre of the British Crown Jewels. When the Cullinan was split up a doctor and two nurses had to be present; indeed the stress was so great that the famous diamond-cutter, on completing his task, was laid low for three months with a nervous breakdown. To this day the house of Asscher is considered one of the most exclusive addresses for diamond trading.

Up until about the 14th c. diamonds were prized less for their beauty than for their hardness and the magic properties ascribed to them. It was not until modern times that their beauty became a foremost consideration with the development of techniques for splitting and cutting them, thereby turning rather unprepossessing stones into "glittering marvels". Thenceforth the diamond took its place as the most precious of all precious stones.

However diamonds did not always bring their owners good luck in the sense that we would understand it today. This is well illustrated by the story of the "Florentine", or "Cursed Diamond", of the Hapsburgs. This stone was stolen from a Buddha statue at Hyderabad in India and came into the possession of the Medici family in Florence, hence its name. Empress Maria Theresia of Austria acquired it when the Medici line died out and presented it to her daughter Marie Antoinette, who died in 1793 at the guillotine during the French Revolution. Robespierre took possession of the stone but died himself at the guillotine just a year later. Napoleon returned the diamond to the Hapsburgs when he gave it to the son of his union with the Archduchess Marie Louise. The son, however, died at the young age of 22 from consumption. The next owners of the stone did not die naturally: Emperor Maximilian of Mexico faced a firing squad at the orders of his adversary Benito Juárez; his nephew, Crown Prince Rudolf, committed suicide with his lover at Mayerling in 1889; his mother, Empress Elisabeth ("Sissy") was murdered by an anarchist in 1898; the wife of the new successor to the throne, Franz Ferdinand, was wearing the diamond when the couple were assassinated in Sarajevo in 1914 – the event that triggered off the First World War. With the passing of the Hapsburg line in 1918, the diamond found its way into various hands, including that of King Farouk of Egypt, who was forced to seek exile in 1952.

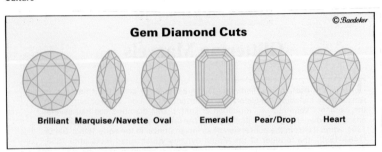

Gem Diamond Cuts © *Baedeker*

Brilliant Marquise/Navette Oval Emerald Pear/Drop Heart

the final one, representing large inclusions which are immediately visible to the naked eye.

Cut

These four valuation criteria are determined by the natural condition of the diamond. The fourth and last one – the cut – is by contrast dependent on human intervention.

Of the types of cut shown, the brilliant cut is the best known and most favoured and consequently all cut and polished diamonds are popularly known as "brilliants", although strictly speaking this term should only be used for diamonds with the brilliant cut, i.e. where the full cut is in 58 facets. The Marquise (Navette), Oval, Emerald, Drop and Heart cuts also have 58 facets. Other cuts are the Baguette (simple cut with 24 facets), Octahedron (16 facets) and Carré (a square cut).

Facets are the surfaces created by cutting, which must be arranged at certain angles to each other in order to obtain the optimum refraction of light. The largest horizontal facet is called the "table".

Whereas raw diamonds used to be split using a diamond chip and a special knife, a low-risk method is used today, the saw technique. The "saw" is a paper-thin phosphor-bronze blade, its edges lubricated with olive oil and diamond grit. The final cut which the stone receives on each facet is carried out with a cast-iron blade which turns with 2500 revolutions and is coated with diamond granules. Nevertheless diamond-cutting is still real precision work. The cleaving of the raw diamond must be carried out taking into account the crystal structure of the stone, i.e. the lattice in which the carbon atoms are arranged in a particular combination, in order that the stone does not literally explode.

Culture

Amsterdam is the country's cultural centre and the main seat of learning and science (including the country's largest university and the Dutch Academy of Science), together with teaching and research. It is the home of world-famous museums such as the Rijksmuseum, with its great collection of old masters, the Stedelijk Museum for modern art, and the Van Gogh Museum, which as a museum sets new standards from the technical and educational point of view.

In the sphere of music the Concertgebouw Orchestra and the Philharmonic Orchestra enjoy an international reputation, as do the Netherlands National Ballet and the Netherlands Dance Theatre. The new opera house on Waterlooplein, Het Muziektheater, which stages opera and ballet, was opened in 1986 and can seat an audience of 1640.

The Holland Festival, which takes place every summer, attracts large numbers of visitors from all over the world with its ballet, opera, music, theatre and folk-dance performances. Furthermore there are many art

The Concertgebouw

galleries and countless events put on by avant-garde music, dance and theatre groups.

Amsterdam's many academies include the Architectural Academy, the National Academy of the Visual Arts, the Gerrit Rietveld Academy (for industrial design), the Dutch Film Academy, the Academy of Drama, the Academy of Cabaret and the Academy of Social Education.

Academies

A number of important scientific institutions have their headquarters in Amsterdam, for instance the Royal Dutch Academy of Science, the Royal Society for the Promotion of Science and the Royal Dutch Geographic Institute.

Scientific Institutions

The University of Amsterdam, founded in 1877, has some 30,000 students. It has eight faculties (divided into subfaculties) and, with its institutes, laboratories and training colleges, is one of the most important in Europe. In 1880 the Dutch Reformed Church set up its university in Amsterdam, "Vrije Universiteit" (Free University), which has five faculties providing education for some 13,000 students.

Universities

Amsterdam also has the Catholic Theological College, teacher training establishments, two conservatoires and a great many research institutes (including the State aviation and aerospace establishment, a nuclear physics research institute, the Royal Tropical Institute, the Institute for Brain Research, the International Archive for Women's Movements, the International Institute for Social History and the Institute of Journalism).

Colleges and Research Institutes

Among Amsterdam's major libraries are the University Library (some 2 million volumes), the Public Library, the art libraries of the Stedelijk and Rijks Museums, the Music Library and the library of the Tropical Museum.

Libraries

Famous People

Karel Appel
(b. 1921)

Karel Appel, who was born in Amsterdam, is one of the most internationally famous and controversial post-war Dutch painters. He received his first major commission in 1949 – a frieze for Amsterdam City Hall entitled "Vragende Kinderen" ("Questioning Children") – which sparked off such a public outcry that the work had to be covered up for a time.

In 1950 Appel settled in Paris, where he joined the international experimental school and was one of the founders of the COBRA group (Copenhagen, Brussels, Amsterdam), composed of artists now enjoying international acclaim such as Corneille, Constant, Alechinsky, Asger-Jorn and Lucebert.

In the fifties Appel took part in many important exhibitions and received international awards and prizes, including the 1954 UNESCO Prize at the Venice Biennale and the Guggenheim Prize in 1960.

Karel Appel's work, much of which can be seen in the Stedelijk Museum, is characterised by an especially expressive and vibrant use of colour.

Hendrik Petrus Berlage
(1856–1934)

Hendrik Petrus Berlage was a brilliant and typically Dutch architect whose highly original style in the building that made him famous, the Amsterdam Exchange (begun 1897), marked the transition between historicism and the 20th c. A great influence on architecture both inside and outside the Netherlands, he was also responsible for the bridge over the Amstel bearing his name and the Gemeentelijk (Municipal) Museum in The Hague, while the furniture he designed assured him a prominent place in the field of applied arts.

Anne Frank
(1929–45)

Anne Frank, a Jewish girl from Germany, achieved fame through her diary which has been filmed and translated into many languages.

The Jewish Frank family fled Hitler's Frankfurt in 1933 and came to Amsterdam, where they went into hiding during the German occupation. Anne kept a diary on their life over this period (June 12th 1942–August 1st 1944), which ended when the whole family was discovered and transported to Germany. Anne, together with her mother and sister, died in the Belsen concentration camp and only her father survived. After the Liberation the diary was found in the family's Amsterdam hideout and published.

Rembrandt
(Harmensz van Rijn)
(1606–69)

Rembrandt, the most famous of all Dutch painters, moved to Amsterdam in 1632, after an early creative period in his native Leiden; in 1634 he married Saskia van Uijlenburgh, the wealthy daughter of a burgomaster. In 1639 he bought the house in the Jodenbreestraat which is today the Rembrandthuis.

During his first ten years in Amsterdam he was much in demand for his portraits, and almost two-thirds of all his commissioned work dates from this period. His portraits were true to life and made no concessions to flattery. Besides his impressive individual portraits (including "Burgomaster J. Six"), his group portraits ("The Anatomy Lesson of Dr Tulp") and self-portraits (with Saskia, the painter as the Prodigal Son), he also painted biblical themes and, later in life, landscapes.

As Rembrandt increasingly declined to subjugate the artistic integrity of his portraits to the wishes of his patrons, the number of commissions declined, and, in fact, the patrons who commissioned "The Night Watch" refused to accept it.

After Saskia's death in 1642 Rembrandt got into personal and financial difficulties and in 1656 was declared bankrupt. Titus, his son by

Saskia, and Hendrickje Stoffels, his common-law wife, formed a company to help Rembrandt's financial situation, but until his death he remained encumbered by debts, and found himself in growing artistic and social isolation (his "Swearing-in of the Batavians under Julius Civilis" for the new city hall in Amsterdam was rejected and replaced by the work of one of his pupils).

When he died in 1669 Rembrandt was buried outside the Westerkerk and was only subsequently reinterred inside the church. Rembrandt left 562 paintings, 300 etchings and 1600 drawings. His best-known works are "The Night Watch" (1642), "The Anatomy Lesson of Dr Tulp" (1632) "Staalmeesters" (1661/62) and "The Jewish Bride" (c. 1665), all of which are in the Rijksmuseum. His best-known self-portrait hangs in the Mauritshuis in The Hague, and almost all of his etchings and many of his drawings can be seen in the Rembrandthuis.

Baruch
(Benedictus)
de Spinoza
(1632–77)

The Dutch philosopher Baruch (or Benedictus) de Spinoza was born in the Jewish quarter of Amsterdam and given a Hebrew education. His independent thinking ran counter to Jewish beliefs and led in 1656 to his excommunication. A considerable influence on Western philosophy, he was above all a rationalist and set out to prove his metaphysical pantheistic doctrines by mathematical demonstration.

His best-known work, "Ethics demonstrated by geometrical methods", written between 1660 and 1675, was not published until after his death.

Spinoza's house in The Hague was taken over by the Spinoza Institute in 1927.

Joost van den
Vondel
(1587–1679)

Joost van den Vondel was the greatest poet of the Dutch Renaissance. His writings ranged from satirical, historical, patriotic and religious poetry to his 32 plays, of which the best-known are "Gijsbreght van Aemstel" (1637) and "Lucifer" (1654). He also translated the Psalms, Ovid and Virgil into Dutch.

Van den Vondel, who played an active part in the political and religious struggles of his times and was converted to Catholicism in 1641, died aged 92 in Amsterdam in 1679. The city's largest park is named after him.

History of the City

1270	A dam is built separating the mouth of the Amstel from the arm of the Zuiderzee called the "IJ".
1275	Floris V, Count of Holland, grants the people of the fishing village of Amstelledamme freedom from tolls on travel and on trade in their own goods within the County of Holland.
1300	Amsterdam receives its charter.
1317	The Bishops of Utrecht transfer the city to Count Willem III of Holland.
1323	The city becomes the point where duty is levied on beer imported from Hamburg, thus leading to increased trade with the Hanseatic towns.
1345	The "miracle of the Host" makes Amsterdam a place of pilgrimage, and pilgrims flock to the chapel built in the Kalverstraat in 1347. When Emperor Maximilian is cured of an illness while on a pilgrimage in 1489, he grants the city the right to bear an imperial crown in its coat of arms.
from 1400	The four Burgomasters are elected annually by the Council of Elders, which gives the city relative independence from the country's rulers.
1421	The city of Amsterdam is almost completely destroyed by a great fire.
1481	Building of a stone city wall.
1535	The city is plunged into the upheaval of the Reformation. Anabaptists run naked in a state of religious ecstasy over the Dam and almost succeed, on May 10th, in occupying the City Hall. The city fathers summon the aid of the Hapsburg Emperor Charles V.
1538	The population of Amsterdam has grown to over 30,000.
1566	During a famine churches and monasteries are stormed by adherents of the Reformation. Philip II of Spain succeeds to the throne of Charles V.
1567	The Duke of Alba occupies Amsterdam on behalf of Philip II and savagely persecutes the followers of the Reformation.
1568	During an uprising by the Northern Provinces of the Low Countries Amsterdam remains pro-Spanish.
1572	William the Silent, Prince of Orange, becomes the leader of the uprising against Spain.
1578	After the city surrenders to William's troops, Amsterdam joins in the Dutch War of Independence from Spain. All pro-Spanish civic leaders, clerics and clergy have to leave the city ("Alternatie"). A new civic administration consists mainly of immigrant Reformed merchants. The "Satisfactie van Amsterdam" lays down that no one may be persecuted for their beliefs.
1578 onwards	Amsterdam becomes one of the most important cities for commerce in the world, a centre for culture and science, a city with flourishing crafts

and a cosmopolitan population. Refugees from the whole of Europe come to settle in the city.

A fleet, financed mainly by Amsterdam merchants, succeeds in finding a sea route to India round the southern tip of Africa.	1595–97
Founding of the United East India Trading Company, with Amsterdam merchants among the major shareholders.	1602
Founding of the Stocks and Commodities Exchange.	1611
The three canals (Herengracht, Keizersgracht and Prinsengracht) are built as part of the fourth project to extend the city with the workers' district of the Jordaan in the west.	1613
The city's population reaches 100,000.	1620
The "Golden Age" of Amsterdam, when the city becomes the most important port in the world.	17th c.
War with England. Amsterdam loses its supremacy at sea.	1780–84
End of the rule of a number of Amsterdam families. Promulgation of the principles of the French Revolution.	January 19th 1795
The Low Countries become the Republic of Batavia.	1795–1806
Amsterdam becomes the capital of the Kingdom of the Netherlands under Louis Napoleon.	1806
The Netherlands are made part of France. The Continental Blockade, which cuts the city off from its traditional markets, finally ends Amsterdam's position as chief trading city.	1810
After the defeat of Napoleon and expulsion of the French, Amsterdam becomes the capital of the Kingdom of the Netherlands, a constitutional monarchy under William I, although the seat of government is in The Hague.	1813
A railway line is built to Haarlem.	1839
A direct link with the sea is established with the construction of the North Sea Canal. New prosperity for the port.	1876
Social Democrats win a majority on the City Council and Amsterdam is henceforward a stronghold of democratic socialism.	1913
The Netherlands stay neutral during the First World War. Amsterdam is plunged into a series of crises during this time (unemployment, food shortages, influx of refugees).	1914–18
Amsterdam has a population of 647,000	1920
German troops occupy the city. Deportation of Jews is begun.	May 16th 1940
The "February Strike" is organised by the workers of Amsterdam to protest against the deportation of their Jewish fellow citizens.	February 25th 1941
Although the resistance movement is particularly strong in Amsterdam (underground press, direct action against the forces of occupation), by the end of the war approximately 100,000 Jews have been deported and Amsterdam's Jewish community has been almost completely eliminated.	1940–45

History of the City

May 5th 1945	The city is liberated by Canadian troops.
1952	Opening of the Amsterdam–Rhine Canal.
1964–66	Appearance of the anti-Establishment "Provos".
March 10th 1966	Mass demonstrations triggered off by the wedding of Princess Beatrix and Claus von Amsberg lead to the subsequent dismissal of the Burgomaster and Chief of Police.
1970	The "Kabouter" (Gnome Party), successors to the Provos, win five seats on the City Council.
1975	Amsterdam celebrates its 700th anniversary; clashes between the residents of the Nieuwmarkt district and the police. Attempts to prevent demolition of housing to make way for the Underground.
1979	Over 60,000 on Amsterdam's housing waiting list. Many empty houses occupied by the "Krakers".
April 30th 1980	Abdication of Queen Juliana. Queen Beatrix pledges her oath of allegiance to the constitution. Coronation of Queen Beatrix in the Nieuwe Kerk. Riots around the church and palace, away from the heavily protected route of the procession, are directed not so much at the Queen as at the acute housing shortage in Amsterdam.
1981	Law for the registration of empty dwellings. Illegal occupation of premises prohibited.
1985	Amsterdam applies – unsuccessfully – to stage the Olympic Games in 1992.
1986	Amsterdam celebrates its quatercentenary as a diamond centre. Opening of the new opera house "Het Muziektheater" on Waterlooplein.
1987	Amsterdam becomes "European City of Culture" for a year, succeeding Athens and Florence in accordance with the 1983 EC Summit decision.
1988	Opening of Amsterdam's new City Hall, which shares its building – the "Stopera" – with the Muziektheater opera house.
1992	In October more than 200 people die when an Israeli freight plane crashes on the district of Bijlmermeer. The largest shopping centre in the Netherlands, the Magna Plaza, is opened in December in the former Amsterdam customs house.
1995	The outstanding event in Amsterdam is "Sail 95", a giant marine spectacular with a flotilla of old wind-jammers.

Architecture

As a result of the economic prosperity which Amsterdam enjoyed in the 16th and 17th c., secular buildings very early on acquired considerable importance. This has meant that the Amsterdam cityscape is distinguished not only by its churches, but also by its city fortifications, its city hall and above all by the many private houses which were built in the 17th and 18th c. – no other city in Europe is as well endowed in this respect.

No traces have survived of the very first houses which were built in the 13th and 14th c. after the construction of the dyke at the estuary of the Amstel. The wooden dwellings were destroyed by terrible fires in 1421 and 1453. As a result the decision was made increasingly to use brick as a building material. Only two wooden houses have survived to the present day. One of these is Begijnhof No. 34 (dating from 1460).

Even the city's first church building was made of wood – the Oude Kerk, built around 1300. Not long after, however, in 1306, work began on a stone church, which had acquired its present dimensions by the middle of the 16th c. The Late Gothic Nieuwe Kerk was begun at the beginning of the 15th c. but was not completed until 1490, the building suffering damage on several occasions from fires in the vicinity. Because of the limited loadbearing capacity of their foundations, both churches – in common with many others in the Netherlands – have vaulting made of wood rather than stone. Other characteristics of Gothic church buildings in the northern Netherlands include the use of bricks (instead of stone), the choir ambulatory, which recalls the style of French sacred buildings, the economy of the decorations and the pronounced simplicity of the interior furnishings.

Gothic

The Renaissance, which took a very special form in the Netherlands, showed discernible influences as early as the first half of the 16th c. (e.g. the tower of the Oude Kerk).

Renaissance

The most important architect of this period was the Utrecht-born Hendrik de Keyser (1565–1621), who worked in Amsterdam from 1591. He designed the city's first Protestant church, the Zuiderkerk, built between 1603 and 1611, and the Westerkerk, which was begun in 1620. Whereas the Zuiderkerk and the Westerkerk still display a large number of Gothic elements, the Noorderkerk (1620–23) shows the architect bringing new ideas to his concept of religious buildings. Thus he gave the church an extremely simple central section (a Greek cross with arms of equal length), which became the norm for later Protestant churches.

The Renaissance style was also the main influence on gentlemen's houses until well into the 17th c. The houses built along the canals were usually given stepped gables, but these were always extremely varied and sumptuously decorated. The canal houses designed by Hendrik de Keyser show, with their columns and pilasters, an espousal of antique architectural forms (for instance the Bartolottihuis).

The Renaissance was superseded by a period when a much severer style of architecture held sway. The first half of the 17th c. (c. 1620–40) saw the arrival of the Classical Style (otherwise known as Baroque Classicism) in Amsterdam's architecture, with architects turning to the models of Greek and Roman antiquity. The outstanding building dating from this period is the City Hall, today the Royal Palace on the Dam, which was designed by the Haarlem architect, Jacob van Campen (1595–1657). With his judicious and uncomplicated interpretation of

Classical Style

27

Baroque Classicism van Campen's buildings continued the style of the Italian architect Andrea Palladio.

Also worthy of note are Adriaan Dortsman (c. 1625–82), who designed the Lutheran Church on the Singel with its circular ground-plan (1668–71), and Philip Vingboons (1607–78). During this period Vingboons was the leading architect of private houses. Instead of the curved or stepped gables he introduced the neck-gable. The façades of the canal houses designed by him are frequently divided up by pilasters. The houses running from Nos. 364 to 370 on the Herengracht, which now house the Bible Museum, are good examples of Vingboons' architectural style. The designs of the magnificent Trippenhuis (1662) are the work of Vingboons' brother, Justus.

Towards the end of the 17th c. and more especially in the 18th c. the French influence on Dutch architecture became increasingly evident. This development was promoted in no small part by the Huguenot Daniel Marot (c. 1660–1752), who worked in Amsterdam mainly between 1705 and 1717. The canal houses designed by him display, in common with those of the brothers Hans Jakob and Hendrik Husly, ornate Baroque forms. After 1750 the cousin of the Husly brothers, Jakob Otten Husly, occupied a pre-eminent position among the city's leading architects. His achievements include the designs for the house on the Keizersgracht (1788), built for the "Felix Meritis" organisation.

The first half of the 19th c. saw a stagnation in Amsterdam's architectural development. As in the rest of Europe, there was an intensification of the so-called Neostyle, following the eclipse of the Classical Style.   Historicism

The leading architect of this time was P. J. H. Cuypers (1827–1921). His most famous buildings include the Rijksmuseum (1877–85) and the main Railway Station (1881–89). Both of these brick buildings have unmistakable echoes of Dutch Renaissance architecture, but also exhibit Gothic elements. In contrast to many other buildings of this period, which are frequently overblown and at times tending to the monumental, those designed by Cuypers stand out for their moderation.

The Concertgebouw, built between 1882 and 1888 by A. van Gendt, also brings together various stylistic elements. While the window and door frames recall the Renaissance, the portico, dominated by its triangular gable, shows a Neo-Classical influence.

The link between historicism and the modern period is represented by Hendrik Petrus Berlage (1856–1934). Berlage still employed Romanesque and Renaissance forms in his buildings, but he always modified them in such a masterly way that what emerged was completely new. With his simple logical designs and his functional use of materials he is a precursor of 20th c. architecture. Berlages's most important work is the Stock Exchange (Koopmansbeurs; 1897–1903).   Beginning of the Modern Period

The Art Nouveau movement had only a limited impact on the architecture of Amsterdam. The American Hotel on Leidseplein was built between 1898 and 1902 and incorporates typical art nouveau elements (e.g. façade walls and window openings in varying shapes and sizes), but also recalls Berlage's Stock Exchange building.   Art Nouveau

Buildings characteristic of the art nouveau style include the former insurance company building at No. 174–176 on the Keizersgracht (built in 1905 by G. van Arkel) and the Tuschinski Picture House (built in 1918–21 by H. L. de Jong).

The Amsterdam School is a term used to denote a group of architects who designed buildings in the first and second decades of this century which show extensive parallels with the German expressionist move-   Amsterdam School

◀ *Typical house on the canals: cultured living behind old façades*

Canal Architecture

The main sightseeing attraction in Amsterdam is undoubtedly the old city centre with its criss-cross of canals. These tree-lined waterways boast picturesque bridges and almost 7000 gentlemen's houses under preservation order. They confer on the city its unique charm and justify its appellation "The Venice of the North".

The oldest settlement occupied the area between the present-day Oude and Nieuwezijds Voorburgwal. The first extension of these limits occurred towards the end of the 15th c., but an actual planned expansion did not come about until 1612 when the famous canal belt began to be established. With the Singel as the outer limit, the Herengracht, Keizersgracht and Prinsengracht were laid out in semicircular fashion to the west of the city centre. In 1657 the ring of canals was extended from

Stepped gable   Beak gable   Neck gable

the Leidsegracht to the Amstel, and finally, bearing the names Nieuwe Herengracht, Keizersgracht and Prinsengracht, the three main canals were continued on the far side of the Amstel. The area was connected to the old centre by radial canals and streets. So it was that Amsterdam acquired its highly characteristic layout.

Although they were initially established for defensive purposes, the canals were soon playing an important role as transport routes for the movement of goods from and to the merchant houses of the rapidly expanding city. The canals, which were generally 2m/6½ft deep and 25m/82ft wide, were additionally used as a canalisation system. To the left and right of each canal there was limited space for building; a plot of this fenland, which could be built on only with difficulty, was extremely expensive, as were the building costs, the houses having to be constructed on stilts.

ment. An outstanding example of the style, with its wealth of forms and three-dimensional effects, is the Shipping House (Scheepvaarthuis; built in 1912–16 and 1926–28) on Prins Hendrikkade. The architect was Johann Melchior van der Mey (1878–1949), who was assisted by Michel de Klerk (1884–1923) and Piet Kramer (1881–1961). Many of the decorative shapes on the exterior and interior of the building are motives derived from Christian seafaring themes.

In later buildings Michel de Klerk, who assumed the mantle of leader of the Amsterdam School, and his fellow architects adopted clearer, more distinct forms, but retained their love of imaginative detail. The Amsterdam School reached its peak in the 1920s, with whole areas of the city coming into being under its architects' inspiration. For them it was important to create dwellings which enabled working people to live their lives in a more humane and dignified way. (e.g. Hembrugstraat and Amsterdam–Zuid).

Baedeker Special

Between the canals two rows of building plots, each 50m/55yd deep, were laid out. The gap between the backs of the two houses had to measure at least 48m/53yd. Thus the canal houses are high and narrow, but also quite long.

These magnificent gentlemen's residences – most of which date from Amsterdam's heyday in the 17th c. – contribute to the city's colourful image with their red and brown tinted façades and white window frames. Moreover, the ornate gables ensure that each house is quite different from its neighbours. There are in fact six main types of gable shapes, but these are always imaginatively embellished with an endless stock of variations.

The relatively unadorned beak gable was mainly used in simple storehouses. At the end of the 16th c. and beginning of the 17th the vast majority of

Bell gable

Classic gable

Flat façade

buildings were embellished with the stepped gable. The neck gable, also sometimes known as the bottle gable, is a transitional style which led to the bell gable, the favoured shape at the middle of the 17th c. Neo-Classical variations appeared around 1770. The central section of the gable was generally richly decorated, or, alternatively, a flat façade, or last gable, was chosen.

Most gables and façades tilt outwards slightly. This "gable overhang" was a regulation at the time that the canal houses were built. The reason for it was probably less to do with aesthetic considerations than the fact that furnishings, fittings and loads could be transported up more easily, the narrow steep stairs within the houses being totally unsuited for this purpose. Such operations were carried out with the help of a hoisting beam in the roof ridge.

Alongside the expressive Amsterdam School, the geometric-rational building style known as "De Stijl" dominated Dutch architecture in the early 20th c. Steel, concrete and glass were the preferred materials of this functional style of architecture. The form of the building was dictated by the demands of the individual rooms. Whereas many important examples of the "De Stijl" architectural movement are to be found in other parts of the country, in Amsterdam itself the architects of the Amsterdam School enjoyed more popularity.

De Stijl

During the Second World War building activity in Amsterdam to all intents and purposes came to a standstill. At the end of the war the devastated areas had to be cleared and then large areas of new dwellings were planned in the 1960s. A good example is the district of Bijlmermeer with its 30 ten-storey blocks of apartments, most of them several hundred metres long (14,000 dwellings). On their completion,

Postwar Period and Present Day

Koopmansbeurs

Art Nouveau house on the Keizersgracht

however, the enormous high-rise blocks, placed among extended green areas, attracted as many opponents as supporters.

In the 70s attention was turned with renewed zeal to the redevelopment of the inner city areas. New buildings were designed so that in size and materials they blended in with the existing architecture. Even in the 80s the planners adhered to the principle that the quality of life in the city centre had to be enhanced (e.g. the houses around the Zuiderkerkhof). New housing developments were built according to the precept of winding streets flanked by low-rise houses in individual styles. Even the more recently erected public buildings do not follow any single unified architectural trend. Impressive examples of contemporary architecture include the double-building of the Stopera, the NMB Bank (1987) and the "Entrepot West" housing development, which was ready for occupation in 1992.

Amsterdam in Quotations

In some Places, as in Amsterdam, the Foundation costs more than the Superstructure, for the Ground being soft, they are constrain'd to ram in huge stakes of Timber (with Wool about it to preserve it from Putrefaction) till they come to a firm Basis; so that, as one said, Whosoever could see Amsterdam under ground should see a huge Winter-Forest.

James Howell
(1593–1666)

Familiar Letters, 1645

It was on a Sunday morning about 11, that I purposely went to the Bourse (after the sermons were ended) to see their Dog-market, which lasts till two after-noone. I do not looke on the structure of this Exchange to be comparable to that of Sir Tho: Greshams in our Citty of London; yet in one respect it exceeds, that ships of considerable burthen ride at the very key continguous to it, and really it is by extraordinary industry, that as well this Citty, as almost generaly the Townes of Holland are so accomodated with Grafts, Cutts, Sluces, Moles and Rivers, that nothing is more frequent then to see a whole Navy of Marchands & others environ'd with streetes & houses, every particular mans Barke, or Vessell at anker before his very doore, and yet the streetes so exactly straite, even, & uniform that nothing can be more pleasing, especialy, being so frequently planted and shaded with the beautifull lime trees, which are set in rowes before every mans house, affording a very ravishing prospect.

John Evelyn
(1620–1706)

Diary, August 1641

Had long a full view of Amsterdam, its roofs & towers intermixed with masts – less in the water than Venice, & rather running along a green level shore. – Went up & down the streets. Plate glass in the windows Magnificence of the Merchant's houses –... The shops richly furnished & from their neatness & the brightness of the window-panes not to mention the proprete of the figures within, in many respects surpassing most in London, & far those of every City, not excepting Paris.

Samuel Rogers
(1763–1855)

The Dutch, by planting trees wherever water ran, have given a chearful charm to a Morass – Canals they love to a madness – they make them where they don't find them – along the side of every road – round every villa – every one has a canal of his own & builds as near the public canal as he can – & thro' every orchard & garden.

Went in an open carriage along canals to Brock (Broek in Waterland), a village like a succession of scenes in a new comic opera – the houses as painted yesterday – almost all wood & in various colours – the windows bright – the courts pebbled in mosaic figures – the public walks (all foot-ways) swept & smooth as in a pleasure ground.

Italian Journey, April 1815

On a desolate marsh overhung by fogs and exhaling diseases, a marsh where there was neither wood nor stone, neither firm earth nor drinkable water, a marsh from which the ocean on one side and the Rhine on the other were with difficulty kept out by art, was to be found the most prosperous community in Europe. The wealth which was collected within five miles of the Stadhous of Amsterdam would purchase the fee-simple of Scotland.

T.B. Macaulay
(1800–59)

History of England, 1849–55

Plan of the Inner City

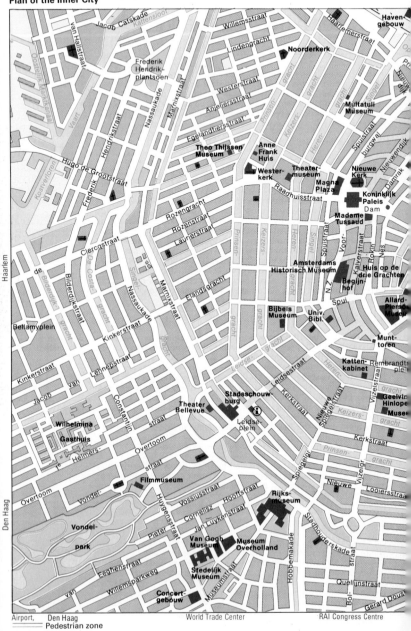

Haarlem

Den Haag

Den Haag

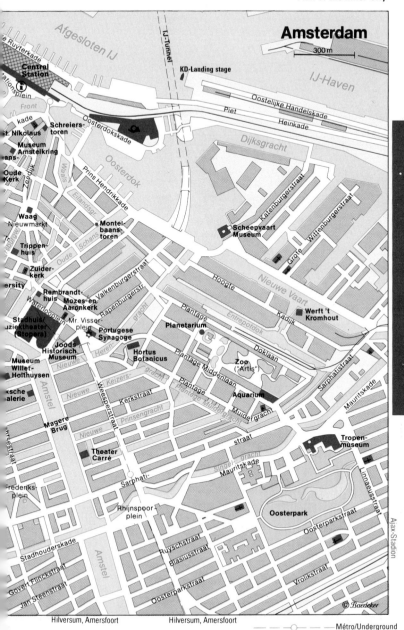

Amsterdam

300 m

Amsterdam A–Z

Aalsmeer Excursion

The district of Aalsmeer (Province of North Holland) on the canal round
the Haarlemmermeer polder is part of Randstad Holland (see Facts and
Figures, General Information). Over one third of its area comprises water,
the "Westeinderplassen". It is internationally famous for its flower auctions, which are the largest in Europe.

In the Middle Ages Aalsmeer owed its importance to peat, fishing and
cattle breeding, but since about 1450, with the growth of nearby Amsterdam and the 19th c. draining of the Haarlemmermeer, it has become
increasingly given over to horticulture.

The flower-growing began with lilac; later the emphasis shifted to pot
plants and cut flowers. Today Aalsmeer has over 600 flower-growers, their
glasshouses cover an area of 600ha/1490 acres and the annual turnover
from the auctions is about 400 million guilders (the Netherlands are the
world market leaders in flower-growing and dealing, ahead of Colombia
and Israel, and control 65% of world trade, more than half their flower
exports going to Germany).

Location
12km/8 miles
south-west

Buses
Stop opposite
the Centraal
Station

Auctions of cut flowers and pot plants take place on Mondays to Fridays
(6.30–11am; visitors can view from 7.30am) in the auction building, built in
1928 (Vereinigde Bloemenveilingen; Legmeerdijk 313). Some 10 million
flowers are sold daily – not just "tulips from Amsterdam", but also carna-
tions from the Negev (Israel), exotic blooms from Kenya and orchids from
Bangkok. The buyers conduct their transactions in silence. Everything is
controlled by headsets and push-buttons. The auctioneer fixes a high
opening price and then gradually comes steadily down. Whoever indicates
his wish to buy by pushing his button then has his bid accepted. The details
of the purchase and the identity of the buyer are kept on computer. The
flowers are placed with an invoice in a crate, taken to the 800m/880yd long
refrigerated hall and then coupled up with other flower consignments
ordered by the same buyer, before being loaded onto air-conditioned
containers.

★Flower
Auctions

Achterburgwal (Oudezijds Achterburgwal) H/J 6 (B/C 2/3)

The Oudezijds Achterburgwal was excavated in about 1385 behind the
Oudezijds Voorburgwal as a second defensive canal, and stretches from
the Grimburgwal to the Zeedijk. It is the narrowest "burgwal" and used to
be one of the "better" residential areas.

Location
Centre

Metro
Nieuwmarkt

Proof of this is to be found on the gable-stone of the "Huis op de drie
Grachten" (House of the Three Canals), where Grimburgwal, O. Z. Voorburgwal and O. Z. Achterburgwal meet. Its inscription "Fluweelenburg-
wal" alludes to the fact that the prominent citizens of the 17th c. dressed in
silk and satin. The three-canal house, which was built in 1610, has regained
its original appearance thanks to restoration work undertaken at the beginning of the 20th c.

The house at No. 47 is also particularly worth seeing. Nowadays the
property of the Salvation Army, it used to be the house of the Lieutenant in
Rembrandt's painting "The Night Watch".

Huis op de drie
Grachten

◀ *Royal Palace on the Dam*

Alkmaar

Oudeman–
huispoort

Opposite the "Huis op de drie Grachten" an arcaded walkway known as "Oudemanhuispoort" links Oudezijds Achterburgwal with Kloveniersburgwal. A number of antiquarian bookshops and bookstalls are to be found here, behind which "oude mannetjes" (old men) stand. (Market times: Mon.–Sat. 10am–4pm.) The covered gallery was originally the entrance to an old people's home, as the name "Old Men's Gateway" indicates. Over the entrance symbolic allusions to age can still be found: a pair of spectacles and two old men.

Alkmaar   Excursion

Location
37km/23 miles
north-west

Rail
from Centraal
Station
(3 times
an hour)

Alkmaar is the ancient centre of North Holland. It lies 8km/5 miles from the North Sea coast on the North Holland canal (in the province of North Holland). Today its major industries are metals, paper, cocoa and carpets.

The town received its charter from Count William II in 1254. In 1517 it fell victim to plundering by a band led by "Big Piet". Alkmaar played a special role in the Dutch struggle for independence from the Spanish by being the first to succeed in routing the son of the Duke of Alba, Frederick of Toledo, who was besieging the town. This took place on October 8th 1573 when the sluices were opened and the surrounding area was flooded. Alkmaar flourished after the war of independence, owing partly to local land reclamation. Wars of religion raged in the town between 1609 and 1621 but after the lifting of the siege by the French (1810–13), Alkmaar, as an inland town, enjoyed a more peaceful fate than the towns on the Zuiderzee.

★Cheese Market

Alkmaar's number one tourist attraction is its cheese market, held, strictly in accordance with tradition, between 10 and 12 every Friday morning from

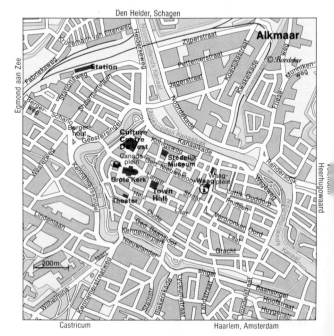

mid-April to mid-September in front of the weigh-house. The cheese porters are dressed in white and wear hats bearing the colours of the guild. They carry the cheeses (sometimes 80 Edam cheeses at a time) on litters, to the scales for them to be weighed and then load them on to carts. (In fact all this is just for show; the actual cheese market is held in the exchange.)

Alkmaar's impressive townscape, with its many 16th–18th c. historic buildings, guild-houses and gentlemen's homes, has been preserved intact. A delightful way of getting to know Alkmaar is to take a canal tour (departure: Mient, near the weigh-house; April–October). The finest and most important historic buildings include:

★Townscape

The Grote or St Laurens Kerk (Kerkplein), built 1470–1516, is a Late-Gothic cruciform basilica with a famous organ (1645) by Jacob van Campen. The carillon in the crossing-tower dates from the late 17th c.

Grote Kerk

The Late-Gothic eastern section and the tower of the town-hall (Langestraat) were built at the beginning of the 16th c., while the western section dates from 1694. The interior is well worth seeing (open: Mon.–Fri. 9am–noon, 2–4pm).

Stadhuis

The weigh-house, which was converted in 1582 from the former Church of the Holy Ghost, boasts a beautiful tower which was added in 1599. The carillon dates from 1688.
  Inside the weigh-house is a cheese museum (open: Apr.–Oct. Mon.–Thur., Sat. 10am–4pm; Fri. 9am–4pm) which recreates before the visitor's very eyes the cheese and butter-making techniques of previous centuries. Information is also given on present-day dairy production and the Netherlands dairy industry.

Weigh-house

The municipal museum (Doelenstraat 3) is housed in a building which served as a militia guild in the 17th c. – up until the beginning of this century this organisation was responsible for law enforcement. Apart from some 16th/17th c. paintings, the museum is worth visiting for its toy collection (open: Tues.–Fri. 10am–5pm; Sun. 1–5pm).

Stedelijk
Museum

Amstel

The River Amstel, which originates in the low-lying Amstellands, gave Amsterdam its name. It flows through the city from south to north and at the spot where it used to empty into the IJ a dam was built in 1270. Today, however, the Amstel ends near the Muntplein and its waters go into the canal system which branches off here in all directions.

Course
Centre and
southern area
of the city

In the city centre near the Stopera (see entry) the canalised river is spanned by the Blauwbrug (Blue Bridge). It gets its name from an earlier bridge which was built at this spot. The existing bridge was built in 1884 and was modelled on one of the bridges across the Seine in Paris.
  From the Blauwbrug one can look across to the Magere Brug (see entry), one of the most photographed views in Amsterdam.

Blauwbrug

The dominating architectural feature at the northern end of the Amstel is the "two-in-one" building of the Stopera (city hall and opera house; see entry). Also of interest, besides the many charming canal houses, is the Theater Carré (see entry) on the east bank of the Amstel.

Stopera
Theater Carré

Further south (by Sarphatistraat) is the impressive Grand Hotel Amstel, re-opened in 1992 after extensive renovation work. This Neo-Renaissance building was conceived in the French château tradition and erected in 1863–67.

Hotel Amstel

On the Amstel river

Amsterdamse Bos (Amsterdam Wood)   C–F 9/10

Location
Nieuwe Kalfjes-
laan, Amstelveen

Bus
70 (Bosbaan)

The Amsterdam Wood was created in 1934 during the Depression as the result of a "job-creation scheme", designed to guarantee work for 1000 men over five years. In the 900ha/2000 acre area on the south-west edge of the city (twenty times as big as the Vondelpark (see entry) in the city centre and larger than the Bois de Boulogne in Paris) grow 150 types of tree from Canada, Japan, China, the Himalayas and North America, as well as shrubs and trees native to the Netherlands. The fauna of the wood is just as varied: there are some 200 species of bird and 700 different beetles (although to see them will require both luck and infinite patience!).

The wood is very popular with the people of Amsterdam and offers many sporting facilities, including riding, walking, cycling, jogging, fishing, swimming, rowing and sailing as well as restaurants and cafés.

Anyone wishing to stay longer here can make use of the camp site (see Practical Information, Camping).

Not to be missed is the Bosmuseum (Koenenkade 56; open: daily 10am–5pm), an information centre for visitors to the Amsterdamse Bos. As well as providing information about different leisure events and activities, it also presents the history of how the wood was established and the various ways in which it is now being put to commercial use. Stuffed animals are on display in the diorama.

★Amsterdams Historisch Museum   A 3

Location
Kalverstraat 92

This museum has been housed in the former municipal orphanage on the St Luciensteeg since 1975, when Amsterdam celebrated its 700th anni-

SECOND FLOOR

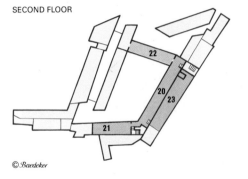

© Baedeker

Amsterdams Historisch Museum

in the former municipal orphanage

SECOND FLOOR

20 Handicrafts and trades in the 17th and 18th c.
21 Archaeology
22 Room for lectures and film shows
23 Reception room for groups

FIRST FLOOR

© Baedeker

FIRST FLOOR

8 Work through trade (17th/18th c.)
9 Magnet for artists (17th c.)
10 Religious freedom
10A Clock room
11 Rich and poor (17th/18th c.)
12 The 18th c.
13 Art in the 18th c.
14 House furnishings (18th c.)
15 Street pictures (18th c.)
16 "Gentle" revolution/capital of the Netherlands (19th c.)
17 Lead-in to the present
18 Copperplate engravings (temporary exhibitions)
19 Library

GROUND FLOOR

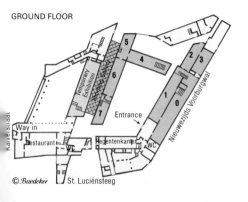

© Baedeker St. Luciënsteeg

GROUND FLOOR

0 Cloakroom, Bookshop, Information
1 In the course of time
2 Origins of the city
3 Commercial city/place of pilgrimage (14th/15th c.)
4 Growth and development in the 16th c.
5 On the world's seas (17th/18th c.)
6 Powerful city (17th/18th c.)
7 Prosperity and war in the 17th and 18th c.

41

Amsterdams Historisch Museum

Doorway of the Historical Museum

Exterior of Anne Frank's house

Tram
1, 2, 4, 5, 9, 16, 24, 25

Opening Times
Mon.–Fri.
10am–5pm,
Sat., Sun.
11am–5pm.
Closed Jan. 1,
Apr. 30, Dec. 25

versary. The name Luciensteeg harks back to the monastery of St Lucia, founded in 1414, which, besides a chapel and a brewery, also had a farm (today restaurant and museum). After the dissolution of the monastery this was the municipal orphanage from 1578 to 1960. A reminder of this past is provided by a saying of Joost van den Vondel over the gateway at the entrance from Kalverstraat: "... Do not pass through this gate without helping us to bear our burden". On the relief above the motto, orphan children are depicted, next to a dove symbolising the Holy Spirit. The gateway with its arms of the city was built in 1581 by Joost Beeldsnijder.

The entrance from St Luciensteeg is also noteworthy. Here 47 "façade stones" have been inserted into the museum wall. Similar types of stones decorated with symbols and inscriptions are usually to be found halfway up on the façades of canal houses. Until the end of the 18th c. they served not only as an embellishment, but also indicated who lived in the house and what his profession was. The façade stones in the museum wall all come from buildings which have no longer been preserved or have been completely renovated.

The buildings of the former orphanage, which are grouped around spacious courtyards, were completely renovated between 1963 and 1975. The outer façades to a large extent retained their original appearance. An exception is the so-called "marksman's gallery", a kind of "museum passage" which is open to anyone. Enormous group portraits of members of the militia guild hang here.

The museum itself uses modern methods to illustrate the past. The visitor can learn about the constantly changing position of Amsterdam in the country and in the world, the growth of the city and the port and the life of its citizens in its streets and in the home. The exhibits range from prehistoric finds and the town's original charter, to items from the present day. Reclamation of the land from the sea is explained by means of slides. Special exhibitions illustrate particular aspects of Amsterdam's varied history.

The library possesses a rich collection of literature on the history of the city. In addition graphics, drawings and the Fodor Bequest can be inspected by arrangement.

Library

A less well-known way of reaching the museum is by crossing the medieval Begijnhof (see entry), which links directly with the inner courtyard of the museum.

Begijnhof

★Anne Frank Huis (Anne Frank's House)　　　H 5

Prinsengracht No. 263 is the house where the Frank family, Jewish refugees from Frankfurt, and their friends hid from the Germans between 1942 and 1944. Here Anne Frank wrote her famous diary, which has been translated into 55 languages. In it she describes the life they led in the inner reaches of the building, their loneliness and fear. The last diary entry is dated August 1st 1944. On August 4th the fugitives were arrested and taken to concentration camps. Only Anne Frank's father, Otto Frank, survived; Anne Frank herself died two months before the end of the war in the Bergen–Belsen concentration camp (see Famous People).

In 1957 the house was given by its owner to the Anne Frank Foundation, who had it restored. In the front part of the house, where Otto Frank had his business, space was created for exhibitions, while the inner part of the house, where the Frank family took refuge, was to a large extent left exactly as it was. The rooms, however, are no longer furnished, the contents having been confiscated by the Nazis, and Otto Frank, when the matter was broached to him in 1962, preferred that the furnishings should not be reconstructed. Nearly 600,000 visitors every year since then have unfortunately taken their toll, and it is therefore planned to build a new extension by 1998 to house exhibitions and offices (the museum will remain open during this period).

The tour of Anne Frank's House begins with a video-show, which among other things gives some idea of how the family lived in the house. A revolving bookcase – specially designed and constructed for its purpose – gives access to the inner part of the house (the ascent is extremely narrow!). A glazed corridor finally leads back into the front part of the house. Here an exhibition provides information on the story of Anne Frank and her family against the background of National Socialism in Germany. The original diary can be seen in a display-case.

There is additional documentation dealing with the history of National Socialism and anti-Semitism, which resulted in the tragic death of six million Jews. Other temporary exhibitions, however, make it clear that persecution of minorities sadly still takes place even now and present-day manifestations of fascism, anti-Semitism, racism and discrimination are examined.

Location
Prinsengracht 263

Buses
21, 67

Trams
13, 14, 17

Opening times
Mon.–Sat.
9am–5pm,
Sun. 10am–5pm
(June–Sept.
until 7pm)

★Artis (Zoo Natura Artis Magistra)　　　J/K 6

Amsterdam Zoo was set up by a private association calling itself Natura Artis Magistra ("Nature is the instructor of Art"), from which the zoo got its name. The aim was to give city dwellers a better understanding of the world of nature by means of exhibits and live animals. In 1838 a site was acquired in the Plantage Middenlaan and the zoo that was built there came to be known as Artis, an abbreviation of the Latin name.

There were few animals to start with but their numbers soon grew, for example by purchases from travelling menageries. In its first hundred years the zoo was open only to members of the Association, who came here for Sunday walks and attended the concerts held here in the summer months. When the Association got into financial difficulties the city of

Location
Plantage
Kerklaan 38–40

Trams
7, 9, 14

Opening times
daily 9am–5pm

Amsterdam Zoo – a pleasure not only for children

Amsterdam and the Province of North Holland bought the zoo in 1937 and rented it to the Association for the nominal annual sum of one guilder, since when the zoo has been open to the general public.

From the start the site has been continuously extended and modernised. Most of the animals live in outdoor enclosures which correspond as closely as possible to their natural habitats. The zoo's main attractions are the aquarium – with 700 species of fish the second largest collection in the world (after Berlin) – and the nocturnal animal house.

In 1988 a planetarium was opened on the Artis site as an additional attraction, followed in 1992 by the Geological Museum (the entry ticket to the zoo also entitles the holder to visit the museums and planetarium). There is a special "hands-on" zoo for small children, while adults will probably find more of interest in the hothouses.

Zoological Museum

The Zoological Museum (closed Mon.) is housed in the same building as the aquarium and has collections of insects, birds, amphibians and reptiles. A diorama gives a three-dimensional picture of a dune landscape with its rich diversity of flora and fauna. Temporary exhibitions are concerned mainly with comparisons between animal and human behaviour.

Geological Museum

The Geological Museum possesses an extensive collection of fossils, minerals and rocks. The visitor is also confronted in a graphic way with the beginning and development of life on earth, from single-cell forms of life, through the dinosaur period to the emergence of mammals. Another exhibition room provides information on natural forces, volcanoes, earthquakes, continental drifts and many other topics.

Artis Expres

Amsterdam Zoo can also be reached by boat. The "Artis Expres" plies between the Centraal Station and the zoo. On board a video is shown which gives the visitor a foretaste of what to expect at Artis. A short halt is made at the Scheepvaart Museum (seafaring museum).

1 Bird house	12 Chimpanzees	23 Elephants
2 Flamingoes, Waterfowl	13 Penguins	24 Wolves, Hyenas
3 Zebra	14 Guanacos (wild llamas)	25 Tigers, Panthers
4 Gibbons, Waterfowl	14 Brown Bears, Polar Bears	26 Lions
5 Ibex	16 Gorillas	27 Flamingoes, Ducks
6 Small mammals	17 Tapirs	28 Pelicans, Cormorants
7 Kangaroos, Mufflon	18 Hippopotamus	29 Reptile house
8 Antelope, Birds	19 Cranes	30 Monkey house
9 Pheasants	20 Bison	31 Bird house
10 Ibis	21 Chamois	32 Camels, Yaks
11 Wolves	22 Giraffes, Antelope	33 Monkey Rock

★ Begijnhof (Beguine Court)   A 3

The Begijnhof is a tiny idyllic spot in the centre of the city where nowadays elderly ladies without families and young women students live for a very low rent.

The green lawn of the inner courtyard is surrounded by houses which include some of the oldest in Amsterdam.

In 1346 the buildings, which at that time still lay outside the city boundaries, were endowed for pious Catholic girls (begijnen) who wanted to live in a religious community but not in the seclusion of a convent. They devoted themselves to the care of the poor and sick. In a "Begijnhof" they were not called upon to abandon their personal freedom and could leave whenever they wished. They had their own accommodation and were not required to renounce personal possessions.

When Amsterdam went over to Protestantism the "begijnen" had to make their church over to the English Presbyterian community and hold their services in secret in a small chapel opposite the church. The Begijnhof was turned into almshouses but the "begijnen" retained the right to be buried in their "old" church. The last "begijn" died in 1971.

Location
Gedempte
Begijnensloot
(entrance in
Spui)

Trams
1, 2, 4, 5, 9, 16, 24,
25

Beurs van Berlage

See Koopmansbeurs

Centraal Spoorweg Station (Main Railway Station)   H/J 5 (C 1)

More than 1000 trains, including 50 international ones, travel in and out of Amsterdam's central station every day. Its architect was P. J. H. Cuypers (also architect of the Rijksmuseum – see entry) and it was built on three artificial islands and 8687 piles. On the north side of the station (de Ruij-

Location
de Ruijterkade

Begijnhof: an idyllic retreat in the centre of the city

Centraal Spoorweg Station: built on three artificial islands

terkade), facing the harbour, are the moorings of numerous motor-boats and ferries.

The need for the station became apparent when in 1860 Amsterdam was linked to Alkmaar and Den Helder to the north. The public joined in its opening in 1889 with considerable enthusiasm and bought as many as 14,000 platform tickets for the occasion.

The station building was conceived in the historicist style and shows clear echoes of Neo-Classical palace architecture. Many of the decorations point to the Renaissance. The art nouveau first-class waiting room is especially worth seeing.

The station building even attracted international attention: when in 1900 the Japanese were looking for a model for Tokyo station their choice fell on Amsterdam.

Buses
18, 21, 22, 28, 31–36, 39, 91, 92, 94, 100 and others

Trams
1, 2, 4, 5, 9, 13, 16, 17, 20, 24, 25

Metro
Centraalstation

Concertgebouw   G 7

The building of the most famous concert hall in the Netherlands was inspired by a German. In 1879 Amsterdam music-lovers invited Johannes Brahms to conduct his third symphony. After the concert Brahms commented: "You are good people, but bad musicians!" The people of Amsterdam took this harsh criticism to heart and formed a society to establish an orchestra and a concert hall which would seat about 2000. Work on the building, which was designed by A. van Gendt, began in 1882 and in 1888 the concert hall was officially opened. At that time it actually lay outside the city boundaries.

The 65-member orchestra was entrusted to Willem Kes, who laid the foundations for the fine reputation both of the orchestra and of the concert hall. Kes's successor was the 24-year-old Willem Mengelberg, who was associated with the Concertgebouw Orchestra for 50 years. Under his direction it developed into one of the best orchestras in the world and it was Mengelberg who introduced the symphonic music of Mahler and Richard Strauss.

Richard Strauss dedicated his "Ein Helderleben" to Mengelberg, while the 1920 Mahler music festival became a high point in the history of the concert hall. The composers Reger, Debussy, Ravel, Hindemith, Milhaud and Stravinsky conducted performances of their own works in the hall.

In the early 80s, however, there were fears for the future of this great concert hall when the building, weighing about 10,000 tonnes and underpinned by 2000 posts, threatened to subside into the muddy subsoil. New foundations were the saving of the building, which also got a new glass foyer as part of the renovation works (completed in 1988). The actual hall itself, whose acoustics are considered to be among the best in the world, remained unaltered.

Location
Van Baerle-straat 98

Buses
63, 170, 179

Trams
3, 5, 12, 16

Dam   H 6 (B 2)

The Dam, with the Royal Palace (see Koninklijk Paleis), the New Church (see Nieuwe Kerk) and National Monument, is no longer either geographically or administratively the centre of Amsterdam, but has remained the heart of the city. It was the dam which gave the city its name: built about 1270 it separated the Amstel from the IJ (an arm of the Zuiderzee; see entry). Amsterdam's history began here with the founding of the original settlement trading in fish and cattle. As in the past, the people of Amsterdam still assemble on the Dam for official events.

In the early days of the square a market grew up here, known, in accordance with medieval custom, as the "Plaetse", and today the square still retains its market character.

Since 1991 Madame Tussaud's Scenerama (see entry) has been situated on the Dam.

Location
west of the city centre

Trams
4,9,16,24,25

Madame Tussaud's

Nationaal Monument (National Monument)

The National Monument, a 22m/72ft high obelisk, was erected on the Dam after the Second World War. This memorial to the victims of the war and monument to the Liberation and peace was designed by J. J. P. Oud and decorated with sculptures by J. W. Rädeler symbolising, among other things, War (four male figures), Peace (woman and child) and Resistance (two men with howling dogs). Embedded in the obelisk are urns containing earth from the eleven provinces. A twelfth urn contains earth from the cemetery of honour in Indonesia.

The monument was dedicated by Queen Juliana on May 4th 1956, the national day of remembrance, and since then the Dutch Queen and her consort have laid wreaths here every year on that day. A two-minute silence is observed throughout the Netherlands at 8 o'clock that same evening. The rest of the year the Liberation monument is a favourite gathering-place for young people from all over the world, who come and sit on the steps to discuss things and make music.

Delft   Excursion

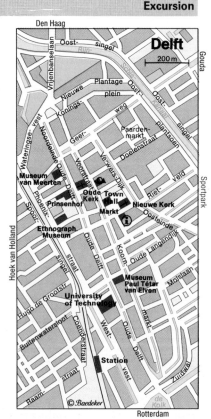

Location
60km/37 miles south-west

Rail
from Centraal Station

Delft lies on the River Schie in the province of South Holland. This town of princes is famous for its blue Delft earthenware and for its annual art and antiques fair.

Delft received its charter in 1246 and from the 13th c. onwards brewing and carpet-making were of considerable importance. Prince William of Orange made Delft his seat in 1580. Chiefly as a result of its earthenware production, the town reached the peak of its prosperity in the 17th c. when it had 30 tile potteries (1650–1760), but by 1854 only the Royal Delft China Factory "De Porceleyne Fles" remained, and this won a new claim to fame as the manufacturer of Delft-blue china (Rotterdamse Weg 196; can be visited).

★Townscape

A visit to Delft will concentrate on its picturesque old town which is enclosed by a network of canals. The following historic buildings should on no account be missed:

The Nieuwe Kerk (New Church) is a Gothic cruciform basilica situated in the market square. Its high tower (ascents possible from April to September) has a carillon dating from 1663. In the choir will be found the magnificent tomb of William of Orange (dating from 1614–21), one of the masterpieces of Dutch Baroque sculpture, which was the work of Hendrik de Keyser. In the summer months organ concerts take place in the church.

Nieuwe Kerk

Hendrik de Keyser was also the architect of the Stadhuis (town hall), which occupies the west side of the market square. Its gable is decorated by a sculpture of Justitia. The interior contains some 16th–18th c. paintings.

Stadhuis

A short distance to the north-west of the Stadhuis stands the Oude Kerk (Old Church), which was built in 1250 but has subsequently been altered on a number of occasions. The slightly leaning tower, originally dating from the 14th c., was given four corner turrets and a pyramid-shaped main section in 1450. The artistic treasures to be found inside include a magnificent chancel (1548) and the tomb of Piet Hein (d. 1629), who defeated the Spanish fleet in 1628.

Oude Kerk

Opposite the Oude Kerk stands the Prinsenhof. Originally founded as the Convent of St Agatha around 1400, it was secularised after the Reformation. From 1575 it was for many years a residence of the House of Orange. The Prinsenhof has a tragic place in Dutch history for it was here that Prince William of Orange, the architect of Dutch independence, was assassinated in 1584 (the mark left by the bullet can still be seen on the stairway leading to the former refectory).

Prinsenhof

The picturesque group of buildings is occupied by the Stedelijk Museum (open: Tues.–Sat. 10am–5pm, Sun. 1–5pm). It is devoted mainly to the 80-year war between the Dutch and the Spanish. The oldest part of the convent contains a double-galleried cloister unique to the Netherlands.

The Prinsenhof is the venue for the annual antiques fair at the end of October as well as its famous concerts.

The Museum Huis Lambert van Meerten (open: Tues.–Sat. 10am–5pm, Sun. 1–5pm), situated to the north of the Prinsenhof, occupies two storeys and boasts an important collection of furniture and paintings, as well as a rich selection of Delftware.

Museum Huis Lambert van Meerten

Also of interest is the Museum Paul Tétar van Elven (open: mid-April–October: Tues.–Sat. 11am–5pm), which is set up in an 18th c. gentleman's house. The museum has brought together the collection of the painter Paul Tétar van Elven (1823–96), who taught at the former Polytechnic School (now the Technical University). His studio, old furniture and Delft pottery convey a vivid impression of the 19th c. world in which he lived.

Museum Paul Tétar van Elven

Driegrachtenhuis (House on three canals)

See Achterburgwal

Edam

The historic town of Edam in North Holland is situated in the polder region adjoining the IJsselmeer and is world-famous for its red and yellow-skinned cheeses. The town's inhabitants work in industry, agriculture, cattle-rearing and fishing.

Location
15km/9 miles north

Edam grew up near the dam in the River Ee which linked the little River Purmer with the Zuiderzee. When in 1230 work was begun on damming the rivers flowing into the Zuiderzee (see General Information, Land Reclamation and also Zuiderzee · IJsselmeer), merchandise was transported here.

Buses
Depart from opposite Centraal Station

Soon customs duties were levied and the township became a trading centre. As early as 1357 Edam received its charter, but the town enjoyed its heyday in the 16th to 18th c. when shipbuilding, herring fishing and cheese brought economic prosperity to the town. (The warships with which Admiral de Ruyter defeated the English were built in Edam's shipyards.) In 1573 William of Orange granted Edam the right to its own weigh-house as a reward for its bravery and services in helping to lift the siege of Alkmaar.

Grote Kerk

The Grote or St Nicolaas Kerk, as it is also known, (Grote Kerkstraat; open: April–October daily 2–4.30pm) is a Late-Gothic church with a 15th c. tower and wonderful stained-glass windows dating from the 17th c. The interior furnishings of the church also date predominantly from the 17th c.

Stadhuis

The Stadhuis (town hall) is on Damplein and was built in 1737. The registry office still has sand on the floor as it did in the Middle Ages. The council chamber is well worth seeing and contains a small exhibition of paintings.

Speeltoren

From the 15th c. tower of the now demolished Church of the Virgin Mary the oldest carillon in the Netherlands (1560) rings out.

Stedelijk Museum

The municipal museum (Damplein 8; open from Easter to mid-October: Mon.–Sat. 10am–4.30pm, Sun. 1.30–4.30pm), in a house dating from 1540 with an attractive façade (1737). The floating cellar is in the shape of a ship.

Note

The stretch of water between the two bridges on Spuistraat is known as "Boerenverdriet" (farmers' dismay), because the farmers' boats often used to get stuck here. In July and August boat trips can be made on the IJsselmeer.

Entrepotdok   J/K 6

Location
east of the
city centre

Buses
31, 22

Tram
7

Wharf Museum

Some years ago the old storehouses on Entrepotdok were transformed into one of the most sought-after residential areas in Amsterdam. The houses, which date back to the 18th and 19th c., were originally temporary storage places for dutiable goods. They were completely renovated and turned into both owner-occupier and council dwellings. The present-day residents have a view of the grounds of Artis (see entry) to the south.

The best way to reach Entrepotdok is via a bridge near the entrance to Artis. Since its creation the district has developed a special atmosphere all of its own: artists have set up their studios in some of the houses and bars have been opened.

Just to the north-east of Entrepotdok is the Wharf Museum (Werft t' Kromhout; see Practical Information, Museums).

Haarlem   Excursion

Location
18km/11 miles
west

Buses
Depart opposite
Centraal
Station

Haarlem, the capital of the province of North Holland, lies between Amsterdam and the North Sea on the tiny River Spaarne (hence its other name "Spaarnestad") at a distance of 7km/4 miles from the coast. This typically Dutch town is part of Randstad Holland and forms a continuous built-up area with the neighbouring communities of Heemstede, Bloemendaal and Zandvoort. Haarlem is the cultural centre of southern Kennemerland. Visible signs of this function are a Roman Catholic and an Old Catholic diocese and several research institutes, educational establishments and libraries. In addition Haarlem is important as an industrial town, with its most significant activities being its docks, railway works, printing works, machine and vehicle building, as well as basic and luxury foodstuffs.

The town has achieved fame, however, through the growing and selling of bulbs, such as tulips, hyacinths, crocuses and narcissi. Haarlem bulbs are shipped all over the world.

Entrepotdok: old warehouses now provide comfortable living accommodation

In the 17th c. Haarlem was the scene of lively artistic activity and many painters lived here, including Frans Hals, Jacob van Ruisdael, Philips Wouverman and Adriaen van Ostade. The town's architect, Lieven de Key (*c.* 1560–1627), founded a school of architecture, the achievements of which are amply demonstrated by the public buildings and numerous old gabled houses in the old town.

The old part of the town, which dates from earlier centuries, has as its centre the Grote Markt. Ten separate streets lead into it and this lively shopping area is closed to cars. In the middle of the market place stands a statue of L. J. Coster, a contemporary of Gutenberg, who is thought to be the person who actually invented printing.

★ Townscape, Grote Markt

The most striking building on the Grote Markt is the 140m/460ft long Grote or St Bavokerk, a Late-Gothic cruciform basilica with a slender 80m/260ft high crossing-tower. The building's long history began with the construction of the choir in the 14th c. In the middle of the 15th c. the transept, by the Antwerp architect Spoorwater, was added. Around 1425 the original nave was replaced by one 125m/410ft long. Two low and narrow side aisles are located on either side of it. In 1520 the crossing-tower was completed, with its beautiful Hemony carillon which peals every evening. In 1536 the wooden vaulting in the choir and nave were finished. The artistry with which the cedarwood ceiling of the main nave is fashioned could have only been found in a land of shipbuilders. The ceiling is borne on 28 round pillars. After the Reformation the church was extended with a baptistry on the south side (1593) and a consistory (1658).

★ Grote or St Bavokerk

The larger part of the interior dates from before the Reformation, including the choir with its choir-desk (1499), the beautifully carved choir-seats (1512) and the copper choir-grille (1509–17). Also of interest is the organ, built in 1735–38 by Christian Müller with its monumental panelling

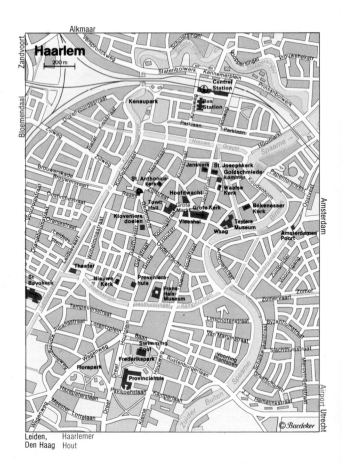

Leiden,   Haarlemer
Den Haag   Hout

by the wood-carver and sculptor, Jan van Logteren. Händel, Mozart and Albert Schweitzer all performed on this instrument.

Stadhuis

On the other side of the market place stands Haarlem's town hall. The oldest parts of the building can be traced back to a hunting-lodge belonging to Count William II (1250), King of Germany. At the end of the 13th c. the Dominicans gained the permission of Count Floris V to build a monastery behind the hunting-lodge, with a chapter-hall, cloisters and a church.

The chaos caused by the independence struggle and later during the wars of religion led to the town hall, monastery and church being severely damaged. In 1579 the latter two came into the possession of the town. In 1590 part of the monastery was turned into the prince's court and used as accommodation befitting the rank of governors and other guests.

The Flemish refugee Lieven de Key was appointed municipal architect in 1593 and in 1597 was charged with designing an exterior staircase. Between 1620 and 1622 he built the building's north wing which adjoins Zijlstraat. A few years later (1630–33) the façade was restored in Neo-Classical style. Around 1860 another storey was added to the cloisters. The prince's court was used as a municipal archive until 1936. In the ensuing period another new wing was added along Koningstraat and Jacobijnenstraat

To the right stands the Hoofdwacht (police station). It is one of the oldest buildings in the town and its front gable dates back to 1650. This used to be the town's main police station and was probably also the earliest town hall in Haarlem.

Hoofdwacht

On the south side of the market place is the Meat Hall, built by Lieven de Key in 1602–03. It is generally considered to be the most outstanding example of northern Renaissance architecture and used to serve as a slaughterhouse and butchers' guildhall all in one. Today it is an annexe of the Frans Hals Museum.

Vleeshal

Near the Grote Kerk stands the Vishal (fish hall), also built by Lieven de Key, which was formerly used by traders in seafish and now houses the modern art section of the Frans Hals Museum. The building has a red and white façade and is crowned by a stepped gable as well as attractive decorative gables on the roof.

Vishal

By following the Jansstraat, which goes north from the Grote Kerk, the visitor will see the Janskerk (14th c.) on the left-hand side. Formerly a convent church, the building is now the town archive.

Janskerk

Not far from the market place across the Begijnhof is the Goudsmidspleintje with the goldsmiths' chamber. A gable-stone in the façade indicates that this was where the Haarlem silver and goldsmiths had their headquarters in the 17th and 18th c.

Goudsmitkamer

Further south in the middle of the Begijnhof stands the 14th c. Waalse Kerk, originally the Begijns' convent church, with its 16th c. sacristy. Since the Reformation it has been a Walloon church.

Waalse Kerk

Just a short distance back in a southerly direction is Teylers Museum. It was opened in 1778 and is therefore the oldest museum in the Netherlands. Pieter Teyler van der Hulst (1702–78), a wealthy cloth and silk dealer, was interested in art and science. He left instructions for the whole of his fortune to be used to build this museum, the purpose of which was to trace the development of both art and science. The museum's possessions include a large number of hand drawings and paintings by old Dutch masters, Michelangelo and Raphael, as well as a section on natural history.

Teylers Museum

Next to the museum stands the town weigh-house, built from ashlar in 1597–89 by Lieven de Key. It was used until 1915 for weighing goods which were transported across the Spaarne by boat.

Waag

Further east, on the other side of the Binnen Spaarne, stands the medieval Amsterdamse Poort, the only one of Haarlem's original town gates to have survived, dating from about 1400. Alongside the main building are two octagonal towers. On the outside of the building, in front of the canal and next to the gate itself, there are two round-towers. On the inside, at the base of the building, remains of the old town wall can still be seen.

Amsterdamse Poort

The former house for old men in the southern part of the old town (Groot Heiligland 62) is another important building by Lieven de Key (1608). In 1913 the municipal art collection was moved here from the town hall. Today it occupies a pre-eminent position among the country's art galleries. Painters from Haarlem predominate.

★Frans Hals Museum

The main focus of interest in the section of the museum devoted to Old Art is provided by the militia and regent group portraits by Frans Hals (b. between 1581 and 1585, d. 1666), the most vivid and expressive of all Dutch

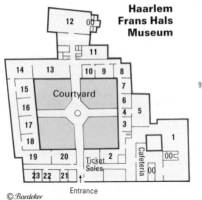

**Haarlem
Frans Hals
Museum**

1 Modern art
2 15th/16th c.; Mostaert, etc.
3 16th c.: Scorel,
van Heemskerck
4 16th c.: van Haarlem, etc.
5 Academy Hall
6 17th c.: Vroom, van Dyck
7 17th c.: Molenaer
8 17th c.: van Goyen
9, 10 18th c.: Regents' Room
11 Chapel
12 Marksmen's portraits
13 Renaissance Room
14 Gilded Leather Room
15 Regents' portraits
16 Verspronck, Heda
17 De Braj, Jan Steen, etc.
18 Regents' portraits by Frans
Hals
19 18th century
20 19th century
21 Miniatures
22 Old Pharmacy
23 Glass Cabinet

© *Baedeker*

painters. In addition there are a large number of portraits from the 17th c., still life pictures, genre paintings and landscapes with works by Adriaen van Ostade, Jacob van Ruisdael, Johannes Verspronck, Jan de Bray, Pieter Claesz and Willem Heda. A selection of Haarlem silver, an old dolls' house and a reconstructed chemist's shop with Delftware can also be seen. The collection of modern and contemporary art includes paintings, sculptures, textiles, ceramics, graphics and objects by artists from Haarlem and the surrounding area, such as Isaac Israël, Jan Sluyters, Karel Appel, Reinier Lucassen and Herman Kruyder (open: Mon.–Sat. 11am–5pm, Sun. 1–5pm).

Proveniershuis

In the Grote Houtstraat, one of the most important shopping streets in the town, stands the Proveniershuis (No. 144), built in 1591, with its richly decorated gable and large gateway. In 1700 dwelling-houses for old men were built around the inner courtyard.

Nieuwe Kerk

From the Raamvest a right turn leads into Korte Annastraat, which contains a square brick building, the Niuewe Kerk. After the original building on this site was burnt down, a new church in the same style was designed by the architect Jacob van Campen and erected between 1645 and 1649. The graceful Renaissance tower built by Lieven de Key in 1613 is, however, still preserved. Of interest is the magnificent Baroque marble tomb of William of Orange, which was fashioned by Hendrik and Pieter de Keyser in 1614. In the cemetery next to the church the painter van Ruisdael and Wouwerman are buried.

**St Bavo
Kathedraal**

The Catholic diocesan church, St Bavo Kathedraal, is located at Leidsevaart 146 in the west of the town. This three-aisled cruciform basilica (100m/330ft long, 42m/138ft wide and 60m/200ft high) was built by J. Cuypers in 1895–1906 and is a good example of the transitional period which ushered in modern architecture. It also brings together Neo-Gothic and even Moorish elements. The tower was not added until 1927–30. The interior contains a treasury with valuable silver tools and instruments and a reliquary (including relics of St Bavo).

★ Haven (Port)   E–M 2–6

Location
north and east
of the centre

The port of Amsterdam is 18.5km/12 miles from the open sea and, thanks to the IJmuiden sluices, is unaffected by the state of the tide. Several thousand ships call here annually, trans-shipments amounting to some 31 million tonnes per year. The port is also important for passenger transport, with more than 100,000 passengers being processed each year.

The port installations were begun in 1872 in conjunction with the construction of the North Sea Canal, the aim being to restore the former importance of the capital city, which was being overtaken by Rotterdam. It is well worth taking one of the cruises through the canals, "Steiger" (de Ruijterkade) and harbour areas. The service is continuous during the summer months and at regular intervals in winter. The trip is especially impressive in the evening when the houses and bridges are illuminated.

The entire dock area was reclaimed from the IJ. Its channel was deepened and artificial islands with landing quays were built alongside. On the south bank of the IJ there is a series of large wet-docks including the Westerdok (with the quay of the Holland–America Line, Stenenhoofd, on the far side), the Oosterdok and the IJhaven, as well as important dockyards.

West of the Westerdok lie the Houthaven (timber), the Minervahaven, the Coenhaven and the spectacular Petroleumhaven, which gives access to the North Sea Canal.

Further west are the Westhaven docks with loading facilities for coal, crude oil, ore and grain, and with oil storage tanks, refineries and chemical plant.

On the north bank of the IJ there are several smaller docks and the locks of the North Holland Canal. Just west of the central station stands the 13-storey Port Administration building, built in 1958–60 by Dudok van Heel, which is 60m/200ft high and has a restaurant with a panoramic view. The Scheepvaart Museum (see entry), the Dutch maritime museum, is located on the Oosterdok.

At the purpose-built Amsterdam Container Terminal container vehicles can be driven straight into the holds of roll-on roll-off vessels. The opening of the Amsterdam–Rhine Canal in 1952 made for considerably improved links with the European hinterland so far as bulk cargo handling is concerned. The free port is used for storing wine, rum, expensive carpets, machine parts and many other commodities.

Buses
18, 21, 22, 28, 31–36, 39, 91, 92, 94, 100, 104 and others

Trams
1, 2, 4, 5, 9, 13, 16, 17, 20, 24, 25

Metro
Centraalstation

Boats
Mooring place "Steiger" (de Ruijterkade)

Heineken Brouwerij (Heineken Brewery)   H 7

The Heineken Brewery, one of the largest in the country, used to have its headquarters on the corner of Stadhouderskade and Ferdinand Bolstraat. The largest production site, however, is now sited in Zoeterwoude near Leiden. However a guided tour through the former brewery buildings, situated on the southern edge of the centre of Amsterdam, is of considerable interest.

The Heineken Brewery was granted its brewing licence in the middle of the last century. At the same time it acquired the old-established "Hoolberg" brewery, which had been in existence since the Middle Ages, when barley brew was the national drink. The rival "Amstel" was bought up in 1968. Today Heineken is the largest export brewery in the world with a whole range of subsidiaries and about 30,000 employees.

The brewery's main product is Heineken lager, produced by the Pilsener method, with a not too pronounced flavour of hops. Heineken also brews a whole range of special beers for its domestic market. The "Amstel" beers, which are also marketed internationally under that name, are noticeably lighter and have a stronger taste.

Entrance
v.d.Helstraat 30

Trams
16, 24, 25

Visits
Mon.–Fri.
9.30 and 11am
(in summer also
1 and 2.30pm)

★★Herengracht   H 5/6 (A/B 1–5)

The origins of the Herengracht go back to the year 1612, when a plan to create a girdle of canals (Heren- Keizers- and Prinzengracht) was made. The project was completed in 1658.

Location
west and south
of the centre

Herengracht

In Amsterdam's heyday (the second half of the 17th c.) the Herengracht was the most elegant residential district. It was such a popular place to live that the magistrate had to confine the width of the aristocrats' houses to 8m/9yd, but of course there were exceptions, such as the "House for a Prince" (No. 54). Behind the aristocratic houses with their magnificent façades (no fewer than 400 houses in the Herengracht are protected monuments), beautiful gardens were concealed, each of them exactly 51.5m/169ft long. The layout of these gardens represented unbelievable luxury for a town which was basically constructed on piles. A law declared that they could not be built on, an exception, however, being made for summer-houses and coach-houses.

Today these gentlemen's houses are mostly occupied by banks and offices, the rents in the Herengracht having become prohibitive. Some of them house museums, which are worth a visit just for their superb architecture. A stroll along the Herengracht could begin close to Raadhuistraat, where the Theatre Museum is located.

Theatre Museum (No. 168)

The façade of No. 168 was designed in 1638 by Philips Vingboons. The building has three wings and is constructed out of light-coloured sandstone. It is dominated by a neck gable. The wall and ceiling paintings in the interior and the stuccoed staircase ensure that the building makes very much the same impression as it must have done when it was designed by Jacob de Wit in the 18th c.

The building has housed the Theatre Museum since 1960. By means of drawings, sculptures, paintings, posters and items of equipment, the history of Dutch theatre is brought to life. As well as the permanent exhibits there are also temporary displays which shed light on individual aspects of theatrical history (open: Tues.–Sun. 11am–5pm).

Herengracht: Bartolottihuis and . . .

. . . house on the corner of Leidsegracht

In the Museum of Cats on the Herengracht

The adjoining Bartolottihuis is also partly used by the Theatre Museum as an exhibition area. The house, whose ground plan follows the curve of the canal, was built in 1622 by Hendrik de Keyser for the brewer Willem van den Heuwel. As his wealth steadily increased, Heuwel gained control of the Bartolotti Bank, and subsequently even made the bank's fine-sounding name his own. The red-brick façade is in the style of Dutch Renaissance architecture, but also displays distinct Italian influences (pillars and vases).

Bartolottihuis
(No. 170/172)

The Huis van Brienen was originally built in 1720 for the Huguenot Frederic Blancard, but in 1781 the house passed into the possession of the van Brienen family. The latter bequeathed it in 1932, after it had stood empty for almost 100 years, to the Hendrik de Keyser Foundation, which was formed with the aim of taking over and restoring historic buildings.

Huis van Brienen
(No. 284)

The Bible Museum has been housed since 1975 in a pair of double-fronted houses which were built for Jakob Kromhout in 1662. The interior is the work of Jacob de Wit. The museum's collection can be divided into three areas: the "biblical archaeology" section displays finds from Egypt and the Middle East; under the motto "Temple and Tradition" another section shows how man in various civilisations has expressed his beliefs in architectural forms; the section "1000 Years in the Mother Tongue" offers an overview of the history of the Bible in the Netherlands (open: Tues.–Sat. 10am–5pm, Sun. 1–5pm).

Bijbels Museum
(No. 364–370)

The most noteworthy section of the Herengracht is the "golden bocht" or "golden bay", going from No. 436 to No. 464 (between Leidsestraat and Vijzelstraat). Along with various other well-to-do Amsterdam gentlemen or "heren" (hence the canal's name), the richest citizen of his time, the banker Jan Balde, used to reside here. His neighbour was a slave-trader, to which two black heads on the gateway testify.

Golden Bocht
(No. 436–464)

Hoorn

Kattenkabinet (No. 468)	A 17th c. building (which, however, underwent extensive alterations in 1874) houses the museum of cats (Kattenkabinet), which was opened in 1990. It is worth visiting the museum just for the interior decorations and furnishings, which were the work of Jacob de Wit from 1745–47. The exhibits (mainly photos, pictures and sculptures) are all connected with the theme of cats; there are temporary exhibitions on the ground floor (open: Tues.–Sat. 11am–5pm, Sun. noon–5pm).
Deutzhuis (No. 502)	This gentleman's house, which originally dated from earlier in the 18th c., was altered in 1792 for Deutz van Assendelft. The central entrance is flanked by two Doric columns. Since 1927 the building has been the official residence of the Burgomaster of Amsterdam.
No. 527	The house at No. 527 Herengracht has a special history. Of the original building, which was erected in 1667, only the high roof survives. The façade which we now see dates from 1770, while the windows were altered around 1800.
	The illustrious residents of this house have included Peter the Great of Russia, who stayed here during his stay in Holland. After the Tsar's visit, the house was in such a dreadful state, that the owner felt obliged to sell it. In 1808 it became the property of King Louis Napoleon, who lived here for some time. Today the house is occupied by the Incassobank.
No. 605	A delightful conclusion to a walk along the Herengracht is provided by a visit to the Museum Willet-Holthuysen (see entry) at no. 605.

Hoorn Excursion

Location 50km/31 miles north	The town of Hoorn, in the province of North Holland, is well worth visiting from Amsterdam. Situated on a bay in the IJsselmeer, the former capital of West Friesland has as its main claim to fame the fact that it used to be an international port, as its many historic buildings testify.
Buses depart from opposite the Centraal Station	Today Hoorn is an important shopping, leisure, cultural and educational centre and it is expected that the "Staatenpoort" will become more important as a residential town because of its excellent communications with Alkmaar and Amsterdam.

In the 14th c. Hoorn rapidly became the market centre of West Friesland and received its charter in 1356. In the second half of that century Hoorn already overshadowed the older towns of the Zuiderzee, Enkhuizen and Medemblik, and in the 16th c. the town became the major international port on the Zuiderzee. By the middle of the 17th c., however, Hoorn was already starting to decline in economic importance.

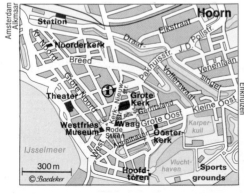

Hoorn numbers among its famous sons Willem Schouten, who sailed round the southern tip of America in 1616 and named it "Kap Hoorn" (Cape Horn) after his home town; Count Philip van Hoorn, a Knight of the Order of the Golden Fleece, who, together with Count Egmont, was executed in Brussels on June 5th 1568 for his part in the Dutch Wars of Independence against Spain; and Jan Pieterszoon Coen, Governor of the Dutch East Indies and founder of Batavia (now Djakarta, Indonesia).

An old Dutch market (Rodesteen) is held every Wednesday in July and August where ancient handicrafts are demonstrated by local people in period costume.

With its noteworthy 17th c. canal houses, Hoorn boasts a highly attractive townscape. The harbour scenery is also delightful with its harbour tower (16th and 17th c.) and the dyke (view of the IJsselmeer).

★Townscape

The Stadhuis, or town hall, stands in Nieuwstraat; built in 1402, it originally housed the St Cecilia convent. The council chamber (1787) occupies what was once the convent chapel and contains a painting by Blanderhoff (1633) of the sea-battle of 1573. In 1613 the façade of the convent building was given a new gable and a double staircase. The building was used by the town administration from 1796 although today it houses the Tourist Office.

Stadhuis

At the end of Nieuwstraat, on the Kerkplein, stands the Grote Kerk, dating from 1883, and the former St Jansgasthuis (1563) with an early Renaissance-style façade.

Grote Kerk, St Jansgasthuis

The old weigh-house of 1609 stands on Rode Steen. The building was designed by Hendrik de Keyser and was originally built of blue ashlar stones, but these were replaced by grey ones when restoration work took place in 1912.

Weigh-house

Opposite the weigh-house stands the Proostenhuis of 1632, formerly the seat of the West Friesland council, now the West Frisian Museum. It is noteworthy for its richly decorated façade of natural stone with the coats of arms of seven West Frisian towns, the arms of West Friesland and Orange. The façade was completely restored between 1908 and 1911. The museum includes exhibits (from the 16th to 18th c.) relating to the history of the town and the surrounding area, as well as a large number of pictures connected with shooting and hunting.

Westfries Museum

North-west of Rode Steen is the Late-Gothic Noorderkerk, which was begun in 1426 and finished in 1519. The interior contains an oak spiral staircase (1497), a choir screen (1642) and choir stalls in Renaissance style, which are all of considerable interest.

Noorderkerk

The Late-Gothic former Oosterkerk (begun in 1450) stands on Grote Oost. The choir and transept were added in 1519; the two-aisled nave was replaced by a simpler one (with a beautiful Renaissance façade) in 1615. The wooden crossing-tower and the glass painting date from the same period (1620). The sea-battle of Gibraltar (1607) is depicted beneath the West Frisian coat of arms. Also worthy of mention is the Bätz organ of 1764. Since the church's restoration many cultural events now take place here.

Oosterkerk

At the end of Kleine Oost, which adjoins to the east, a left turn leads to the Oosterpoort, part of the old town walls dating from the 16th c.

Oosterpoort

Hortus Botanicus (Botanical Garden)

J 6 (D 4)

The botanical garden of the municipal university contains over 6000 exotic flowers, trees and plants. Only a short time ago an extensive hothouse was built on the site. The garden's special treasures include a cycas palm (an genus of palm which is almost extinct) and an agave, which at almost 2000 years old, is one of the oldest pot-plants in the world. Another attraction is the herb garden, which is laid out in the 17th c. manner. However it is not necessary to be a botany specialist to gain pleasure from a visit to the botanical garden; anyone wishing to find an oasis of greenery amid the hustle and bustle of Amsterdam will enjoy coming here. The café housed in the old orangery is a pleasant place to sit.

Location
Plantage
Middenlaan 2

Tram: 9

Opening times
Mon.–Fri.
9am–4pm,
Sat., Sun.
11am–4pm
(in summer 5pm)

The botanical garden's history goes back to the time when monasteries and convents had herb gardens. In 1554, as a result of a book on plants appearing which dealt with the plants for their own sake and not just for their healing properties, the Botanical Garden of Vlooienburg came into being (with some 2000 indigenous trees, plants, herbs and shrubs). The garden was moved and extended on several occasions and in 1877 made over to the university.

IJsselmeer

See Zuiderzee

IJtunnel   J 5

Location
north-east of
the centre

Over 100 years ago people were looking at ways of linking Amsterdam with the opposite bank of the IJ in the north (link with North Holland). A tunnel was being considered even at that time (plans for a suspension bridge are even older), since the ferries to and from North Holland caused considerable delays. For a long time, however, such plans were thought unrealistic, and it was not until the beginning of this century that the city council was prepared seriously to examine the idea of a tunnel. From 1930 to 1950 countless designs were discussed and rejected but it was finally decided to build a tunnel for road vehicles only. Cyclists and pedestrians still have to use the ferries. On May 25th 1955 the first pile was driven into the ground but the project was dogged by organisational and financial problems and it was years before the work was completed at a total cost of over 20 million guilders. In October 1968 the tunnel was opened to traffic.

Jodenbuurt (Jewish Quarter)   J 6 (C/D 3/4)

Location
Around the
Waterlooplein

Trams
9, 14

Metro
Waterlooplein

The former Jewish quarter extends from the Houtkoopersburgwal in the north to the Binnen-Amstel in the south. The first Jewish refugees came to Amsterdam at the end of the 16th c. and settled in the area around the Waterlooplein (Jodenbreestraat, Valkenburgerstraat, Oude Schans). They were mostly from Portugal (see Portuguese Synagogue), but also from Germany and Poland. The Jewish quarter had a special charm, with its countless little second-hand shops, haberdashers and greengrocers.

A market used to be held on the Waterlooplein on Sundays, although it is hard to see how the dealers could make a living from selling their second-hand goods. After the Second World War hardly anything was left of what had once been the charming Jewish quarter around the Waterlooplein. Deportation robbed the quarter of its inhabitants – of the 140,000 Jews who lived in Amsterdam before the war only a fifth survived the Holocaust.

In the sixties the building of an expressway drastically changed the face of the quarter, then a cutting was made for the building of the Metro, leaving only a row of houses on the Amstel, until these too were demolished in 1976.

The Waterlooplein has made a comeback, however. Today it is the site of Amsterdam's opera house, "Het Muziektheater", which shares its building with the new city hall (see Stopera), and the Jewish past is recalled in the Joods Historisch Museum (see entry). The latest addition is the "Holland Experience" (see Practical Information, Museums), which was completed in September 1996.

Vlooienmarkt

Except for a gap of several years during the 1980s, the Waterlooplein has been the venue since 1886 of the Vlooienmarkt, Amsterdam's famous flea market (market times: Mon.–Sat. 10am–5pm).

"Whether there are fleas in the flea market in Amsterdam is hard to say; there is certainly everything else. Threadbare clothes, once the height of fashion, and factory surplus lie side by side waiting for buyers, to be gaped at, smiled at, scoffed at – unsold.''

This is one writer's description of the scene on the Waterlooplein, where traders large and small offer their wares for sale on stalls or simply on the ground – a colourful jumble of junk and handy bits and pieces, a tatty treasure trove. Although new goods are on sale as well, the emphasis is still on second-hand goods.

★Joods Historisch Museum (Jewish Historical Museum)　　　D 4

In 1987 the Jewish Historical Museum moved into its new premises – four redundant synagogues next to the Waterlooplein.

The first of the four synagogues, the Grote Synagoge or Grote Sjoel, was built in 1670 but soon after its consecration was already proving too small. In 1686, therefore, a second, smaller synagogue, the Obbene Sjoel, was built behind the Grote Synagoge and over the kosher slaughterhouse. The third synagogue, the Dritt Sjoel, was added in 1700 and finally, in 1752, the new synagogue, the Neie Sjoel. The whole group of buildings was sold in its entirety to the City of Amsterdam by the Jewish Community in 1955. In the mid-seventies the city decided that it should be put to a new use. The buildings were restored at a cost of over £10 million, and joined together using steel and glass to create a very attractive, highly accessible building that now houses what is probably the most important Jewish museum outside Israel.

The tour of the museum complex begins in the New Synagogue where the visitor is introduced to "Aspects of the Jewish identity". Here the five crucial elements are seen as being religion, Zionism, persecution and survival under the Nazis, culture, and the influence of the Dutch environment. The Great Synagogue houses the ritual objects in the collection –

Location
Jonas D.
Meijerplein
2–4

Trams
9, 14

Metro
Waterlooplein

Opening times
daily 11am–5pm

The Jewish Historical Museum

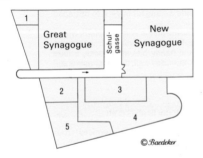

Jewish Historical Museum

1 Mikwa (ritual bath)
2 Third Synagogue
3 Upper Synagogue, Café, Bookshop
4 Temporary exhibitions
5 Mediathèque/Library

silver Torah containers, Torah robes and decorated Torah head-dresses, hangings and baldachins – and on the eastern wall of the synagogue, pointing towards Jerusalem, the white marble "Holy Shrine".

The permanent exhibits are supplemented by temporary exhibitions. The museum also has a mediathèque full of books, tapes and audio-visual material, and in the Upper Synagogue, the Obbene Sjoel, there is a kosher restaurant.

Dock Worker Memorial

On the square between the Jewish Historical Museum and the Portuguese Synagogue (see entry) stands the statue of "The Dock Worker" (by Mari Andriessen). The memorial commemorates the dockers' strike on February 25th 1941, when they refused to co-operate with the deportation of their Jewish fellow citizens. To this day, on the evening of February 25th every year, large crowds of people assemble in front of the statue as a tribute to the dockers' courage.

Jordaan G/H 5/6

Location
Between Prinsengracht and Lijnbaansgracht

Trams
7, 10, 13, 14, 17

To the west of the city centre, between Prinsengracht (see entry) and Lijnbaansgracht, lies the Jordaan, the working-class district made famous as the subject of many songs. It came into being when the city was extended in the early 17th c. and many small craftsmen set up shop here. Refugees settled in the quarter during the Thirty Years' War and artists (including Rembrandt) were so attracted by the Jordaan that they made their homes here.

There are many theories about the name "Jordaan". The most likely is that it comes from the French word "jardin", meaning "garden", but whether or not the district owes its name to its many little front gardens and backyards there were certainly many Walloons and French living here when the Jordaan got its name.

Life in the Jordaan is still largely lived out on the streets. Originally this was for practical reasons (large families, small houses) but nowadays it is on grounds of sociability. The Jordaan still has its own special atmosphere, with convivial corner drinking-houses, sweet-shops kept by little old ladies, and tiny boutiques. Artists and eccentrics are consequently irresistibly drawn to this quarter, where many long-established Amsterdamers can still be encountered.

Kalverstraat H 6 (A/B 2–4)

Location
Between Dam and Muntplein

Kalverstraat is the meeting place for half Amsterdam. Its smart boutiques and perfumeries make it the city's best known shopping street, although the P. C. Hoofstraat has overtaken it as the most exclusive address.

First mentioned in 1393, it gets its name from the calf-trade. There is no proof that cattle-markets were actually held in this street, but cattle were certainly driven through Kalverstraat to the calf-market which in the 16th c. took place on the Dam. Needless to say, the first businesses to settle in Kalverstraat were butchers, later followed by craftsmen, including cobblers and basket-makers. In the mid-18th c. there were already more than 200 shops of all kinds here, as well as coffee-shops and boarding houses.

Nowadays Kalverstraat is a pedestrian precinct and attracts up to 100,000 shoppers a day. On Saturdays the crush is frightening. It can take at least half an hour to walk from Muntplein to the Dam instead of the usual 10 minutes – that is, if you can manage to get there at all and are not swept along by the crowd in quite a different direction. In the evenings walking along Kalverstraat is not very enjoyable, once the shops have closed, as the proprietors pull down their protective grilles, thereby denying the passer-by even the smallest glimpse of the goods on display.

Trams
1, 2, 4, 5, 9, 16, 24, 25

★Keizersgracht   H/J 5/6 (A–C 1/2/4)

Of Amsterdam's three main canals, the central one, the Keizersgracht, which was laid out in 1612 as part of the city's expansion, does not quite come up to the elegant standards of the Herengracht (see entry). Nevertheless it is a memorable experience to walk along the Keizersgracht, which gets its name from the Emperor Maximilian I (1459–1519), who was Holy Roman Emperor from 1508.

The finest houses are the odd-numbered ones between Westermarkt and Vijzelstraat. This is the part which was famed in the last century for the "slipper parade", which took place here on Sundays after church when, between two and four o'clock in the afternoon, most of Amsterdam strolled up and down here in their Sunday best in order to see and be seen.

Location
West of Centraal
Station to the
south of
Rembrandtsplein

Houses on the Keizersgracht

Keukenhof

Huis met de
Hoofden
(No. 123)

The House with the Heads (No. 123) dates from 1622 and is one of the finest gentlemen's houses in the city. The gable is decorated with six helmeted heads, but there is also popularly supposed to be a seventh female head. The story goes that the house was the home of a rich merchant who had a deaf serving-maid in his employment. One day, when the maid was alone in the house, thieves broke in but were all beheaded by the maid. Today the house is occupied by offices.

Nos. 174–176

The house at Nos. 174–176, built in 1905, is a fine example of art nouveau architecture. Today it is the headquarters of the environmental protection organisation Greenpeace. An image in ceramic high above the façade commemorates the previous owners, a life insurance company. A "guardian angel" stands for the security which the company sought to offer its members.

House with the
Golden Chain
(No. 268)

The House with the Golden Chain (No. 268; today a hotel) is an old gentleman's residence from which a golden chain hangs. There are many legends purporting to explain the significance of this chain. According to one story, a maid was accused of stealing a golden chain from her mistress but the chain was discovered in a crow's nest so the maid was re-instated. Another story tells of a captain who lived in the house and had grown weary of going to sea. When forced to set sail again for financial reasons, he swore to bring back a golden chain if fortune smiled on him and an iron chain if she did not. Obviously fortune smiled, hence the golden chain.

There are other similar legends, but the truth seems to be that the house was the home of a goldsmith and the golden chain, which has hung in front of the house since 1643, served as his trademark.

Felix Meritis
(No. 324)

The building at No. 324 is extremely characteristic. This Neo-Classical house, with its façade adorned by four Corinthian columns, was built in 1788 by Jacob Otten Husly for the organisation "Felix Meritis" ("Happiness through effort"), whose aim was to promote science and the arts and to make them accessible to a wider group of people.

The most beautiful room in the house is the Oval Room, which was one of the city's most illustrious concert-halls in the 19th c. In 1808 Napoleon himself attended concerts here. The Oval Room served as a model for the Small Hall of the Concertgebouw (see entry). In the end "Felix Meritis" had to sell the building for financial reasons, and it subsequently had a number of different owners. In 1932 it was almost completely destroyed in a fire, but afterwards was rebuilt, to a large extent exactly as it was originally.

Fodor Museum
(No. 609)

The Fodor Museum is at No. 609. Its temporary exhibitions display the work of contemporary artists, with the emphasis being on those actually living in Amsterdam. When it was first opened in 1863 the museum housed the collection of a coal merchant by the name of C. J. Fodor, although this is now housed in the Amsterdams Historisch Museum (see entry). (The Fodor Museum is open daily from 11am to 5pm.)

Van Loon Museum
(No. 672)

The building at No. 672, which today houses the Van Loon Museum, is also particularly worth seeing. The house was built for a Flemish merchant in 1672 and became the property of the Van Loons in 1884. The interior is furnished in typical mid-18th c. style and besides various objets d'art includes a gallery of over 50 family portraits from the 17th and 18th c. The museum also has a lovely formal rococo garden (open: Mon. 10am–5pm, Sun. 1–5pm).

★★ Keukenhof   Excursion

Location
Lisse

The Keukenhof, in the heart of the Dutch flower-growing area between Haarlem and Leiden, some 35km/20 miles south-west of Amsterdam, has

Keukenhof: Holland's flower paradise

since 1949 been a special place for an excursion; the National Flower Exhibition takes place here every year from the end of March to the end of May on a 28ha/69 acre site. Apart from every imaginable type of bulb the Keukenhof also has shrubs such as rhododendrons and azaleas. Even before the flowers in the grounds are in bloom, hundreds of thousands of crocuses, hyacinths, narcissi and, above all, tulips can be admired in huge greenhouses (5000 sq.m/53,820 sq.ft) from nine in the morning until sunset. In the Juliana and Queen Beatrix Pavilion exhibitions and other events are held.

From the second half of April until the beginning of May the five million flowers in the grounds of the Keukenhof are at the height of their splendour and there is a magnificent view of the site from a windmill.

The nearby 19th c. castle is also worth seeing.

Rail
from Centraal Station to Haarlem or Leiden

Opening times
End of March to end of May: daily 8am–7.30pm

Castle

★★ Koninklijk Paleis (Royal Palace)

A 2

The Royal Palace on the Dam (see entry), formerly the city hall, constitutes an impressive central point in Amsterdam. Nowadays it serves as the Queen's residence when she is in the city.

Building began on January 20th 1648 with the sinking of the first of 13,659 piles for the new city hall. Its architect was initially Jacob van Campen, but he was unable to complete it, and in 1654 Stalpaert took on the task. In the meantime the costs had risen so steeply that it was necessary to suspend work on the building of the tower for the Nieuwe Kerk (see entry). The city councillors were able to have to work resumed on the hall just a year later in 1655, but it was not completely finished until 1665.

For some two hundred years this imposing building, the masterpiece of Dutch Baroque Neo-Classicism, represented the political centre of the city

Location: Dam

Buses
21, 170–172

Trams
4, 9, 16, 24, 25

Opening times
in summer: daily 12.30–4pm;
in winter: Tues., Wed., Thur. 1–4pm

Baedeker Special

A House for a Tulip Bulb

Tulipa Bononiennsis

"**H**ow much is a tulip bulb worth?" "As much as a house on the canals in Amsterdam!"

Back in 1637 this comparison would have been valid, wild speculation in the bulb trade having reached its absolute height. The whole of Holland was immersed in tulip fever, with Dutchmen longing to gain possession of a tulip bulb – at that time a very scarce commodity. Historically these plants had not existed in the Netherlands. Then in the autumn of 1593 the first tulips in the Hortus Botanicus of Leiden were planted. The man who first put the bulbs into soil, thereby ensuring that in early 1594 Holland should have its first tulips, was called Carolus Clusius.

Carolus Clusius had acquired his bulbs in Turkey. Tulips of all colours and variations had grown there since the beginning of the 11th c. The plant did not originate there, however, but came from West and Central Asia, notably from Armenia, Persia and the Caucasus. From there the flower found its way to the countries along the eastern Mediterranean seaboard and also as far as China. It was the Turks, however, who were responsible for making tulips so widespread in Europe.

A "tulip mania" took hold of the Netherlands at the beginning of the 17th c. The trade in tulip-bulbs degenerated into mere speculation, with people selling all their possessions in order to be able to afford the astronomical prices for all the much sought-after bulbs, or "bollen" as they are called in Dutch. Even those who could best be described as impecunious clubbed together in order to be able to own just a single bulb. The rise in the price of tulip-bulbs was colossal, especially between 1623 and 1637. As a result the "Semper Augustus" bulb, which is still renowned today, cost just 1200 guilders in 1624, but by 1637 was fetching a phenomenal 10,000 guilders – the same price at that time as a house on one of the canals in Amsterdam.

For those totally unaware of the boom in tulips, the consequences could be dire. A sailor recently returned home was invited to eat at a merchant's house. In order to add, as he thought, a little more flavour to the dish he had been served, he reached for a tulip-bulb, which his host had bought at some expense, and, all unsuspecting, proceeded to eat it!

and the republic. In 1808, however, Louis Bonaparte, the new King of Holland, desired the city hall for his residence. The Empire furniture which he had procured for his new palace still ranks today as one of the finest such collections in the world. When the Napoleonic period of rule came to an end, the city hall came back to the city, which, however, for financial reasons was unable to afford to return the palace to its original use. Instead it was presented to King William I as a short-term residence. In 1935 the state bought the palace for 10 million guilders and organised for it to be completely restored, so that the premises could be used for social and diplomatic functions (and official ones since 1968).

Baedeker Special

The tulip boom brought untold wealth to many Dutch people. Yet it did not last long. Eventually the speculation and deals went too far and the authorities, no longer prepared to countenance such transactions, stepped in and brought the "tulip mania" to a swift end. Day by day the prices for bulbs tumbled and many a person who had gone from rags to riches by speculating in them suddenly found himself back in the poorhouse.

That the end of "tulip mania" might turn out to be the death-knell of tulip growing and trading proved far from being the case. Tulips have remained an essential component of the Dutch economy right up to the present day. Not for nothing do they, along with windmills, symbolise the Netherlands to the rest of the world. And yet, in the rich and varied assortment of blooms which the Dutch cut-flower market has to offer, they by no means occupy first place. (They were ousted from that position for the first time in the 18th c., hyacinths becoming the front runner.) In fact the flower suitable for cutting which is sold the most is the rose, followed by the chrysanthemum, carnation, tulip (only in fourth place!), lily, freezia and gerbera. These are just a few examples of the hundreds of types of flowers which are grown in the Netherlands. Indeed the number is many times higher. For example, there are today 75 types of rose and 150 types of gerbera, while the attempts by growers to create a "black tulip" are the stuff of legend. Almost all flowers originate in other latitudes – the snowdrop being one of the few examples of an authentic Dutch bulb. As well as bulbs, however, the Dutch flower market can also offer pot-plants, the variety of types available exceeding even that of cut-flowers. Green foliate plants such as ficus, dracaena, azalea, begonia and yucca are particularly in demand.

The systematic cultivation of flowers and ornamental plants in the Netherlands began when gardeners in Aalsmeer turned their strawberry fields and tree nurseries over to horticultural production, which at the time was economically attractive. The first heated greenhouse went into service in 1871 (for growing pelargoniums). Roses – today the greatest seller of all – did not feature in this profitable new horticultural industry until just before the turn of the century. In the surrounding towns the produce of this phenomenal new development also started to come on to the market. Today the Dutch flower and ornamental plant industry is heavily dependent on exports, with almost 75% of production going to foreign markets. The share of world exports in flowers for cutting is 63%, for plant exports some 51%. Nearly half the Dutch exports go to Germany.

The Dutch love flowers. In no other country in the world is so much money per head of population spent on cut flowers. Consequently, whatever the time of year, there is always a magnificent array of flowers for the visitor to admire, whether in flower markets, floral processions, auctions (bloemenveilings), in botanical gardens or nature parks and museums.

Exterior The Neo-Classical palace is built on a rectangular groundplan. The main façade and also the rear one are made less severe by a central projection and two corner ones. The central projection overlooking the Dam is crowned by a gable relief displaying the allegorical figure of "Amsterdam" to whom homage is paid by two gods of the sea.

The bronze figures on the gable stand for "justice", "prudence" and "peace". The centre of the building is dominated by the 51m/167ft high tower (with a carillon), whose dome is topped by a weather vane in the shape of a ship. The roof is decorated by another four imperial crowns, one

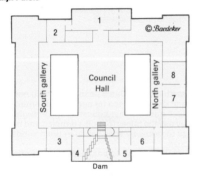

© Baedeker

Royal Palace

1 Jury Room
2 Room of the Commissioner for petty crime
3 Burgomaster's Hall
4 Burgomaster's Chamber
5 Justice Room
6 Aldermen's Room
7 Assurance Room
8 Bankruptcy Room

at each corner (in 1489 Emperor Maximilian I had conferred on Amsterdam the right to use the imperial crown in the city's coat of arms).

Interior

The interior fittings and furnishing are extremely grand and opulent. The apartments are adorned with a wealth of reliefs, ornaments, marble sculptures by the Flemish artists Artus Quellinus and Rombout Verhulst, and wall and ceiling paintings by Ferdinand Bol and Govert Flinck, pupils of Rembrandt.

De Vierschaar (Courtroom)

The tour of the palace begins on the ground floor with the room known as the Courtroom. It was used exclusively for the announcement of death sentences. The judge and jurors would sit on the marble bench on the west side of the room; the secretary, whose task was to record the judgments in writing, used to sit on a chair on the north side opposite the entrance. A board over his chair commemorates the year 1648 when the foundation stone of the palace was laid. The courtroom's decorations were fashioned by Quellinus the Elder in 1650–52.

Council Hall

The largest and most important room in the palace is the Council Hall (34×16.75m/112×55ft and 28m/92ft high). This magnificent hall, one of the finest in Europe, was the venue in 1966 for the ball held on the occasion of the marriage of the then Crown Princess Beatrix to Claus von Amsberg.

Over the entrance on the Dam side of the building sits the patron saint of Amsterdam between the allegorical figures of "strength" and "wisdom". The olive and palm branches held by the patron saint symbolise peace. On the opposite side of the hall "justice" is shown conquering "greed" (King Midas with an ass's ears) and "envy" (a woman with serpents in her hair). "Justice" is accompanied by "death", represented by an hour-glass, and "punishment", carrying instruments of torture.

The inlaid copperwork in the marble floor depicts the two halves of the earth and the northern heavens, thereby indicating Amsterdam's dominant position in world trade in the 17th c. The glass chandeliers date from the Napoleonic period and originally each one had oil lamps hanging from it (electrified in 1937).

Jury Room

The judge and the nine city jurors conducted their inquiries here. The painting over the fireplace is by Ferdinand Bol and depicts Moses descending from Mount Sinai with the tablets containing the Ten Commandments.

South Gallery

Passing through the room used by the commissioners for petty crime (they were responsible for the administration of justice in those cases attracting fines of up to 600 guilders), we reach the South Gallery with its richly decorative sculptures. The figures in the corners of the gallery represent gods of antiquity: Apollo, Jupiter, Mercury and Diana. Rembrandt painted

The Council Hall in the Royal Palace

"The Nocturnal Conspiracy of Claudius Civilis" for this part of the palace in 1661, but for reasons which are not clear it was removed a year later. To this day, however, the South Gallery is still decorated by the paintings "Brinio being chosen as leader" by Jan Lievens and "Bataver's Conspiracy" by Jurgen Ovens.

The painting over the fireplace is the work of Govert Flinck and shows a Roman consul refusing offers of gifts as bribes and eating a simple meal instead.

Burgomaster's Hall

Next to the Burgomasters's Hall there is a small room from which the four burgomasters could look through a window into the Courtroom. The picture over the fireplace is by Jan Lievens. It depicts a meeting between Quintus Fabius Maximus and his father; the latter is honouring his son by dismounting from his horse before speaking to him. The message to burgomasters is: blood kinship is less important than position and rank.

Burgomaster's Chamber

Those sentenced to death were brought to this small room after the judgment had been publicly proclaimed. Here a priest would pray for them for the last time, after which the death sentence would be carried out on a wooden scaffold on the Dam.

Justice Room

The 36 members of the city authority met in this room. The painting "Moses chooses the 70 elders" opposite the window is by Jacob de Wit (1736–38). The paintings over the doors, depicting scenes from the Old Testament, are also his work.

Aldermen's Room

As in the South Gallery, the corners of the North Gallery are decorated by sculptures of gods: Saturn or Chronos, Cybele as goddess of the earth, Venus, the goddess of love, holding in her hand the apple given to her by Paris, and the god of war, Mars.

North Gallery

Koopmansbeurs

Assurance Room

The "Assurance Room" was where the citizens of Amsterdam could safe-guard themselves from various imponderables. Of particular note are the Empire furnishings, which were originally in the private apartments of Louis Bonaparte.

Bankruptcy Chamber

Even here the artistic decorations are in keeping with the use to which the room was put: a relief depicts the fall of Icarus – a victim of his reckless ambitions; the rats, gnawing away at unpaid accounts, can also be discerned.

★Koopmansbeurs (Beurs van Berlage)   B 2

Location
Damrak 243

Trams
4, 9, 16, 24, 25

One of the pinnacles of modern Dutch architecture is the Koopmansbeurs or Beurs van Berlage on the Damrak. It was built in 1897–1903 to plans by Hendrik Petrus Berlage (1856–1934). As a reaction to the prevailing his-toricism, Berlage created a revolutionary and controversial building for the new century, one with clear lines and austere proportions. The most impor-tant building materials which he chose were brick, iron and glass. The interior central hall is vaulted by a construction made of iron and glass.

Amsterdam's first stock exchange was built on the Rokin in 1608 – before that merchants had just met in the open air near the harbour. When the old stock exchange was demolished in 1835, activities transferred to a new Neo-Classical building, which in turn was replaced by Berlage's exchange in 1903.

In the 1970s it seemed as if this modern exchange building was destined for only a short life. Serious problems with its foundations became appar-ent and it was even debated whether it would be necessary to pull it down. However, thanks to a fundamental reconstruction programme, Berlage's exchange was able to be saved. Today it is used as a venue for concerts and also for exhibitions and conferences.

Effectenbeurs

Stock exchange business is conducted as before in the nearby Effecten-beurs (Beursplein 5). The building was constructed in 1913 under the direction of the architect Joseph Cuypers.

Leiden   Excursion

Location
40km/25 miles
south-west

Rail
from Centraal
Station

The old university town of Leiden in the province of South Holland lies alongside the still waters of the Old Rhine, which flows like a canal through the town. For many centuries it was an industrial town and was known in the Middle Ages for its cloth-weaving. Nowadays its major industries are machinery and printing (its far-eastern prints are world-famous).

In the 12th c. the Counts of Holland built first a castle, then a palace (where Floris V was born) on a rise overlooking the Old Rhine. The little town of Leiden grew up between the castle and the palace and received its charter in 1266. In the 14th c. the town became the centre of the cloth industry. On October 3rd 1574 William of Orange freed Leiden from the Spanish siege which, accompanied by plague and starvation, had lasted almost a year, and this event is still commemorated each year. In 1575 the town was rewarded for its bravery by the founding of a university which later became an important European centre of culture. Several important artists and scholars were born here in the 17th c., including Rembrandt van Rijn (1606–69), Jan Steen (1626–79), Gerard Dou (1613–75) and Herman Boerhave (1668–1738).

★Townscape

Leiden is one of the oldest and most picturesque towns in the Netherlands. It possesses some fine old buildings and a large number of museums. The following description covers only the most important.

Burcht

The Burcht or castle (at Burgsteeg 14) was built in 1150 as a place of refuge at times of high water. It stands on an artificial mound about 12m/40ft high

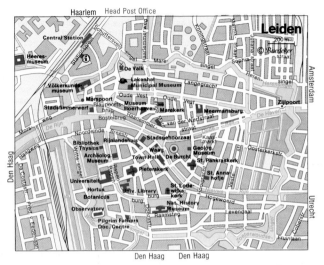

at the confluence of the Old and New Rhine. The castle courtyard inside the encircling wall and battlements is about 35m/115ft across. A tower was planned but never built.

A short distance to the south-west in Breestraat stands the Stadhuis or town hall, with its magnificent Renaissance façade of 1597. The building was almost totally destroyed by fire in 1929, but later partially restored in the old style.

Stadhuis

The foundation walls of the Late-Gothic St Pieterskerk date back to the year 1121 when the town's first church was consecrated here. At the beginning of the 13th c. Rutger van Kampen began building a new and larger church. The choir was completed in 1339, the five-aisled nave during the course of that century. In 1412 the choir was extended by an ambulatory. At the end of the central nave there was a 110m/360ft high tower which unfortunately collapsed in 1512 and was never rebuilt. The wooden barrel vaulting extends as far as the main façade. On the outside stands a small annexe building with a sloping roof. Inside the most impressive things are the pulpit and several of the tombs, including that of John Robinson. He was the man who in 1611 founded the first congregation of Independents (Puritans driven out of England) in Leiden.

St Pieterskerk

As the church congregation kept on shrinking and the necessary repairs to the building could not be financed, a private foundation stepped in and took over the costs, at the same time making the church available for public functions. The church is now used not only for university and school examinations, but also for fairs and exhibitions.

Diagonally opposite the church is the Gravensteen with its Neo-Classical façade, originally a prison used by the Counts of Holland, later by the town. Today it forms part of the law faculty of the university. The oldest parts of the building are the two towers dating from the 13th c.

Gravensteen

The main building of the university, which has over 15,000 students, is situated on the left bank of the broad Rapenburg canal. The medical and natural science faculties have enjoyed worldwide renown for hundreds of years. Since 1581 the university principal's offices have been housed in the former chapel of the Convent of the White Nuns.

University

Hortus Botanicus	Behind the university stretch the Botanical Gardens (Academietuin), which was established as long ago as 1590. The park is a favourite place for relaxation and exercise both with students of the university and the general public. Within the site the visitor will find, as well as exotic plants and trees, a Japanese Garden and also a reconstruction of the first Botanical Gardens which were systematically laid out in the 16th c. (open: Mon.–Sat. 9am–5pm, Sun. 10am–5pm).
Rijksmuseum van Oudheden	The National Museum of Antiquities (Rapenburg 28; open: Tues.–Sat. 10am–5pm, Sun. noon–5pm) has an extensive collection of Greek, Etruscan and Roman sculptures, antique vases and artefacts as well as archaeological finds, chiefly from the Netherlands.
	Since 1979 the museum has owned the Nubian temple of Taffeh, a present from the then Egyptian President Sadat in gratitude for Dutch help in rescuing historic buildings along the Nile which were under threat.
Stedelijk Museum De Lakenhal	The municipal museum (Oude Singel 32; open: Tues.–Fri. 10am–5pm, Sat., Sun. noon–5pm) is in the Lakenhal (Cloth Hall, built in 1639), which formerly housed the guild of the cloth-weavers. Besides important 17th–18th c. works by artists such as Corm, Lucas van Leyden, Rembrandt, Jan Steen, it also has an exhibition relating the history of weaving.
Molenmuseum "De Valk"	Also worth visiting is the mill museum, "The Falcon", situated a short distance to the north (open: Tues.–Sat. 10am–5pm, Sun. 1–5pm). The seven-storey grain mill, built of stone in 1743, stands on a rise and was formerly an essential part of the town's defences. From the early 17th c. 19 windmills stood on this embankment. Today there are still a total of 30 windmills within the town's boundaries. After its restoration in 1964 the mill was turned into a museum (occupying the miller's operation rooms and living quarters).

Leidseplein   G 6

Location On the southwestern edge of the town centre	Amsterdam's second-largest amusement and entertainment centre (after the Rembrandtplein, see entry) caters for all tastes with a theatre, countless cinemas, hotels and restaurants in every price-category, night clubs, bars, cabarets, pubs and, since 1991, a casino (located on the site of the former city prison, De Balie). From Shakespeare to striptease, everything is there
Trams 1, 2, 5, 6, 7, 10	on the Leidseplein, which pulsates with life until well into the night.
	The lively atmosphere of the Leidseplein is not a modern phenomenon. It was here that the farmers used to leave their carts and have their horses looked after when they came into town for the market. Today the square's cosmopolitan atmosphere comes from the Stadschouwburg (Municipal Theatre), the Hotel American and pavement cafés (including the Café Reynders, a meeting-place for artists and journalists) and, last but not least, the many visitors from both home and abroad.
Stadschouwburg	The municipal theatre, or Stadschouwburg, at Leidseplein 26 was built in 1894. It was designed by J. L. Springer in the Neo-Renaissance style. Because of financial constraints many of his original plans for the building could not be realised. When the theatre was finally completed, the vociferousness of the building's critics was so immense that Springer soon afterwards renounced his career as an architect.
	Where the Stadschouwburg now stands, there was originally a theatre of wooden construction, dating from the end of the 18th c. It was replaced by one built of stone in 1876. The present building is used primarily for plays but operas and ballets are also put on from time to time.
Hotel American	The other dominating building on the Leidseplein is the Hotel American. It was built between 1898 and 1902 to plans by Willem Kromhout and, with its art nouveau elements, numerous decorative details and use of brick as a

building material, can be considered as a precursor of the work of the Amsterdam School (see Introduction, Architecture). The bar and the restaurant with its art nouveau interior are favourite meeting-places.

Lieverdje   A 3

The Lieverdje (an Amsterdam street-urchin) on the Spui was originally a plaster figure made by the sculptor Carel Kneulman for a local festival. A manufacturer found the lad so appealing that he had it cast in bronze and donated it to the city. It was unveiled on the Spui on September 10th 1960 and has since proved a favourite rallying point for political action because of its central position near the university, and as an anti-Establishment symbol. In the mid-sixties it was here that the "Provos", the spontaneous young people's movement of that time, mounted "happenings" and handed out their first manifestos.

Location
Spui

Trams
1, 2, 5

Madame Tussaud's Scenerama   B 2

The first Madame Tussaud's outside London was opened in Kalverstraat in 1970 and moved to its new premises on the Dam in 1991. The entrance fee is quite high, but entitles the visitor to see a whole galaxy of historical and contemporary characters, including Willem van Oranje (William of Orange), Peter the Great, Napoleon, Rembrandt, Vermeer, Queen Beatrix, Margaret Thatcher and Marilyn Monroe. As if that were not enough, a whole range of special effects (motion, light and sound) attempt to transport the visitor into another world.

Location Dam 20

Trams
4, 9, 14, 16, 24, 25

Opening times
daily Sept.–June
10am–5.30pm;
July–Aug.
9.30am–7.30pm

★Magere Brug (Mager Bridge)   C 4

Of Amsterdam's thousand or more bridges The "Magere Brug" near Weesperstraat is the most photographed. This simple wooden drawbridge over the Amstel was built in 1671 as a footbridge. After being renovated several times it was demolished in 1929. It was intended that it should be replaced by a modern electrically-operated bridge but the decision was finally made to build a reconstruction of the original wooden one. The building work was supervised by the architect Mager – hence the bridge's name.

Location
Amstel/Nieuwe
Kerkstraat

Tram: 4

Metro
Weesperplein

Marken   Excursion

Marken used to be an island in the IJsselmeer but since 1957 it has been linked to the Nes headland by a 2km/1¼ mile long dyke. This dyke is one of the ring of dykes that will encircle the Markerwaard polder which is to be the fourth area reclaimed from the Zuiderzee (see Introduction, Land Reclamation). Since fishing lost its importance with the damming of the Zuiderzee, tourism has become the main source of income for the peninsula and 80% of Marken's inhabitants work outside the area. In 1232 Marken was a monastic settlement attached to the Frisian abbey of Mariengaard which owned the whole island from 1251 to 1345, when it was bought by the city of Amsterdam. This meant that in the Middle Ages it was often the scene of the quarrels that determined the relationship between Amsterdam and the ports on the opposite bank of the Zuiderzee (e.g. Kampen). In the 17th c. shipping flourished here, and Marken became independent during the French occupation (c. 1811). By the late 19th c. Marken had 17 residential districts, but today there are only seven villages in addition to the main village of Monnikenwerf.

Location
22km/14 miles
north-east

Rail
from Centraal
Station

Buses
depart opposite
Centraal
Station

Magere Brug: the most photographed of all Amsterdam's bridges

Wooden houses on Marken

The principal attractions for tourists in Marken are the architecture of the houses and the folk costumes which are still worn here. Until 1931 the wooden houses were built on piles, but their interiors were also of interest: the visitor will find a good deal of carving and elaborately painted pieces of furniture, including the bed of honour, which is traditionally never actually used. The women wear a "ryglyf", a type of semi-transparent bodice that is either dark blue or embroidered in various colours. The island is still very Calvinist and strangers would not be invited to a winter wedding, which the islanders celebrate on the frozen Zuiderzee – in the traditional costumes, of course, with music and folk dancing, the women dancing together. The people of Marken still hold an Easter procession.

In the local history museum (Kerkbuurt 44–47; open from Easter to October: Mon.–Sat. 10am–4.30pm, Sun. noon–4pm) the visitor can see a vivid representation of the everyday life of islanders of past generations. The museum is housed in the four "lookhuisjes", which did not have a chimney for drawing off smoke, but merely an opening.

Marker Museum

From March to October there are excursion boats at half-hour intervals linking Marken and Volendam (see entry).

Marken-Volendam Express

De Molen van Sloten (Mill of Sloten)   B 8

A 34m/112ft high mill dating from 1847 has been rebuilt at Sloten, a district in the south of the city. It pumps water out of the polder at a rate of 60 cu.cc/4 cu.in. per minute. The mill, which also serves as a community centre, has a display of photographs and tools which illustrate the way of life in previous centuries. There is also an audio-visual show "Rembrant op Zolder" (Rembrandt in the Attic), which is intended to transport the viewer back into the 17th c. with its life-size figures which were originally destined for Madame Tussaud's Scenerama (see entry).

Location
Akersluis 10

Buses
68, 144, 145

Opening times
daily
10am–4pm

In the cheese dairy opposite the mill (open: daily 10am–5pm) one can watch the cheese being made. Visitors also have the chance to taste, and buy, different types of cheese.

Cheese Dairy

Monnickendam   Excursion

Monnickendam is a small old town in North Holland on the banks of the Gouwzee and the IJsselmeer and its location explains why it is best known for its smoked fish and as a centre for water sports. About 70% of Monnickendam's working population have jobs elsewhere and the rest are in business and tourism.

Monnickendam was founded by monks in the 12th c. and was granted its charter in 1335. Its position on the Zuiderzee with its busy shipping trade soon brought the town prosperity but by the 17th c. only fishing remained as an important source of income, and life in Monnickendam had adjusted accordingly. Various catastrophes have also struck the town during its long history: in 1297 it was raided by the Frisians and in 1494 and 1514 large sections of the town were destroyed by fire.

Location
13km/8 miles
north-east

Buses
depart opposite
Centraal Station

Motor-boat
from
Stationsplein or
de Ruijterkade
(only in summer)

The Speeltoren, or belfry, at Noordeinde 4, dates from the 16th c. and possesses a carillon (1596) comprising 18 bells. The tower also houses a museum with archaeological finds from the surrounding area.

Speeltoren

The Grote Kerk or St Nicolaas Kerk in Zarken was built in 1400. It contains a collection of tiles and majolica ware.

Grote Kerk

Stadhuis

The town hall (Noordeinde 5) was built in 1746 as a gentleman's residence. The council chamber is decorated with golden wallpaper and a Rococo ceiling.

Note

Of considerable interest is a visit to one of the eel-smoking factories (Palingroberejen). It is also possible to make trips by boat to Marken and Volendam (see entries).

Montelbaanstoren   D 3

Location
Oude Schans

Buses
22, 31

An arresting sight in the eastern part of the city centre is Montelbaanstoren. The tower was built in 1512 as part of the city's defensive fortifications. It was later given Baroque additions by Hendrik de Keyser in 1606. On top of the fortified lower section of the building three extra levels have been created: one with a clock and above it two decorative storeys housing a carillon.

Today the tower houses the water control centre which is responsible for maintaining water levels in the canals and locks.

Mozes- en Aaronkerk (Moses and Aaron Church)   C 3

Location
Jodenbreestraat

Trams
9, 14

Metro
Waterlooplein

The history of this church goes back to the "Alteratie" (see Facts and Figures, History of the City), when secret churches sprang up everywhere, since Catholics no longer dared to hold services in public.

In 1641 Father Boelenzs purchased the Moses and Aaron House in Jodenbreestraat from a rich Jew and converted it into a church. In the course of time the church was enlarged, and it was consecrated in 1841, after undergoing a transformation into its present Neo-Classical form by a Belgian architect.

For many years now the Moses and Aaron Church has no longer been used for religious services. During the 1980s it was used as a youth club but now, after extensive renovation, it serves as a meeting place and venue for various organised events.

Moses and Aaron Church

Muntplein (Mint Square)   H 6 (B 4)

Location
South of the
centre

The main shopping streets, Rokin, Kalverstraat (see entry) and Reguliersbreestraat, start from the Muntplein. In the 15th c. this square on the Amstel next to the city wall, known at the time as Sheep Square, was where the

The Montelbaanstoren by night

sheep market was held. Its present name dates from 1672 when money was coined in the Mint (the former guardroom next to the Mint Tower). Although the square was officially renamed Sophia Square in the 19th c., the name "Muntplein" was never allowed to die out completely, and the square is nowadays popularly called "de Munt" (the mint).

Trams
4, 9, 14, 16, 20, 24, 25

Munttoren (Mint Tower)

The name "Mint Tower" dates from 1672 when, for two years, Amsterdam was the site of the mint while the French occupied Utrecht where coins were usually minted. The Munttoren is part of the medieval city walls which were almost completely destroyed in the great fire of 1818. The lower part of the tower was left standing. On the remaining stones the city architect Hendrik de Keyser placed a wooden structure (with a carillon by Hemony) and a gilded weather-vane in the shape of an ox, as a reminder of the calf-market which used to be held on the nearby Dam (see entry). When this weather-vane fell from the top of the tower during a storm in 1840 it was replaced by the usual weather-cock.

★Museum Amstelkring   C 2

The Museum Amstelkring with its "underground" Catholic church has the popular appellation "Ons' Lieve Heer op Zolder" ("Our dear Lord in the Attic"). It occupies a private dwelling-house which was built between 1661 and 1663. The house was commissioned by Jan Hartmann, who, in having it built, intended from the outset that it should be possible for a secret church to be installed in the upper storey.

Location
Oudezijds
Voorburgwal 40

Trams
4, 9, 16, 24, 25

Museum Amstelkring

Opening times
Mon.–Sat.
10am–5pm,
Sun. 1–5pm

After Amsterdam had embraced the teachings of Calvin and the Reformation, Lutherans and Catholics were forbidden to hold services. However the practising of other beliefs was to a large extent tolerated. In many places in the city there were "underground" churches in which the faithful came together. It was only with the occupation of the Netherlands by the French in 1795 that religious freedom returned to the city and the secret churches ceased to exist.

In this fine old house on Oudezijds Voorburgwal religious services took place right up to 1888. After that the house and church were set up as a museum by the Amstelkring foundation, with the result that visitors can still feel the special atmosphere of an underground church in the 17th c. In special circumstances the church still fulfils the functions of a house of God, while at the same time being used for concerts.

As well as the original prayer-room, there are also private rooms dating from the 17th and 18th c. which can be viewed. They contain collections of ecclesiastical antiquities, furniture, pictures and copperplate engravings.

De Sael

The grandest of the rooms is "De Sael", set out in the classic 17th c. Dutch style. The symmetrical pattern on the floor, ceiling and walls is characteristic of this period. The walnut cupboard opposite the fireplace was formerly used as a bed.

Secret Church

Although some 200 believers could be accommodated in the secret church – with an emergency exit through the roof if danger threatened – the church is designated as "small" in a list of Catholic meeting places. Its present appearance dates from 1735 and the Baroque altar with its three interchangeable pictues (at the present time the "Baptism of Christ" by Jacob de Wit, 1736). In order to save space the late 18th c. pulpit can be swung into and out of the altar, as the need arises.

The Willet-Holthuysen Museum   *Neiuwe Kerk*

Museum Willet-Holthuysen   C 4

The Museum Willet-Holthuysen is a perfectly restored and furnished gentleman's house on the Herengracht. Built in 1685–90, it has over the years been the home of a succession of distinguished Amsterdam citizens. In 1855 the house was acquired by the businessman Holthuysen who bequeathed it to his daughter Sandrina Louisa (1824–95). She lived here with her husband Abraham Willet (1825–88) and on her death left the house with its art collection to the city of Amsterdam, with the stipulation that the house should be opened to the public under the name "Willet-Holthuysen". In 1896 the new museum was inaugurated.

The house is semi-detached with a frontage five windows wide. The entrance is halfway along and leads into a hall from which the symmetrically arranged rooms lead off to right and left. A tour of the house begins in the basement, where provisions were once stored. It comprises the office, another room thought to have been the servants', and the kitchen, still looking very much as it must have in the 18th c. Stairs lead up to the main floor with its various reception rooms and the dining room (furnishings from the 18th and 19th c.). Of particular note is the Blue Room in 18th c. style. Its ceiling paintings and the picture over the fireplace are the work of Jacob de Wit (1695–1754). On the upper storey are the private rooms of Sandrina Holthuysen and her husband, which are today partly used as exhibition rooms (including a collection of glass ranging from the 16th to 18th c.). On the third floor (not open to the public) there were servants' quarters.

Behind the house there is a pretty garden set out in the 18th c. French style. Today it is more extensive than it was in the last century as up until 1929 the rear section was taken up by stables and a coach-house.

Location
Herengracht 605

Trams
4, 9, 14

Opening times
Weekdays
10am–5pm
Weekends
11am–5pm

★Nieuwe Kerk (New Church)   A/B 2

The Coronation church of the Dutch monarchs (since 1814) lies in the heart of the city next to the Royal Palace (see Koninklijk Paleis) on the Dam (see entry), and its most recent great event (after 22 years of renovation work) was the coronation of Queen Beatrix on April 30th 1980. The church is no longer used for services. Antique fairs, art exhibitions and regular organ concerts take place here.

Despite its name the Nieuwe Kerk is one of the oldest churches in the city. Built in the early 15th c., its foundation letter is dated 1408 when the Bishop of Utrecht granted the city of Amsterdam the right to have a second parish, the first being that of the Oude Kerk (see entry).

A city banker Willem Eggert presented the site. After his death he was buried in the church and his son had a chapel named after him built on to

Location
Dam

Trams
1, 2, 4, 5, 9, 13, 14, 16, 17, 24, 25

Opening times
daily 11am–5pm
(closed
Jan.–Feb.)

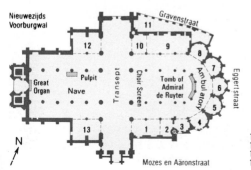

Nieuwe Kerk
St Catherine

1 Sanctuary
2 Eggert Chapel
3 Chapel of Our Lady of the Seven Sorrows (Sills Chapel)
4 Chapel of concealment
5 Meeus Chapel
6 Bricklayers' Chapel
7 Boelens Chapel
8 Cloth-workers' Chapel
9 Crucifix Chapel
10 Chapel of Our Lady
11 Deaconry
12 Old Crucifix Choir
13 Headmaster's house

the church. When Amsterdam was ravaged by fire in 1421 and 1452 the New Church suffered considerable damage, but in each case was quickly restored. Its present aspect dates roughly from 1490. The imposing Late-Gothic cruciform basilica was almost completely burnt down in 1645 owing, it is said, to the carelessness of a craftsman. After its reconstruction, which took about three years, the church was reconsecrated with a service of thanksgiving for the Peace of Münster (1648).

Tower

The church is noticeably lacking in a high church-tower; all it has is a low unprepossessing one. Work was indeed started in the 16th c. on the foundations of an exceptionally high tower along the west front of the church (the congregations of the Oude and Nieuwe Kerk ended up vying with one another for architectural honours!), but the project was never brought to fruition. When the City Hall (see Koninklijk Paleis) began to be built in the mid-17th c., there was not enough money to continue with the church-tower.

Interior

The magnificent pulpit (1649) by Albert Vinckenbrink, a marvel of Baroque woodcarving, is decorated with the four evangelists and figures symbolising Faith, Hope, Charity, Justice and Prudence. The church has a notable organ of 1670, the case of which was designed by Jacob van Campen; an exceptionally beautiful choir screen, cast in bronze by Jacob Lutma (c. 1650); and fine choir-stalls.

Of great significance are the tombs of many famous Dutchmen: in place of the high altar stands the Baroque tomb of Admiral Michiel de Ruyter, who in 1676 succumbed to wounds sustained in the sea battle against the French at Messina. The black marble tomb shows him in full armour. There are also tombs and cenotaphs of the poets P. C. Hooft and Joost van den Vondel, the doctor Nicolaas Tulp and the naval heroes J. H. van Kinsbergen and Jan van Galen.

The stained-glass windows are also interesting: one of them (dated 1650) depicts the granting of the city's coat of arms by William IV; the Royal

The old weigh-house on the Nieuwmarkt

Window (designed by Otto Mengelberg, 1898) commemorates the coronation of Queen Wilhemina.

Nieuwmarkt (New Market)   H/J 6 (C 2/3)

There actually used to be a market on the Nieuwmarkt in the 17th and 18th c. and it was divided up into individual plots for the stalls selling cheese, fish, herbs and cloth. During the Second World War the Nieuwmarkt was widely known for its flourishing black market.

    In 1975 there were street riots in this area when the local people gave vent to their anger at the demolition of many houses for the construction of the Metro (commemorated by a permanent exhibition in the metro station).

Location
Centre

Metro
Nieuwmarkt

Waaggebouw (Weigh-house)

The old weigh-house with its seven towers in the Nieuwmarkt is the former St Anthony's Gate (St Antoniepoort), once part of the 15th c. city wall. It did not serve as just a gate for very long: with the growth of the city it was converted in 1617 into the weigh-house and was used to weigh ships' anchors and ordnance as well as foodstuffs.

    The upper floor served as the guildhall. Each guild (painters, smiths, surgeons, etc.) had its own entrance. The guild of stonemasons was responsible for its internal and external decoration; the chamber of the guild of bricklayers has been kept in its original state. In the 17th c. the surgeons gave their lectures on anatomy here and their entrance can still be recognised today by the inscription "Theatrum Anatomicum" above the doorway. Rembrandt was a frequent guest at these lectures which inspired him to paint his "Anatomy Lesson of Dr Tulp" (Mauritshuis, The Hague) and "Anatomy Lesson of Dr Deijman" (Rijksmuseum, see entry). It was this use that ultimately saved the weigh-house from demolition, since the surgeons needed the building for their work. After 1819 the weigh-house was used for several purposes, including use as a fire-station, for municipal archives and as a museum (see Amsterdams Historisch Museum). It also served as the Jewish Historical Museum (see entry) until its move in 1987. At the present time the building is undergoing extensive restoration work.

Olympisch Stadion (Olympic Stadium)   E/F 8

Amsterdam's most important sports centre is the Olympic Stadium. Built in 1928 when the Olympic Games were staged in the Netherlands, it originally held 40,000 spectators but after being extended in 1936 it now holds 60,000.

Athletic, speedway meetings and cycle races take place in the stadium.

Location
Stadionplein

Trams
6, 16, 24

★Oude Kerk (Old Church)   B/C 2

Amsterdam's oldest church is situated right in the middle of the entertainment and red-light district of Walletjes (see entry). It was built in 1306 as a small cruciform church to replace a wooden church which is thought to have been built here in about 1300. It was the first hall church (i.e. with the aisles the same height as the nave) in North Holland and served as a model for other churches in the region (e.g. the church in Edam). It was dedicated to St Nicolaas, the patron saint of fishermen and seafarers as well as of the city of Amsterdam, by the Bishop of Utrecht.

    There were soon plans for enlarging it and in 1370 two chapels were built on to the choir and an ambulatory added. The church was spared the two

Location
Oudekerksplein 23

Trams
4, 9, 16, 24, 25

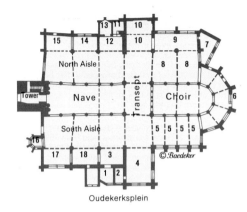

1 South Portal (entrance)
2 Iron Chapel
3 Smiths' Chapel
4 St Sebastian's Chapel
5 Seamen's Chapel
6 Remains of the former Chapel of the Holy Tomb
7 Chamber of the Guild of Our Lady
8 Old Female Choir
9 New Female Choir (stained glass)
10 Tomb of St Joris
11 Holy Tomb
12 Buckwheat Merchants' Chapel
13 Old North Portal (c. 1520)
14 Shippers' Chapel
15 Hamburg Chapel
16 Former Baptistery (c. 1462)
17 Lijsbeth Gaven Chapel
18 Chapel of the Poor

Oudekerksplein

great fires which devastated Amsterdam in the Middle Ages. Other chapels were partly endowed by guilds, the large side chapels being added around 1500. The alterations to the choir in the 16th c. were financed (as was usual in those days) by a lottery. Also dating from this period is a portal on the south side, which bears the arms of Emperor Maximilian I and Philip the Handsome. It gives access to the "iron" chapel, where the documents showing the city's privileges, including the freedom from tolls granted in 1275, were kept behind an iron door, until they were finally transferred to the municipal archives in 1872.

The tower was also remodelled in the 16th c. and the low Gothic tower was replaced by the present high west tower. This has a carillon (by Hemony, 1658) which is among the finest in the country. It is possible to climb to the top of the tower which affords a fine view over Amsterdam.

Opening times
Church
daily 1–5pm
except Sat.
11am–1pm

During the vicissitudes of the 16th c. many of the church's most valuable artistic objects and fittings were lost. This explains the very simple interior of the three-aisled church, which is nowadays a Protestant place of worship. The wooden barrel vaulting is borne on 42 columns. Among the most valuable artistic treasures remaining in the building are the Renaissance glass windows in the New Female Choir, which show scenes from the life of the Virgin Mary. They originally date from 1555, but were substantially renovated in their old form during the 18th c. The large Baroque organ (1724–26) with its rich gold and wood decorations is especially impressive. The elaborate carving on the choir benches dates from the first half of the 15th c. In common with Nieuwe Kerk, the Oude Kerk is the final resting place of many of Amsterdam's famous citizens. Besides admirals (such as Jacob van Heemskerk and Willem van der Zaan) and other important figures the church contains the tomb of Rembrandt's wife Saskia (d. 1642).

Interior

Oudemanhuispoort

See Achterburgwal

Oudewater   Excursion

Oudewater in the province of Utrecht has existed as a locality since the end of the 10th c. and at that time belonged to the diocese of Utrecht. In 1265 it received its town charter but in 1280 was given as a pledge to Floris V of

Location
42km/26 miles
south

◀ *Oude Kerk: the oldest church in Amsterdam*

Holland. This pledge however was never redeemed, with the result that until 1970 Oudewater formed part of the province of South Holland. The town served Floris V as a border fortress, which led to an excessive number of battles, uprisings and sieges, even in more recent times.

In terms of religion Oudewater enjoyed comparative peace, so that Oudewater became a place of refuge for many Catholics. In the late Middle Ages the town enjoyed a heyday of trade and prosperity. The historic old town with its narrow canals today derives its living from agriculture, trade and service industries, although some 60% of the workforce is reliant on work based outside the town boundaries.

Heksenwaag

Oudewater is known chiefly for its "witch's scales" (Heksenwaag), to be found at Leeuweringerstraat 2. These scales were used from 1595 to 1754 for weighing alleged witches – who were usually found to be too heavy. Even in those days very few Dutchwomen would have weighed less than 50kg/8 stone on the scales. If a suspected woman weighed more, she could not be a witch because otherwise her broomstick would have collapsed under her weight. This "witch's test" can still be taken today and as a reward the testee receives a special certificate. An exhibition in the Heksenwaag documents the history of the persecution of witches in the Netherlands (open: Apr.–Oct., Tues.–Sat. 10am–5pm, Sun. noon–5pm).

Grote Kerk

The Grote Kerk (Norderkerkstraat 20), a hall church dating from the 15th c. possesses a 14th c. tower with carillon which still has its original saddleback roof intact.

Stadhuis

The town hall (Stadhuis) was built in the Renaissance style in 1588. It was burnt down in 1968 but has since been completely restored. The interior contains a painting depicting the many atrocities perpetrated by the Spanish in 1575 (not open to the public).

Portuguese Synagogue with the dock-worker's statue

Portugese Synagoge (Portuguese Synagogue)   D 3/4

The Portuguese Synagogue, the largest of the Jewish houses of worship on the J. D. Meijerplein, is reached through a forecourt surrounded by small houses (including the sexton's house, the Tes Haim library and the Livraria Montezinos). The finest building of the Jewish faith in the Netherlands, it is also the only synagogue still in use for religious services. The synagogue complex opposite has housed the Joods Historisch Museum (see entry) since 1987. The Portuguese Synagogue was reopened to the public in the summer of 1993 after a two-year period of restoration work.

The dark-red brick building, completed in 1675 and facing south-east towards Jerusalem, was modelled on the temple of Solomon. The rectangular interior is divided into three aisles by four Ionic columns. The roof above each of the three aisles consists of wooden barrel-vaulting. The synagogue contains an Ark of the Covenant made of rare Brazilian wood and splendid menorahs. When a service is held, there is room for 1200 men and – separated from them, on a gallery – 440 women, although these days that number of people hardly ever come to worship. When the synagogue was consecrated in 1675, 2500 Sephardic Jews were living in Amsterdam (a distinction is made between Sephardic Jews coming from Spain and Portugal and Ashkenasic Jews coming from Central and Eastern Europe). In 1941 they numbered 3800 but only 500 of them survived the persecutions of the Nazis.

Location
J. D. Meijerplein

Trams: 9, 14

Metro
Waterlooplein

Opening times
Mon.–Fri.,
Sun. 10am–4pm
(in winter, Fri.
until 3pm, Sun.
until noon)

★ Prinsengracht   G/H 5–7

The Prinsengracht is less elegant than either the Keizersgracht or the Herengracht (see entries) and therefore livelier and busier. The rents of the houses here are much more reasonable; there are relatively fewer banks and offices but many pleasant cafés which in summer put tables and chairs out on the pavement overlooking the canal. That section of the canal to the north of the city centre, which has the low-numbered houses, is also where many houseboats are to be seen. Most of these have been turned into comfortable and individual homes by their owners.

Location
between
Prinsenstraat
and Amstelveld

The Noorderkerk is situated along the Prinsengracht at the Noordermarkt. The church was designed by Hendrik de Keyser and constructed between 1620 and 1623. The ground plan which he chose for the building was an unusual one at that time: a Greek cross with annexes between the equal-length arms (subsequently many evangelical churches were built after this model). The point of intersection of the arms of the cross is marked by a low clock-tower. The four façades are all of identical design and impress the observer with their severity and simplicity. The hall-like interior with its wooden barrel-vaulting is also extremely austere in appearance.

Noorderkerk

The buildings with the house numbers 187–217 are in fact old storehouses. The goods were hoisted by means of pulleys under the gables.

Storehouses

Other places of interest along the Prinsengracht are Anne Frank Huis and the neighbouring Westerkerk (see entries).

Anne Frank
Huis, Westerkerk

The Paleis van Justitie is situated at Prinsengracht No. 436. The city architect de Greef had this Neo-Classical building erected between 1825 and 1829. Building materials from an orphanage which had stood on the site were incorporated into its construction.

Paleis van
Justitie

The Amstelkerk on the corner of Prinsengracht and Reguliersgracht is a wooden building dating from 1688, thought to have originally been put up as a temporary construction. Today, however, the cube-shaped church is still in use for services of the Dutch Reformed Church. The Café Kort is housed in an adjoining building.

Amstelkerk

Cafés and restaurants along the Prinsengracht

The Amstelveld, the square in front of the church, is the scene of much hustle and bustle in the summer months, particularly on Monday mornings when a flower market is held here.

★Rembrandthuis (Rembrandt's House)   C 3

Location
Jodenbree-
straat 4–6

Trams
9, 14

Metro
Waterlooplein

Opening times
Mon.–Sat.
10am–5pm,
Sun. and public
holidays 1–5pm

This house on the Jodenbreestraat, now the Rembrandt museum, is where Rembrandt (see Famous People), with his wife Saskia, spent his happiest and most successful years, the time when pupils and commissions came to him in a steady stream. It was in this quarter, where Jews had settled (see Jodenbuurt) from all over the world, that he found the models for his Biblical themes. Here he painted what he had seen during the day on his outings along the canals and the Amstel.

The house in which Rembrandt lived for some 20 years was built in 1606. Rembrandt bought it in 1639 for 13,000 guilders – an exhorbitant sum at that time. He used the lower floor for living quarters and turned the upper floor into his studio. The rooms in the attic were used as studios by his pupils (Ferdinand Bol and Govert Flinck both worked here for a time). When Rembrandt lived here, his own works, as well as those of his masters and friends, used to hang all over the house. An inventory from the year 1656 listed more than 100 paintings. In order to meet the demands of his creditors Rembrandt was forced to sell the house in 1657–58. Shortly afterwards the building was enlarged, acquiring an additional storey, and right up until this century it was actually divided into two separate dwellings. In 1906 the house was bought by the city of Amsterdam, restored and returned in good measure to how it was in Rembrandt's time. Since 1911 it has been open to the public as Rembrandt's house. Around 250 of Rembrandt's etchings and some of his drawings are on display. In addition various paintings by Rembrandt's teachers and pupils are kept here.

Rembrandtsplein (Rembrandt Square)   H 6 (B 4)

With the Leidseplein (see entry), the Rembrandtsplein is the most important entertainment area in the city. There are cafés and restaurants here,
but also numerous night clubs and strip-tease establishments.

Location
Centre, near
the Amstel

Thanks to a comprehensive programme of renewal over the last few
years, the status of the Rembrandtsplein has been considerably enhanced.
The central green area contains a statue of the great artist, which was cast
in bronze by R. van Royer in 1852. Sitting in one of the terrace cafés the
visitor can enjoy watching the world go by and perhaps even listen to a
barrel-organ player as he draws captivating sounds from his huge brightly-
painted instrument.

Trams
4, 9, 14

The square, in which the butter market used to be held, has always been a
centre of social interaction. When fairs were held here it swarmed with
people in search of the abundance of entertainment to be found in the
booths and at the many stalls. When the butter market was discontinued in
the mid-19th c. the square retained its atmosphere as somewhere to stroll
and find amusement. In 1876, with the erection of the Rembrandt statue, it
acquired its present name.

★★Rijksmuseum (National Museum)   G/H 7

This world-famous museum of art dates back to the time of King Louis
Napoleon who wanted to make Amsterdam a centre for art and science. In
1809 he set up the Grand Musée Royal in his palace (see Koninklijk Paleis)
on the Dam (see entry). Works from the National Museum in The Hague,
which had been opened in 1798, and a few pieces belonging to the city,
including Rembrandt's "Night Watch", formed the basis for the museum,
which grew rapidly with the purchase of various new collections. Soon the
palace rooms could no longer hold all the works, so eight years after its
foundation the museum, now known as the "Rijksmuseum", was transferred to the Trippenhuis (see entry). More purchases and gifts over the
next few years made another move inevitable. It was finally decided that a
museum building appropriate to the purpose should be built on the Stadhouderskade (1877–85) and P. H. J. Cuypers was appointed architect. Only
two years after the building was completed it was clear that further space
must be acquired to house the rapidly growing collections. The South
Wing, also designed by Cuypers, was linked to the main building by a
narrow corridor. Extensive renovation of the South Wing was carried out in
1993, and this section of the museum has again been open to the public
since April 1996.

Location
Stadhouders-
kade 42

Trams
2, 5, 6, 7, 10

Opening times
daily 10am–5pm

The Neo-Gothic building, which also has many Renaissance elements, is
particularly noteworthy for its carillon. Some of the 24 bells date back to the
15th c. The gardens surrounding the museum are laid out in 17th c. style.

Today the Rijksmuseum has about 7 million works of art, including 5000
paintings housed in over 250 rooms, a library with some 100,000 volumes
and about 30,000 auction catalogues. Apart from its unique collection of
old masters, it offers an exhaustive account of the development of art and
culture in the Netherlands and is especially rich in old Dutch handicrafts,
medieval Dutch sculpture and modern Dutch paintings.

The print room specialises in Dutch 16th and 17th c. and French 18th c.
drawings and prints. In the library the visitor can inspect all the prints from
the national collections, such as Rembrandt's etchings.

Print room

This department displays paintings, model ships, flags, costumes, documents, curios and other items illustrating the political and military history
of the Netherlands (in all about 3000 exhibits). The exhibition is not a
chronological account but highlights interrelated topics (which are in
chronological order) of fundamental importance in the country's history.
The period covered ranges from the late Middle Ages to the present day.

Dutch history

Rijksmuseum

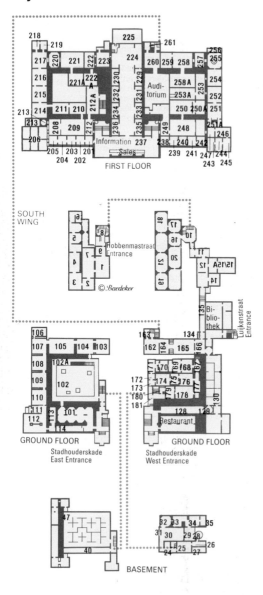

The Rijksmuseum

Sculptures and handicrafts	The wide-ranging exhibition of liturgical robes, furniture, tapestries, jewellery, pottery, costumes, dolls' houses, Delft pottery, lace, snuff boxes, etc. presents a picture of life in various periods from the Middle Ages to the early 20th c.
Oriental art	The visitor can see Chinese porcelain and objets d'art from India, South-East Asia and the Far East. Japanese prints are to be found in the print room.

Painting collection

The painting section offers a superb collection of Dutch masters from the 15th to 19th c. (in particular the 17th c., the golden period of Dutch painting). The non-Dutch painters are arranged by country; among these the most prominent names include Fra Angelico, Crivelli, Bellini and Mantegna, Veronese, Tintoretto and Bassano, Goya, Velázquez, Murillo, Cano and Cerezo.

Without in any way intending to detract from the other masterpieces hanging in the Rijksmuseum, the following pages deal solely with the major works of Dutch painting from the 15th to 17th c. in chronological order. As the paintings are often moved around, there is no attempt to indicate in which room they are to be found.

Late-Gothic Painting (15th c.)

The origins of the old Dutch art of painting lie in the miniaturists of the late 14th c., who were influenced by French models. The detail of their realism combines during the course of the 15th c. with a striving towards an individual and physically accurate representation of the human form and the illusionistic reproduction of space and landscape, along with decorative and genre-style elements. Allied to this goes a gradual turning away from the medieval-religious view of the world, with its preoccupation with the hereafter, in favour of a much greater awareness of contemporary ways of life. The painting of this period enjoys its greatest triumphs in the southern provinces of the Low Countries – Ghent, Bruges and Antwerp – with the works of the van Eyck brothers, Rogier van der Weyden, Hugo van der Goes, Hans Memling and others. The northern provinces, on the other hand, for a long time remained outside this ferment of artistic activity and it was not until the end of the 15th c. that some notable painters also appeared there.

Geertgen tot Sint Jans (1460/65–1488/93), despite his early death, represents the main exponent of the Late-Gothic Haarlem school of painting. His panel painting "The Holy Family" depicts his subjects sitting among the columns of a Gothic basilica. On the left is Saint Anne, framed by Joseph and James with Mary and the baby Jesus. On the right is Saint Elizabeth with the child John on her lap, surrounded by Mary, wife of Cleopha, and Mary Salome, whose children are playing on the floor of the church. The altar in the background of the picture is decorated by a sculpture depicting the sacrifice of Abraham, while the choir screen and column capitals have figurative embellishments based on the theme of salvation through God. Representations of the Holy Family were particularly popular among the Brotherhoods of Anne in the 15th and 16th c.

Geertgen tot Sint Jans

What is unusual and looks forward to 17th c. painting is Geertgen's choice of a church interior as the setting of his painting, the introduction of still life elements such as the basket of bread at Saint Anne's feet and the faithful reproduction of materials in detailed colours rich in nuances. In addition Geertgen shows himself to be an expert in central perspective, something which was not encountered again for another 60 years. The device enables him to create a symmetrical and harmonious composition in his pictures with an extraordinary effect of depth. Figures are not arranged according to strict hierarchy nor placed in a row next to one another, but instead are placed together in small groups with the appearance of little formal organisation. As a result the whole scene makes a very everyday and familiar impression.

The "Master of the Virgo inter Virgines" (active between 1470 and 1500) was responsible for the altar picture "Mother of God with child and four saints". It has led to the unknown painter being referred to as the "Master of the Virgin among Virgins", because the depiction of a slim woman figure with high hairline, heavily domed forehead and melancholy drooping eyelids – without lashes – occurs in all the works ascribed to him.

Master of the Virgo inter Virgines

Another important work of the Late-Gothic period following Geertgens is the "Seven Works of Mercy" (1504) by the Master of Alkmaar which are conceived in glowing colours with imposing architectural backdrops. They depict in great detail the feeding of the hungry, the giving of water to the thirsty, the clothing of the naked, the burying of the dead, the sheltering of the homeless, the caring of the sick and the visiting of the prisoners.

Master of Alkmaar

Renaissance and Mannerist Painting (16th c.)

The most important early work of Dutch Renaissance painting is the "Adoration of the Magi" (1515–20) by Jan Mostaert (1475–1555/56), in which the subject-matter is transported directly to the present. The kings and Mary are conceived in the manner of individualised portraits and are fashionably clad in garments of fur and brocade. The ruin of a fortress and the farmhouses of a Dutch village can be discerned in the background. The extreme spatial disparity between the large figures in the foreground and the tiny details of the background is palliated by an arched gateway in the centre of the picture. This serves as a frame for a picture within a picture, a rustic

Jan Mostaert

scene showing the kings' travelling party with horses, grooms and peasants. Mary with the baby Jesus has been moved to the middle of the picture. From a compositional point of view her central position has been enhanced by the gate pillar which is embellished by grisaille figures and paintings which allude to the symbolism of the stem of Jesse.

Jacob Cornelisz
van Oostsanen

Jacob Cornelisz van Oostsanen (before 1470–1533) is a representative of the school of Amsterdam Renaissance painting with his triptych of the "Adoration of the Magi" (1517), which he sets in a courtly-ceremonial style with opulent colours. On the side panels appear founder figures with their many children. They are being commended to the Mother of God by their patron saints. A fantastic and grotesque world of figures, reminiscent of Hieronymus Bosch, coupled with flickering colours, distinguish Jacob Cornelisz's unusual representation of "Saul with the Witch of Endor" (1526), which is derived from the Book of Samuel and describes how the Israelite king Saul, no longer having the ear of God, seeks counsel in order to ward off the threat of the Philistines.

Lucas van
Leyden

With his triptych, the "Adoration of the Golden Calf", created in about 1530 for the house of a wealthy townsman, Lucas van Leyden (1494–1533), shows himself to be the master of the early Mannerist style, which is characterised by its curved lines, restless outlines and flickering colours. He creates a monumental picture with a naturalistic landscape which spills over on to the side panels. Into this is incorporated, mainly on the central panel, a lively country scene, while the main religious event, that of Moses receiving the holy tablets on Mount Sinai, takes place almost unnoticed in the background of the picture. While Moses, in the face of the godlessness of his people, is even on the point of shattering the tablets, a carefree feast of eating and drinking is being enacted in the foreground. Thus the moral message of the picture, not to offend against the first commandment, is heavily obscured.

Jan van Scorel

Jan van Scorel (1494–1562) made a pilgrimage to Rome and thus was one of the few Dutchmen to become acquainted at first hand with the masterpieces of the Italian High Renaissance and to take back the essentials of their style to his homeland. This can be seen in his "Saint Mary Magdalen" (1528) which, while having many of the qualities of a portrait, shows the Italian influence in the highly plastic and at the same time monumental conception of its figures. The beautiful penitent is positioned in the middle, between a clump of rocks on the left and a tree motive on the right, thereby emphasising the equal claims of the picture to be a portrait and a landscape study. Dressed as a flighty seductress in elaborate garments, she exudes a sensuousness which is only further emphasised by the soft colours and the intentional contrasts between light and dark.

Maerten van
Heemskerck

Portraits of great psychological understanding were painted by Maerten van Heemskerck (1498–1574), including the "Portrait of Anna Codde" (c. 1530). By excellent use of light he is able to achieve at the same time a high degree of plasticity in his figures and the illusion of space. The young woman sitting dreamily at the spinning-wheel captivates by her charm and sheer vitality.

Pieter Aertsen

Pieter Aertsen (1509–75) depicts in his painting of 1557, the "Egg Dance", an earthy rustic scene of everyday life, in which a young man is watched eagerly by a group of onlookers as he tries, to the strains of bagpipes played on stockings, to dance round an egg without slipping and crushing it. In the foreground another man caricatures the fashion of the time by his affected manner.

Joachim
Beuckelaer

The increasing secularisation of religious themes in the 16th c. is shown by the work of Joachim Beuckelaer (c. 1530–73), a nephew of Pieter Aertsen who worked chiefly in Antwerp. His painting, "Christ in the house of Mary and Martha", is first and foremost a magnificent kitchen scene. It is an astonishing composition, in which the main scene of the picture, involving Jesus, takes far away in the background, but is made the main centre of the observer's attention, by being projected over the confusion of meat, poultry and fruit in the foreground, through the employment of a triumphal arch and extreme spatial contrasts. The balance of the picture is achieved by having a group of people on the left-hand side, offset by a still life arrangement on the right-hand side. The opulence of the foreground composition and the minuteness of the background scene provide a clear contrast between the concepts of transitoriness (the preparation of the meal) and eternity (the appearance of the Son of God), between worldliness (the satisfaction of physical needs) and spirituality (communion, faith).

With his paintings Cornelisz. van Haarlem (1562–1638) made an important contribution to European Mannerist art. His powerful and monumental style is evidenced in paintings such as "Bathsheba in the Bath" and "The Fall of Man" (1592), in which the figures portrayed are both sensual and erotic, and also nude and muscular.

Cornelisz. van Haarlem

The Utrecht-born Anthonis Mor van Dashorst (1520–76), better known as Antonio Moro, enjoyed a Europe-wide reputation as a portrait-painter and as a result spent a lot of time abroad. His "Portrait of Sir Thomas Gresham" (c. 1570) shows its subject, the financial representative of the English court in the Netherlands, fixing the observer with a searching gaze. Although true to life, the picture's main quality is predominantly a cold and lofty detachment.

Anthonis Mor van Dashorst (Antonio Moro)

Pre-eminent among the early landscape painters is Joos de Momper (1564–1635). His "Landscape with a Boar Hunt" (c. 1610), very much a product of the imagination, has a richly varied subject-matter: a hunting scene in the foreground and views of rocks, sea bays with ships, ruins, castles and town which disappear into the blue distance.

Joos de Momper

In his still lifes Jan Breughel the Elder (1568–1625), who worked mainly in Antwerp, seems to delight in bringing the whole gamut of flowers before our eyes. The flowers in his vases are arranged with the utmost taste and with due consideration for colour and form. They show a bewildering wealth of detail, which calls to mind the miniaturists' paintings. Yet while the intoxicating profusion of colours beguiles the observer's senses, there are also faded and wilted blooms and leaves which serve as a reminder of the transitoriness of existence.

Jan Breughel the Elder

In his painting "The Fisher of Souls" (1614), in which countless figures can be seen on either side of a large river and in overladen boats, Adriaen van de Venne (1589–1662) presents the theme of religious wars in the form of an allegorical representation of the jealousy between the various religions, each of which endeavours in its own way to offer salvation to the would-be believer.

Adriaen van de Venne

Baroque Painting (17th c.) · The Golden Age

As a result of the declaration of independence in 1581 by the Calvinist northern provinces of the Low Countries, it is appropriate from this point to talk about separate Dutch and Flemish schools of painting, the Catholic southern provinces, which included the important artistic region of Flanders, remaining under Spanish rule. Around 1600 the religious, political and socio-economic changes in the Low Countries brought about a corresponding new direction in the field of fine arts. Whereas previously works of art had been commissioned by princes and churches, now it was the fashions and buying habits of a newly-emerged and secularised bourgeoisie which had the power to bring specialist artists and painters to the fore. This in turn led to the emergence of various genres of painting which had hitherto not existed independently. Portrait painting, which had always been a preserve of Dutch painters, blossomed as a result of the popularity of group portraits, such as militia and regency groups. Landscape paintings, including marine and animal subjects, were much sought-after additions to the accoutrements of a bourgeois household, as were still life and genre pictures, entertaining society paintings, interior and architectural pictures. These types of picture never achieved the same diversity and mastery anywhere else in Europe as they did in the Netherlands of the 17th c. This, the country's golden age, produced many masters besides Rembrandt, Frans Hals and Jan Vermeer.

Werner van den Valckert

The prelude to all the many group portraits of the 17th c. can be said to be the two representations of the "Regents and Regentesses of the Leper Asylum" by Werner van den Valckert (c. 1585–1627/28). Bourgeois self-confidence and social responsibility are conveyed by these men and women, who are largely portrayed in separate individual portraits in the dark severe costumes of the time.

Frans Hals

It was Frans Hals (1581/85–1666) who first succeeded in translating the feeling of community in a vivid way into his group pictures. In his militia picture "The Company of Captain Reynier Reael and his Lieutenant Cornelis Michielsz. Blaeuw" (1637) it is clear that each member of the Amsterdam militia will have paid to have his own portrait painted and therefore have expected to be portrayed in such a way as to bring out the importance of his rank and status. However this is no longer done just by positioning but by the gently ironic posing of the self-conscious officers in their magnificent uniforms, reinforced by the differentiated "language" of their gestures and demeanour. In addition Hals immerses his group scene in gleaming colours and adds rhythmic accents through colour; for example one should notice the way the arrangement of the shimmering silk sashes skilfully deploys the colour blue throughout the picture. Admittedly certain individ-

Franz Hals "The Merry Drinker"

ual poses are repeated but ultimately this serves to strengthen the balance and unity of the picture. The extravagance involved in these group portraits is demonstrated by the fact that Pieter Codde actually completed this portrait in Amsterdam because the militia members were reluctant to travel from Amsterdam to Hals's studio in Haarlem for sittings, while Hals was similarly disinclined to make the journey to Amsterdam.

"The Merry Drinker" (1628–30), with its subject's beckoning gesture to the observer, expresses *joie de vivre* and high spirits. The laughing face, tilted hat and balanced wine-glass are spontaneous in their conception and are captured on the canvas with a deft use of colour and the painting technique normally associated with a sketch. This "snapshot" of a moment in time, which was so admired by Manet and the 19th c. impressionists, bubbles over with life, and yet it is probably not an actual portrait that Hals was commissioned to paint, but possibly an artistic representation of one of the four temperaments.

As a portrait of old age, "Maritge Voogt Claesdr" (1639), which Hals painted when he was 62, occupies a pre-eminent position. The plain background leads the observer directly to the subject's hands, raised up against the incoming light, and her face. Her dark, severe dress is only softened by her white ruff and bonnet. The latter serves to frame her expressive face and intensifies the observer's concentration on her personal and individual features. With her left-hand clutching the arm of her chair, and a bible in her right hand, the impression of a proud (note the family coat of arms!) and determined member of the bourgeoisie emerges.

Judith Leyster (1609–60), a pupil of Hals and wife of the painter Jan Molenaer, was accepted as the first woman member of the Haarlem guild of painters in 1633. She painted genre pictures, portraits and pictures of birds. Her "Lutenist" (1629) is depicted with powerful, sweeping brush-strokes and a masterly use of light.

Judith Leyster

Pieter Claesz (1597/98–1661) possessed exceptional gifts in the field of still-life painting. His "Still Life" is composed of interlocking elliptical shapes – the tin plate, salt-cellar and large, half-filled goblet. Alongside them are some fish, bread, and fruits, all painted close enough for the observer to feel he could take hold of them.

Pieter Claesz

The captivating beauty of these still-lifes is, however, continually belied by the functional character of their material: the glasses tend to be half-empty, the bread has been nibbled, the fruit partly peeled, thereby providing a stark reminder of the transitoriness of all earthly things.

With his "Winter Landscape with Fun on the Ice", Hendrick Averkamp (1585–1634) was especially successful in translating onto canvas the wintry delights of his native polderlands with their frozen rivers and canals. He was almost certainly inspired by the densely-peopled pictures of Pieter Breughel the Elder, and so in his painting the scene is of countless people bustling around merrily on the ice. Averkamp has skilfully succeeded in capturing in colour the atmosphere of a cold and gloomy winter's day.

Hendrick Averkamp

While nature casts a breath of melancholy with birds clustering on the bare branches of the trees, the human beings in the picture are totally immersed in their various activities and diversions. While some of them are chatting, others are skating or playing ice-golf, eels are being caught through a hole in the ice, reeds are being cut and water fetched for the makeshift drink-stalls. But at the same time the picture can be viewed in a symbolic way, with winter being universally recognised as a metaphor for death, the corpse of the animal in the top left corner of the picture serving to reinforce this idea. The skater right in the middle of the picture, who has fallen over and landed on his nose, illustrates the sort of universal truths that are enshrined in proverbs: notably pride coming before a fall, skating on thin ice, and the fragility of human existence itself. The bird trap on the left in the foreground of the picture reminds us of one of the Bible's teachings: that the devil sets traps for the unwary and seeks to lure them into perdition.

Rijksmuseum

Pieter Lastman

With Pieter Lastman (1583–1633), Rembrandt's teacher, a style of painting which is both academic and pleasing comes to the fore. This highly versatile painter, whose youthful sojourn in Italy was to leave an abiding influence on his work, created an almost theatrical setting with his "The Quarrel between Orestes and Pylades", both by its antique elements and its Mediterranean ambience.

Jan van Goyen

Jan van Goyen (1596–1656) wrestled over and over again in pictorial terms with the watercourses of Holland. His "View of the Dordtse Kil near Dordrecht" is set out as a diagonal composition which begins on the left with the fusion of sky and water in an atmospheric haze, and then ascends to the right, past a group of sailing-boats, up to the highest point, with its towering church tower and, in front, the tall oak-trees, whose plenteous foliage leads the eye up to the billowy cloud formations in the sky. In general van Goyen's landscapes are painted with verve and a lack of inhibition, often depicting wide-sweeping views peopled with peasants who are usually relaxing and enjoying a respite from their toil.

Pieter Saenredam

An outstanding exponent of the architectural picture is Pieter Saenredam (1597–1665). "The Interior of the Church of St. Odulphus in Assendelft" (1649) is set out with a central perspective which has been shifted slightly to the right, thereby giving the spatial structure, in particular the columns and arches, even more emphasis and clarity. In this way the church interior, suffused with light, but, in accordance with Calvinistic ideas, devoid of any decoration, has the impact of a dramatic stage, notwithstanding the precision and detail shown in the rest of the picture's composition. The memorial slab of the poet's father is set into the floor in the foreground, and some way behind, the tomb of the Assendelft family is visible. These memento mori motives give symbolic dimensions to the architecture of the picture.

Bartholomeus van der Helst

Bartholomeus van der Helst (1613–70) conceives "The Banquet in St George's Civil Guardhouse on the Occasion of the Celebration of the Peace of Münster" (1648) (the treaty which ended the Thirty Years' War and brought the Dutch recognition of their nationhood and sovereignty) as a lavish meal in the house of the archery guild in Amsterdam. To the right the captain can be seen with the guild's drinking horn on his knees, symbolically receiving the lieutenant's congratulations. In the centre of the picture appears the standard-bearer, who links up with the group on the left. Fastened to the drum are verses by Jan Vos celebrating the peace. In spite of the men's lively facial expressions and relaxed posture, and notwithstanding the complicated arrangement in which they are grouped, it is impossible not to be aware of a certain stiltedness in their pose. However, the play of colours provided by the fine cloths, magnificent uniforms and striking head-coverings is beautifully handled.

Landscape painting

Dutch landscape painting enjoyed its finest flowering in the second half of the 17th c. As in the preceding decades the most popular subject was the Dutch landscape itself, with its deep horizon, thick clusters of clouds and frequently changing light. Such pictures were very popular with the people, as it was possible for them to identify with them and feel their patriotic feelings being consoled during the long stuggle for recognition of their nationhood, which was not achieved until 1648. In many cases the qualities of stillness and tranquillity dominate these landscape pictures, which are first and foremost intended to be close to nature, but which also admit of symbolic interpretation, notably the moving clouds, flowing water, changing light, with their allusion both to the transitoriness of existence and metaphysical forces influencing nature and man.

Jacob Isaaksz. van Ruisdael

The greatest of the Dutch landscape painters was Jacob Isaaksz. van Ruisdael (1628/29–82). His "View of Haarlem" was painted from the raised dunes of the neighbouring town of Overveen. The observer's gaze ranges over the whitish areas representing Haarlem's linen and damask manufacture, with tiny figures going about their work, past farmsteads and windmills, until the eye is arrested by the silhouette of the mighty St Bavo's Church. Pockets of light and shade cover the fields and give the overall landscape its wonderful feeling of depth. In spite of the extremely narrow strip of land depicted and the vastness of the cloudy heavens, Ruisdael manages to achieve a tense and expressive balance between the flatness of the landscape and the illusion of depth created.

The extraordinary gifts of the self-taught painter Jan Steen (1626–79) are seen at their best in his genre pictures. "The Feast of St Nicholas" (*c.* 1660) shows a family scene on St Nicholas's Day. The contrasting emotions of joy and disappointment on the children's faces, depending on whether they are being rewarded for good or bad behaviour, are strikingly juxtaposed. The weeping boy has found only a rod of birch in his shoe, but his grandmother is seeking to console him by beckoning him to look behind the curtain, where something is obviously hidden for him. The little girl, however, is triumphantly pressing her present to her. In the foreground there is a still life composed of all manner of delicacies: nuts, gingerbread and fruit, representing special St Nicholas's Day gifts. The original Catholic festival was not looked upon kindly by the Dutch Reformed Church as it smacked of the sin of gluttony, but even a temporary ban on its celebration did nothing to break the attachment of the Dutch for the tradition. In his sumptuous depiction of the feast-day celebrations, Steen, as a Catholic, was intentionally criticising the uncompromising harshness of the reformed faith. Again and again Steen shows himself to be a perceptive portrayer of family scenes, investing them with his own enigmatic sense of humour. The happy-go-lucky atmosphere which pervades his social genre pieces, such as "The Happy Family" (*c.* 1670), often belies the serious intent of his art, but in this picture the aphorism to be found over the fireplace indicates the real meaning of the picture: "The young will pipe what the old have sung". Since children inevitably imitate their parents, it behoves the latter to set a proper example. But Steen's pictures take us into households where this

Jan Steen

Jan Steen "The Happy Family"

precept is not followed, where children receive lessons in coarse-mannered carousing from depraved and drunken adults. Much of what the children are getting up to in Steen's picture is a play on the word "pipe" (in Dutch: pypen): they are smoking from pipes, piping a tune and drinking from a long drinking-vessel known as a "pyp". The message of the picture is thus quite didactic: children adopt bad habits such as smoking and drinking, if their parents practise them in their presence.

Adriaen van Ostade

Adriaen van Ostade (1610–85), a pupil of Frans Hals, provided, with his "Interior of a Farmhouse with Skates" (1650) a vivid example of the rustic way of life. Bathed in a soft diffuse light, the shabbily-dressed peasants sit round the hearth to keep warm.

The "Fishwife" (1672) is thought to have commissioned her own portrait, for at this time even less well-off people could afford paintings, especially as works of art were increasingly regarded as objects of commerce and were therefore subject to the rules of the open market. As she looks up from her job of cleaning the fish, she gazes straight at the observer, while in the background the business of the market unfolds.

Nicolaes Maes

Nicolaes Maes (1634–93) painted sensitive genre pictures such as the "Old Woman at Prayer" (c. 1655), which captures an emotional yet dignified moment of prayer in every precise detail. The girl at the window, known as "The Dreamer" (c. 1655), impresses with her pensive gaze and melancholy visage, while the window-bay is framed in a one-dimensional decorative way by fruit-bearing branches of an apricot-tree trained along the wall of the house. Soft atmospheric colours add to the picture's effect, while a spatial depth is achieved by the window shutters and the open inner window.

Gabriel Metsu

In his picture "The Sick Child" (c. 1665), Gabriel Metsu (1629–67) lets the observer share directly in personal grief. The mother stoops over the pale tiny girl on her lap with the utmost concern. The composition consists of two diagonal arrangements of figures, with the colours bringing out the theme of illness – the powerful combination of red-green-yellow in the foreground giving way, with the sinking back of the sick child, to an almost monochrome beige-brown background. The stance of the mother and child also evokes associations with the traditional madonna and child motive.

Paulus Potter

Paulus Potter (1625–54) was the most important representative of the Dutch school of animal painting, and indeed was even the movement's instigator. His "Two Horses on the Meadow" (1649) makes it clear that he did not just see animals as additional subject matter for a landscape, but conceived his pictures of them almost as portraits. He was, however, not a painter of the outdoors, but did his compositions in the studio using individual studies which he had taken from nature.

Willem van de Velde the Younger

Given that in the 17th c. the Dutch possessed an important navy and the largest merchant fleet in the world, it is hardly surprising that motives connected with seafaring, for example, sea battles, were very popular, particularly as a way of reinforcing the patriotic consciousness of the people. Willem van de Velde the Younger (1633–1707) achieved a high level of mastery in his sea pictures. In his "Cannon Shot" (c. 1660), which is actually a gun salute, the calm sea with its smooth surface provides a stark contrast to the military action with its gunpowder smoke. A gentle breaking of the waves can be seen making its way to the foot of the picture, thereby creating the impression that the observer is standing on the harbourside, gazing at the harbour surroundings.

Gerard Terborch

Gerard Terborch (1617–81) proved to be an important painter of genre pictures. His "Gallant Conversation," also known as "The Fatherly Admonition" (c. 1654), is intended ironically, as the young officer on the right-hand side is beguiling the young lady with a gleaming coin.

Johannes
Vermeer

The oeuvre of Johannes Vermeer (1632–75) comprises just thirty or so oil paintings, since he worked extremely slowly – small wonder, given the incredibly meticulous detail of his pictures. Form, colour and light fuse with unique effectiveness, giving his painted interiors and people both the stillness of a still-life and a spiritual depth. It is because of this that Vermeer's portrait of the "A Maidservant Pouring Milk" (c. 1658), depicting her at work in a rather shabby room, comes across as such as fascinating scene from everyday life. The painter develops a resonant interconnection of both plasticity and colour between the still-life on the kitchen table and the woman pouring the milk. Rounded shapes are sequenced into the picture to offer both contrast and variety – the bread-basket and the loaf of bread, the earthenware bowl and the opening of the milk jug, even to the rounded shapes of the clothes the woman is wearing on the upper part of her body and her full face framed by the simple head-covering. This array of rounded forms is expressively deployed using subtle gradations of colour, full of nuances, and the gentlest transitions between light and shade. Using the rear of his own house as a vantage point, Vermeer painted a picture of the houses in Delft, known as "The Tiny Street" (c. 1658), and thereby proved himself to be not only a master of realism, but also an artist who in the most striking way combined techniques of composition which were able both to open up spaces and bring surfaces into particular prominence. Thus the picture is basically made up of right-angles but also uses diagonal lines. These achieve both spatial-perspective and one-dimensional decorative effects.

The early-morning atmosphere in "The Letter Reader" (1662/63) is conveyed by a colour symphony of blue, ochre, and greenish-white. The picture depicts a pregnant woman lost in thought as she peruses a letter, presumably from the man she loves, most likely the father of the unborn child, who is far away from home, as suggested by the map in the background.

"A Maidservant pouring Milk" . . .   . . . "The Letter Reader" (detail)

Pieter de Hooch

Pieter de Hooch (1629–84) portrays in his picture "At the Linen Cupboard" (1663) a domestic scene with the washing being put away. The interior of the room is depicted in warm colours, giving the picture its snug atmosphere. On the other hand, for de Hooch, painting the view looking through a room involves important principles of composition and the most skilful mastery of light and shade, so that the interior opens up as a sequence of several interconnecting rooms with views leading inwards, outwards and right through the middle of the picture.

Emanuel
de Witte

The range of the architectural picture was greatly enriched by the work of Emanuel de Witte (1616/18–92). "The Interior of a Gothic Church" is a severe, central-perspective composition, with masterly use of light to bring out and delineate the spatial divisions of the subject. The open tomb with the gravedigger can be seen as a memento mori, a warning of the transitoriness of life, while the heraldic plaques and flags point to the high regard enjoyed by the deceased even after death.

"The Interior of the Portuguese Synagogue in Amsterdam" (1680), a building which has survived to this day unscathed, also makes delightful play of contrasts between light and shade. In all his paintings de Witte attaches great importance to the precision with which architectural features are copied.

Philips Koninck

One of the most outstanding landscape painters of the second half of the 17th c. was Philips Koninck (1619–88). In his "Flat Landscape with Huts along a Road" (c. 1655) he offers a magnificent panoramic view obtained from an elevated vantage point.

Rembrandt van Rijn and his Pupils

Rembrandt's
early work

Rembrandt van Rijn (1606–69) is represented in the Rijksmuseum with masterpieces from all his different creative phases. His early works from the Leiden period include "Tobias accuses Anna of the theft of a kid" (1626), a human situation depicted with the utmost psychological insight, in which both the face and posture of the old and blind Tobias express his total bewilderment, while resentment and horror are written on the face of the unjustly accused Anna, who has used her wages as a spinning-woman to acquire the little goat quite legitimately. What is outstanding is the precision and subtlety with which the characters are delineated down to the last

detail, including Tobias's worn coat and the superb use of light, which contributes to the enlivening of the scene. The powerful contrasts of light and shade which are so characteristic of Rembrandt also distinguish his impressive "Self Portrait" (1628) and the painting "Jeremiah mourns the destruction of Jerusalem" (1630).

"The Night
Watch"

One of Rembrandt's greatest commissions during his creative period in Amsterdam was "The Deployment of the Militia Company of Captain Frans Banning Cocq and his Lieutenant Willem van Ruytenburch" (1642), popularly known as "The Night Watch" because the colours of the picture darkened considerably during the 19th c. The subject of the painting, however, has no nocturnal connections. The deploy-

"The Night Watch" (detail)

ment takes place in a shady side-street in daylight, though it is not based on any real event. It is a visual memento for these soldier-citizens of their shared activities, each member of the militia actually paying for his own individual portrait, and it was intended to be hung in the militia's large assembly room. Perhaps, in his composition of this picture, Rembrandt let himself be inspired by the parades organised on the occasion of the Queen of France's visit to Amsterdam in 1638. At all events it broke with the previous tradition of militia group pictures for, unlike all the painters before him, Rembrandt does not arrange his group in any kind of clichéed pose, but has them moving at full speed. Originally the militiamen gave the impression that they were marching straight towards the observer. Unfortunately, when the picture was rehung in the Amsterdam City Hall in 1715, the painting had about 1m/3ft chopped off on the left-hand side and about 30cm/1ft on the right-hand side. This was so that the picture could fit between two doors, but it has had the result that the central group of the captain and lieutenant today seem much more static than they would have done in the original composition.

Rembrandt's painting of the militia deployment is a vivid and fascinating piece of theatre in glowing colours and with the most varied dramatic details. Special lighting is employed to pick out a small girl who is carrying a chicken at her belt, the claws of which are brought strikingly into relief. They can almost be thought of as the mascot of the kloveniers' guild, as kloven means rifle-butt, but also has a similarity with the word "klauw" (claw). Accordingly both claw and rifle form the emblem of the militiamen's organisation.

The original 275×200cm/9×6½ft "Anatomy Lesson of Dr Deyman" (1656) was severely damaged in a fire in 1723 in the surgeons' guildroom where it was hanging. Only a section 100×134cm/3¼×4½ft was preserved. After his first anatomy lesson picture "Anatomy Lesson of Dr Tulp" (1632; The Hague, Mauritshuis), Rembrandt's second one is dedicated to Dr Tulp's successor, Dr Joan Deyman, who was praelector of the Anatomical Theatre in Amsterdam. It shows the famous doctor with the skull in his hands, carrying out a public brain autopsy on January 29th 1656 on a criminal who had been hanged the day before.

"Anatomy Lesson of Dr Deyman"

The original arrangement of the figures in this group portrait was rather conventional – no doubt following the terms of the commission – with the anatomist Dr Deyman right in the centre of the picture. Highly impressive, on the other hand, is the foreshortened representation of the corpse, which looks back to famous Italian depictions of the dead Christ in the "Mourning of Christ" by Mantegna (late 15th c.) and that of Orazio Borgianni (c. 1615).

Rembrandt's last group portrait – and a magnificent example of the genre – is "The Leaders of the Clothdyers' Guild", known as "Staalmeesters" (1662). These men were chosen for a year to check the quality and colours of the cloths. The painting was formerly hung high on the wall in the Staalhof, the hall of the dyers' guild. The five guild leaders – the man without a hat is a servant – are captured in the most vivid fashion, right down to their individual body movements, whether looking around, looking up, standing up, bowing or leaning back. Even the various movements of their hands have been translated onto canvas. But all these details are totally dependent on one another and what is so impressive is the unity of both conception and execution to which the painting can lay claim.

"Staalmeesters"

The "Self-portrait as the Apostle Paul" (1661) is a highly expressive portrait of Rembrandt in old age. In his 100 or so self-portraits Rembrandt affords the observer insights into his eventful life – insights which penetrate to the innermost depths of his soul.

"Self-portrait as the Apostle Paul"

Rijksmuseum Vincent van Gogh

"Jewish Bride"

The double portrait of a man caressing his wife has been known as the "Jewish Bride" (c. 1665) since the 19th c. and is thought to be of the Jewish poet Don Miguel de Barrios and his wife Abigael de Pina, with allusions to the biblical world, principally Isaac and Rebekah. What is noticeable in Rembrandt's late works is the paste-like application of colour, which sometimes give a relief-like quality, so that the warm brown shades, the reddish and yellow-gold hues have an even more intense and glowing impact.

Ferdinand Bol

Ferdinand Bol (1616–80) was a pupil of Rembrandt's who painted "The Four Governors of the Amsterdam Leper Asylum" (1649). Both the lighting and the expressive vividness of the figures' gestures are deployed in masterly fashion as unifying elements within the composition. The special emphasis given to the people's hands and faces is reminiscent of Rembrandt's group portraits.

Gerrit Dou

Gerrit Dou (1613–75) achieved particular distinction through his night pictures. "The Evening School" (before 1665) is painted using highly effective techniques of light and shade. Not only do the children's eager faces shine in the candlelight, but the whole spatial area of the picture is brilliantly opened up with the flames of just four candles as the only source of light. Moreover, the light acquires a symbolic significance – the "light of understanding" or enlightenment. "The Hermit", the depiction of an old man at prayer, impresses by its masterly reproduction of detail and its excellent use of light.

Govert Flinck

Of all Rembrandt's pupils it is Govert Flinck (1618–80) who with his "Isaac blesses Jacob" (1638) comes closest to his master. This representation of the old and blind Jacob, feeling with his hands for his son's hair, is distinguished by its emotional directness and the consummate skill of its characterisation.

Late 17th c.

The 17th c. bows out with the enigmatic genre pictures of Frans van Mieris (1635–81), the historical pictures of Gerard Lairesse (1641–1711), including "Cleopatra's Banquet", and the animal pictures of Melchior d'Hondecoeter (1636–95), e.g. "Pelican and other fowls by a water-basin" (c. 1680). In the period which followed, Dutch painting tended to draw much closer to the mainstream of European art and it was not until the end of the 19th c., with Vincent van Gogh, and the beginning of the 20th c., with the De Stijl movement, that it attained new fame and importance.

Rijksmuseum Vincent van Gogh

See Van Gogh Museum

Scheepvaart Museum (Maritime Museum)   J/K 6

Location
Kattenburger-
plein 1

Buses
22

Opening times
Tues.–Sat.
10am–5pm,
Sun. noon–5pm

The Dutch Maritime Museum possesses one of the largest collections of its type in the world and offers a comprehensive coverage of the history of Dutch seafaring from its earliest beginnings up to the present time. The visitor will be fascinated by its 500 scale models of ships and a host of nautical charts, navigational instruments, paintings, weapons and photographs, set out in chronological order.

The Maritime Museum is housed in a building which was erected in 1655 to plans by the city architect Daniel Stalpaert and was designed as the admiralty arsenal. It was renovated in 1791 after a fire. The building was vacated by the admiralty in 1973 and after extensive restoration work it has been open since 1981 as a museum with a library, book and souvenir shop and café.

"Amsterdam"

The entry price to the museum includes a tour of the sailing-ship, the "Amsterdam", which has stood at anchor at the museum quayside since

The Maritime Museum

1991. The ship is a copy of a ship belonging to the Dutch East India Company. The original ship went down off the coast of southern England on its maiden voyage in 1749, and has lain there ever since. As a result of a work scheme for the unemployed in the 1980s a copy of the ship was constructed. The visitor to the ship is transported back in time to the 18th c. People dressed in historical costumes give a vivid impression of how life on this 48m/150ft long and almost 12m/40ft wide three-master must have been.

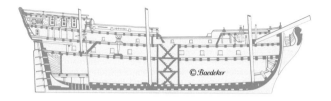

Schiphol Airport (Luchthaven Schiphol)   A 10

Schiphol Airport is situated 13km/8 miles south-west of Amsterdam in the middle of the reclaimed Haarlemmermeer polder, about 4m/13ft below sea level. Charts of 1610 designate this area "Shipp Holl", which implies that many ships must have foundered here when it was the Haarlemmermeer.

Schiphol was first used by military aeroplanes for take-off and landing in 1917. In 1920 KLM (Koninklijke Luchtvaart Maatschappij) started flights to London and thus brought Schiphol into the international air traffic network.

Location
10km/6 miles
south-west

Rail
from Centraal
Station (every
20 mins)

103

On May 10th 1940 Schiphol was destroyed by bombing but soon after the war it was rebuilt and extended.

Today over 80 airlines fly from Schiphol to 205 destinations in 87 countries. With some 21 million passengers coming here each year, Schiphol ranks fifth among European airports. In order to cope with the increasing number of passengers, work on an extension to the existing airport facilities was begun some time ago. It is anticipated that by the year 2003 the airport will be able to process 30 million passengers a year.

Schipol airport is renowned for its high standards of comfort and service. At the end of 1993 a new office and conference centre opened its doors, and a leisure centre offers spectators the use of a sauna and solarium as well as the opportunity to try their skill on 24 "different" golf courses by means of a simulator.

There are magnificent views of all the runways on the roof of the 370m/405yd long and 18m/20yd wide central concourse where passengers board their planes. Part of this walkway is covered. There are also good views from the comfort of the "Aviorama" restaurant.

Visitors to Schiphol should also take a look at the "Aviodome" aviation museum (see Practical Information, Museums).

Schreierstoren (Wailing Tower)   C 2

Location
On the corner
of Prins
Hendrikkade and
Geldersekade

Trams
1, 2, 4, 5, 9, 13,
16, 17, 24, 25

Metro
Centraalstation

On the corner of Prins Hendrikkade and Geldersekade, near the main station (Centraal Spoorweg Station), stands the Wailing Tower, a fragment of the medieval city wall (built in 1480). It was the office of the harbourmaster until 1960 when he moved into the Port Administration building. The tower stood empty for some considerable time but now it houses a ship's chandlers.

There is some controversy about the real meaning of the name: a gable stone bearing the date 1569 shows a woman crying, which gave rise to the idea that this was where the sailors' wives took leave of their husbands when they were about to go back to sea. A second version suggests that the name stems from the fact that the tower stands astride (schrijlings) a wall called the Kamperhoofd.

In 1927 a bronze plaque was placed on the tower to commemorate Henry Hudson, who set off from here on April 4th 1609 in his ship "De halve Maan" (Half Moon) on a journey which was to end in the founding of New Amsterdam (New York).

Singel   H 5/6 (A/B 1–4)

Location
Centre

No. 7

**Ronde Lutherse
Kerk (No. 11)**

The Singel (not to be confused with the Singelgracht) was originally a moat. The city used to run on the inner side, where the odd-numbered houses now stand. On the other side of the wall lay Amsterdam's vegetable gardens and meadows (the Torensluis is one of the former passages to the gardens). When the city was enlarged and the wall lost its defensive function, it was demolished (c. 1600) and houses were built on the site.

A walk along this canal will afford the visitor many delightful points of interest: the house at No. 7 is no wider than a front door and can therefore claim to be the narrowest house in Amsterdam.

The Ronde Lutherse Kerk (Circular Lutheran Church) was built in 1668–71. In 1822 it burnt right down to its foundations and was subsequently rebuilt in its original form. As is usual in Protestant churches, the white interior gives a very sober impression. The seats in the galleries are arranged in an echelon formation and call to mind a theatre rather than a church.

Since 1935 religious services have no longer been held in the Ronde Lutherse Kerk and today it is used for concerts and occasionally conferences (Sonesta Koepelzaal).

The cat boat moored in front of the house at No. 44 has developed into a real tourist attraction. Countless homeless cats have found board and lodging here. Visitors are more than welcome, but should be ready to make a contribution to the upkeep of this animals' sanctuary.

Pilasters with Ionic capitals give relief to the façade of the Veerhuis de Zwaan, which was built in 1652. The house takes its name from a former owner.

Of particular architectural interest are the houses at Nos. 140–142, which were designed by the architect Hendrik de Keyser in 1600. This is where Banning Cocq, the principal figure in Rembrandt's "Night Watch", lived for a while.

A tower once stood on the widest bridge across the Singel (at the junction with Oude Leliestraat). In the 17th c. it was used as a prison and it gave the bridge its name. Just above sea level there was a dungeon which is supposed to have been used at one time as a sobering-up cell (for men and women separately). Since 1987 the bridge has had a monument to the Dutch writer Multatuli (1820–87).

Just after the university buildings on the Singel, the visitor comes to the Flower Market, partly accommodated on house boats (Mon.–Sat. 9am–5pm). Innumerable types of cut flowers and pot plants are on sale here. Every conceivable aid to growing and tending flowers is available here: garden peat and earth, fertiliser and seeds, watering cans and flower pots.

The flower market has not always been on the Singel: during the 17th c. it was held every Monday in the summer on the St Luciensteeg, near the present Amsterdams Historisch Museum (see entry). As regards the goods on sale, even then it was just as large as it is now – so much so that

The old and new buildings of the Stedelijk Museum

someone at that time complained that it would be wearisome to have to list all the names of the shrubs and plants that one could buy there.

★★ Stedelijk Museum (City Museum)   G 7

Location
Paulus Potter-
straat 13

Trams
2, 3, 5, 12, 16

Opening times
daily
11am–5pm

The City Museum (founded in 1885) is one of Europe's most important modern art museums. Its collection mainly covers 19th and 20th c. Dutch and French painting.

The main part of the Stedelijk Museum is a red and white brick building, built in 1895 in the Neo-Renaissance style. The statues in the niches represent important Dutch artists and architects (including Hendrik de Keyser and Jacob van Campen). In 1954 the modern south wing was added.

The museum owes its existence to the appreciation of art and the generosity of leading citizens of Amsterdam. Its collection is based on the gift of

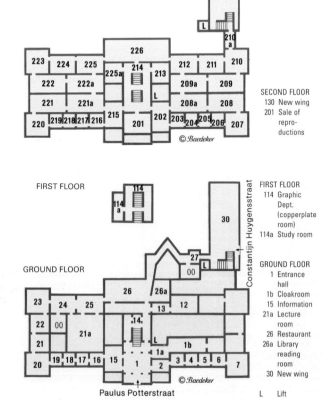

**Stedelijk
Museum**

SECOND FLOOR

N

SECOND FLOOR
130 New wing
201 Sale of
    repro-
    ductions

FIRST FLOOR

GROUND FLOOR

FIRST FLOOR
114 Graphic
    Dept.
    (copperplate
    room)
114a Study room

GROUND FLOOR
1 Entrance
  hall
1b Cloakroom
15 Information
21a Lecture
    room
26 Restaurant
26a Library
    reading
    room
30 New wing

L   Lift

Paulus Potterstraat

© Baedeker

Constantijn Huygensstraat

Stedelijk Museum: Karel Appel "Couple" (1951)

the widow Suasso-de Bruin ("Sophia Augusta Foundation"). Chr. P. van Eeghen's collection of contemporary art was added to this as well as other collections not confined to contemporary works. These were later transferred to other museums, since in accordance with its original concept the City Museum specialises in modern art from the mid-19th c. onwards.

The following are some of the movements and artists represented:
De Stijl (Van Doesburg, Mondriaan, Rietveld), Cobra (Karel Appel, Corneille, Jorn), Colourfield Painting (Kelly, Louis, Newman), Pop Art (Rosenquist, Warhol), Nouveau Réalisme (Armand, Spoerri, Tinguely); painters such as Chagall, Dubuffet, De Kooning, Malevich and Matisse. The museum also possesses a large number of sculptures, including those of Rodin, Moore, Renoir, Laurens and Visser, and some of these are to be found in the sculpture garden.
The City Museum has its own library and puts on showings of avantgarde films, concerts and exhibitions.

Stopera (City Hall and Opera House)

J 6 (C 3/4)

Much of the former Waterlooplein (see Jodenbuurt) is today taken up with a modern building which houses both Amsterdam's city hall, the "Stadhuis", and its opera house, "Het Muziektheater" – hence the name "Stopera". Although the Muziektheater was opened in 1986 the Stadhuis was not occupied until 1988.

Wilhelm Holzbauer, an Austrian, was responsible for the original plans for this massive building. He had already won a competition for designing the city hall in 1968. At that time a separate building for the opera house was envisaged. Heated controversy about both buildings delayed the start of construction and it was not until 1979 that the decision was made to combine both projects within a communal building. This plan finally came to fruition on the Amstel in the 1980s.

The L-shaped city hall wraps around the opera house, which bulges out, crescent-shaped, towards the river and which, with its unusually wide

Location
Waterlooplein
(Amstel 1–3)

Metro
Waterlooplein

107

Stopera: a modern complex housing the City Hall and Opera House

stage (22m/72ft) and correspondingly large arena-type auditorium, is the venue for the Dutch national ballet and opera companies, plus guest performances.

On the ground floor of the Stopera there is a café which provides a fine view – from the terrace in summer and through large windows in winter – of the houses along the Amstel and the Zwanenburgwal.

Normaal Amsterdams Peil

In the arcade between the city hall and the opera house and against the background of a 25m/82ft long sectional view of the Netherlands there is a replica of the "Normaal Amsterdams Peil", the NAP. This shows the average water level of the North Sea. The genuine article is actually below the paving in front of the Royal Palace, the Koninklijk Paleis.

Theater Carré   J 6

Location
Amstel 115–125

Trams
6, 7, 10

When Amsterdam lost its fair, Oscar Carré, director of the Carré Circus, which was extremely popular at the turn of the century, began to look for a permanent site in Amsterdam. He found a suitable spot on the Amstel and obtained a temporary permit to build a wooden marquee. However he ignored the official requirements and had a stone roof put on his marquee. When the municipality ordered him to demolish it he applied for a permanent permit. Eventually he met with success and the Carré in the form we know it today was opened in 1887.

After Oscar Carré's death in 1911 it was converted into a theatre, but this was not as successful as the circus, and in the end the Carré family had to sell the building. It changed hands several times before being transferred in 1927 to a company whose manager, Alex Wunnink, succeeded in re-establishing its importance in Amsterdam's theatrical life.

Today a wide variety of artistes appear here: ballet and operetta companies, The Russian State Circus, as well as internationally famous pop stars.

Tropenmuseum: the interior . . .   *. . . and one of the exhibits*

Trippenhuis (Trip House)   C 3

This elegant mansion, on the corner of the Amstel and the Nieuwmarkt, was built by the Trip brothers (immensely rich cannon manufacturers) and today houses the Dutch Academy of Sciences.

When the two "cannon kings" moved to Amsterdam they wanted an imposing house to live in. In 1662 they were able to move into the "Trip House". Its chimneys are shaped like the mortars to which the brother owed their wealth.

The Royal Institute for Science, Literature and Fine Arts, today the Dutch Academy of Sciences, moved into the Trip House in 1808.

Tradition has it that one of the family's servants was heard to say, "Oh, if only I had a house as wide as your front door, I should be happy!" One of the Trip brothers overheard this and had a little house built of the same materials and in the same style opposite the Trip House. This little Trip House is still there today at No. 26.

Location
Kloveniers-
burgwal 29

Metro
Nieuwmarkt

Little Trip
House

★Tropenmuseum (Tropical Museum)   K 6

The Tropical Museum, with its displays of artistic and everyday objects from tropical and sub-tropical areas, is part of the Royal Tropical Institute. Both old and new exhibits are displayed in authentic surroundings. For example faithful copies have been constructed of a street in a North African town, an Indian village, a Javanese house and an African market. Other sections of the museum deal with such subjects as handicrafts (e.g. textile manufacture), technology and economics, religion, music and theatre. In

Location
Linnaeus-
straat 2

Tram
9

Opening times
Mon.–Fri.
10am–5pm,
Sat., Sun.
noon–5pm

addition the Tropical Museum provides a continuous series of temporary exhibitions, regular concerts of Oriental or Asiatic music, as well as a comprehensive library. The original purpose of the Royal Tropical Institute, successor to the "Koloniaal Instituut", was to provide information about the Dutch colonies (Surinam, Indonesia and the Dutch Antilles). Nowadays its prime concern is the problems of the Third World.

TM Junior

The TM Junior children's museum is the junior branch of the Tropical Museum. It is specially intended for children between the ages of six and twelve. Open Wed. afternoons and weekends, and Mon.–Fri. during school holidays.

Universiteit van Amsterdam (University)   A 3

Location
Spui

Trams
1, 2, 5

The Amsterdam City University, endowed in 1877 and therefore comparatively young, was the first university in the Netherlands after the war to set up a faculty of social and political sciences. It has the reputation of being progressive.

One of the main university buildings is the former old people's house on the Oudemanhuispoort (see Achterburgwal).

The "Vrije Universiteit", opened in 1880, is a Christian-oriented university in which teaching is based on the Reformed faith.

★★Van Gogh Museum   G 7

Location
Paulus Potter-
straat 7

Trams
2, 5

Opening times
daily 10am–5pm,

The Van Gogh Museum contains the largest Van Gogh collection in the world (a donation from van Gogh's brother Theo and his nephew V. W. van Gogh). Originally housed in the Stedelijk Museum (see entry), it has been at its present purpose-built location (designed by Gerrit Rietveld) since 1972. The collection comprises some 200 paintings, 500 drawings and 850 letters. Also on display are works by those contemporaries of van Gogh who either influenced him or were influenced by him.

On the ground floor of the building are paintings by artistic precursors and friends of van Gogh: these include Delacroix, Pissaro, Monet, Corot, Toulouse-Lautrec and Gauguin.

The upper floor has the works of Vincent Willem van Gogh (1853–90), arranged in chronological order. The first graphic pieces (on display on the second storey) date from 1878–80, during the time that van Gogh was working as a missionary in the Belgian mining district of Borinage. In the end he was forced to admit that he was not suited to such work and he gave it up, moving to Brussels in 1880 to pursue his artistic studies. Largely self-taught, he learnt his craft from the works of Frans Hals and Rembrandt. In his early pictures from the years 1880–87 he carried on the established Dutch tradition. This phase of his work is typified by realistic paintings in very dark hues, the subjects he chose being mainly peasants and working people (main work: "Potato eater", 1885)

Van Gogh received financial support from his brother Theo, who in 1886 took him to Paris. Here he began in earnest to get to grips with the works of the impressionists. In February 1888 he moved to Arles, where he created his most famous works. The period between 1887 and 1890 is distinguished by glowing colours full of contrasts; the paintings with their broad brushstrokes show clear impressionist influences ("Vase with Sunflowers", "The Yellow House", "The Sower", etc.). In Arles van Gogh began by living with Paul Gauguin but, inevitably, with two such profoundly different artists, this attempt at co-existence soon foundered. After repeated nervous breakdowns and mental disorders (in December 1888 van Gogh cut off his left ear) he was taken to the Saint-Rémy sanatorium. Nevertheless his creative activity did not flag ("Van Gogh's Room", etc.). At the beginning of 1890 van Gogh moved to Auvers-sur-Oise, where he came

Van Gogh Museum

under the protection of the doctor and art connoisseur Paul Gachet. During these last few months van Gogh created some of his most profoundly expressive pictures, including "Wheat-field with Ravens", "The Garden of Daubigny" and just before his death, "Crows over the Cornfield"). On June 29th 1890 van Gogh ended his life with a revolver shot – his brother Theo only survived him by a few months.

Van Gogh's drawings and graphic work are displayed on the second storey of the building, while special exhibitions are held both here and on the third floor.

The museum also has a library which contains literature concerning Vincent van Gogh and his times. The museum also boasts a studio, where students can take advantage of the active instruction provided (there are courses in photography, painting and various printing techniques).

Volendam

Excursion

The village of Volendam is part of the district of Edam and lies on the IJsselmeer. As elsewhere, its fishing industry has been hard hit by the damming of the Zuiderzee.

Volendam is the Catholic counterpart of Marken (see entry). It is famous in the Netherlands for its folk costumes, so that it is not surprising that tourism has become its main source of income. The older inhabitants still wear their costumes with pride: for the men this consists of baggy woollen breeches, while the women wear flowered dresses with striped aprons, coral necklaces, and in cold weather blue-and-white-striped shawls. During the week the women usually wear a simple cheesecloth cap, but on Sundays and holidays this is replaced by the famous lace headdress. (At the harbour it is possible to have oneself photographed in the traditional Volendam costume.)

Location
20km/12 miles
north-east

Buses
Departure
opposite
Centraal
Station

Vondelpark

Besides the harbour (boat trips to Marken and Monnickendam (see entries)
and the picturesque old houses, the following are of interest: the collection
of paintings in the Hotel Spaander by the harbour, with more than 100
works by old masters; the Volendam Museum (Zeestraat 37; open: Apr.–
Oct.: daily 10am–5pm) with folk costumes and models of fishing vessels;
"De Gouden Kamer" (Oude Draaipand 8; open in the season: daily
9am–6pm), which is papered with millions of cigar bands assembled to
make pictures such as New York's Statue of Liberty.

Marken-Volendam
Express
From March to October there is a daily boat service between Marken (see
entry) and Volendam, leaving at half-hourly intervals.

Vondelpark — F/G 7

Main entrance
Leidseplein

Trams
1, 2, 3, 5, 6, 12

This green lung in the heart of Amsterdam is named after Joost van den
Vondel, Holland's most famous poet (see Famous People). His statue was
unveiled in the park in 1867. The park, Amsterdam's Bois de Boulogne, as
one newspaper called it when it was opened, covers approximately
48ha/119 acres and is landscaped on English lines, with sandpits and
playgrounds, ponds and fountains, flower-beds and lawns, a rose-garden
and a little tea-house, a wealth of different types of tree, and hedges
providing homes for many birds.

During the 1960s and 1970s the Vondelpark was a favourite haunt of
hippies. However, when drug-pushing and the negative phenomena associated with it started to get out of hand, the authorities decided to forbid
sleeping in the park at night.

During the summer months the park is the venue for the Vondelpark
Festival and many other programmes of music, drama and children's
events.

Film Museum
On the edge of the Vondelpark can be found the Film Museum (see Practical
Information, Museums) with its terrace café, from which there is a delight-
ful view of the park.

Waaggebouw

See Nieuwmarkt

Walletjes (City district) — B/C 2/3

Location
Centre

In the oldest part of Amsterdam, between the Oudezijdsvoorburgwal and
the Achterburgwal (see entry), in the triangle formed by the central station,
the Dam and the Nieuwmarkt, lies the area known as "de Walletjes", the
red-light district.

The "oldest profession" was officially sanctioned here as far back as the
14th c. Along the romantic canals and in the small side alleys the prostitutes
sit in their "shop-windows" and offer their services. If the red light is not on
and the curtains are drawn, the ladies are busy.

"De Walletjes" seem strangely innocuous with their bizarre mixture of
scantily-clad girls, sex-shops and little old lady shopkeepers, tourists and
locals (not all of whom are clients by any means).

Waterlooplein

See Jodenbuurt

★Westerkerk (West Church)   G 5/6

The Westerkerk, in which the magnificent wedding of Princess (now Queen) Beatrix to Claus von Amsberg took place in 1966, is the most popular church in the city. Its tower, popularly known as "Langer Jan" (tall John), which at 85m/279ft is the highest in the city, is a symbol of Amsterdam.

After the city went over to Protestantism Hendrik de Keyser began the building of the church in 1620. After his death the work was completed by Jacob van Campen in 1630 and the tower was added. In 1631 the church was consecrated with a Whitsun service. The people of the surrounding Jordaan district (see entry) stayed away at first because of the gentry from along the canals who came here to worship. They wanted a church of their own which they finally acquired with the Noorderkerk.

From an architectural point of view, the Westerkerk can be seen as a continuation of what de Keyser had attempted in the Zuiderkerk (see entry).

Location
Westermarkt

Trams
13, 14, 17

Opening times
Mon.–Sat.
10am–4pm;
tower:
Apr.–Sept.:
Mon.–Sat.
10am–4pm

Westerkerk

At 29m/95ft wide and 28m/92ft high, the Westerkerk is the largest Protestant church in the Netherlands. It was constructed in the Dutch Renaissance style, but also contains many elements which recall the Gothic period (e.g. the high sweeping vertical lines). The tower soars up from the middle of the west façade and at its highest point bears the imperial crown: in memory of Emperor Maximilian of Austria, who was cured of an illness in Amsterdam and as a result in 1489 gave the city both his protection and the right to carry the imperial crown in its coat of arms. The carillon inside the tower is the work of François Hemony. The largest of the bells weighs 7500kg/7¼ tons, while the hammer alone is 200kg/440lb. The carillon plays every Tuesday between noon and one o'clock.

Exterior

The interior of the church is exceptionally plain. The central aisle and the two transepts have wooden barrel-vaulting, because the soft foundations of the building hereabouts would not have allowed them to be made of anything heavier. On the other hand, the two side aisles have stone groin-vaulting. It was not until the end of the 17th c. that it became customary for the members of the congregation to be accompanied by an organ when they sang and in 1689 the church was given its organ, the instrument then being enlarged in 1727. During a general refurbishment undertaken between 1988 and 1991, an attempt was made to restore the organ to how it was when it was built. The side-panels of the organ were decorated by Gerard Lairesse with painted biblical motifs and musical instruments (the church's other organ is used exclusively for the performance of Bach cantatas).

The Westerkerk also contains the grave of Rembrandt, who was interred here on October 8th 1669. Where exactly he was buried, however, has never been established. In 1906, close to the place where the artist's son Titus had his final resting place, a memorial stone dedicated to Rembrandt was added to one of the columns.

Interior

Zaanse Schans

De Drie
Driehoken

In 1987, on the Westermarkt, at the corner of the Keizersgracht, a memorial by Karin Daan was consecrated, as a lasting reminder of the persecutions suffered by homosexuals during the period of Nazi rule. The memorial consists of three triangles fashioned out of pink granite – homosexuals were forced to carry a pink triangle on their clothing to mark them out.

★Zaanse Schans   Excursion

Location
15km/9 miles
north-west

Rail
from Centraal
Station

Opening times
daily 10am–5pm
(some museums
close in winter)

About 15km/9 miles out of Amsterdam one comes across a little piece of "picture-book Holland": the reconstruction of a Zaanland village as it would have looked about the year 1700. This open-air museum was privately set up in 1948. The Zaanse Schans Foundation managed to rescue old buildings that stood in the way of industrial expansion and typical 17th and 18th c. wooden houses and windmills were dismantled to be re-erected here. That this open-air museum gives the visitor such a true-to-life picture of the past is due in no small measure to the fact that almost all of the carefully restored houses are inhabited.

At the beginning of the 18th c. this area had about 500 Dutch windmills. Half of them ground mustard, oil, cocoa, spices and tobacco as well as flour. The other half were saw-mills, since the timber industry was very important in this area in the 17th c. Among the few mills still maintained in Zaanse Schans an oil-mill, dye-mill, mustard-mill and saw-mill can be visited; there are also a cheese-dairy, an old bakery, an old grocery, a clogmaker's and a pewterer's, as well as the Zaans Museum of Clock-making (Zaanse Uurwerken Museum) with a collection of old Dutch clocks.

The old houses and windmills form a delightful backdrop to a boat trip on the Zaan.

Zaanstad   Excursion

Location
10km/6 miles
north

The various villages and localities grouped around the River Zaan, about 10km/6 miles north of Amsterdam, are collectively known as the municipality of Zaanstad. It is a densely-populated and highly industrialised belt of land. The first timber saw-mills were built here in the 16th c. and they led to the development of wood-processing and shipbuilding industries.

Zaandam

For four months in 1697 Peter the Great, Tsar of Russia, worked here incognito as a carpenter and shipwright under the name of Peter Michael (an event commemorated by Lortzing in his opera "Zar und Zimmermann"). Those times are recalled by the Tsar Peter House (Krimp 24) and the Tsar Peter Monument on the Dam presented to the town by Tsar Nicholas II in 1911. Also worth a visit are the Old Catholic Church, 1695 (Papenpad 12), the old "Held Josua" sawmill (behind the station), and "De Oolevaar", a watermill dating from 1640 on the southern side of the Julia bridge.

The Zaanse Schans open-air museum (see entry) lies just outside Zaandam.

Zaandijk

The Zaanlandse Oudheidkamer (Lagedijk 80; open: Tues.–Fri 10am–noon and 2–4pm, Sun. 2–4pm) contains costumes, toys, model ships and other 17th and 18th c. objects and is well worth a visit. There is also the Weefhuis (weaving house) or "house with the picture garden" (Lagedijk 39), the "Death" corn-mill (Lagedijk 29), built in 1656, and the Town Hall (Lagedijk 104), an old merchant's house with antique furniture and wall-paintings.

Koog aan de
Zaan

The Moolen Museum (Museumslaan 19; open: Tues.–Fri. 10am–noon and 2–5pm; Sat., Sun. 2–5pm) gives visitors an insight into 17th and 18th c.

mills using scale models and documents. A visit to "Het Pink", the old oil-mill of 1610 on the Pinkstraat, completes the picture.

Westzaan

Places of interest: the Great Church (Torenstraat) with temporary exhibitions in July and August; "Het Prinsenhof" (Weelsloot), a mill dating back to 1722; "De Schoolmeester" (Guisweg, built in 1695), the only paper-mill in the world still in operation; the Stadhuis (Kerkbuurt), a former courthouse in the style of Louis XIV, with a cupola (1781); and the "Zuiderver-maning" church (Zuideinde 231), built in 1731, which has an exceptionally fine interior.

Krommenie

Krommenie has a watermill dating from 1640 and known as "De Woudaap".

Graft

The oldest village on the island of Schermer is mentioned as early as 1325. Its town hall (1613) is worth seeing.

De Rijp

De Rijp is the birthplace of J. A. Leeghwater (1575–1650), inventor of the diving bell. The "Wooden House" museum (Jan Boonplein 2; open from Easter to May and Sept./Oct. Sat., Sun. 11am–5pm, June–Aug.: Mon.–Wed., Fri.–Sun. 10am–5pm) has displays of tiles, ceramics, old sea-charts and the skeleton of a whale. The Waaggebouw (Kleine Dam 2) dates from 1690 and was designed by Jan van der Heiden. The building is adorned by 24 stained-glass windows.

Purmerend

Purmerend has been an important market town since 1484. The main attraction for tourists is the cheese-market held every Tuesday from July to September, but the Koepelkerk, with its famous Garrels organ, is also worth seeing.

Broek in Waterland

Broek in Waterland is one of the Netherlands' most prettiest villages, its 18th c. wooden houses grouped around a large pond. The village still has two cheese-makers and one clogmaker.

Zandvoort

Excursion

Zandvoort is situated in North Holland directly on the North Sea and has an international reputation as one of the main Dutch seaside resorts. During the summer months on fine days thousands of people are attracted to the endless expanses of sandy beach (almost 9km/5½ miles long). Attractive dunes, covering an area of 3600ha/14 sq.miles, skirt the beach and are popularly known as "Amsterdam's Waterworks".

The range of sports on offer in Zandvoort is immense, as can be imagined: mini-golf, golf, tennis and riding can all be enjoyed. The resort is also famous for its motor-racing circuit, opened in 1948, which hosts both car and motor-cycle races (in recent years it has had to be reduced in size for noise prevention reasons).

In spite of its many attractions as a modern resort, Zandvoort tries to preserve its old character. By renovating the northern part of the town it has sought to retain the atmosphere of the old fishing village which in 1828 only had 700 inhabitants.

Besides its seaside and wide beaches Zandvoort's attractions include: the 60m/197ft high observation tower, with a restaurant, the dolphinarium (Burgermeester van Fenemaplein 2) with dolphins and sealions.

The Zandvoort Casino (Badhuisplatz 7), which is on the 18th floor of the "Bouwes" is the highest point on the Dutch coast (it is open from 2pm to 2am).

Location
25km/16 miles
south-west

Rail
from Centraal
Station

Zoo

See Artis

Zuiderkerk (south church)   C 3

Location
Zandstraat

Metro
Nieuwmarkt

Opening times
Mon.–Fri.
noon–5pm,
Thur. until 8pm;
tower:
June–Sept.
Wed.–Sat.
10am–4pm

The Zuiderkerk, built between 1603 and 1611 (tower completed 1614) was the first Protestant church to be built in Amsterdam after the Reformation. Its architect was Hendrik de Keyser, who is also buried here, according to a memorial with verses by Joost van den Vondel (see Famous People). The rectangular basilica-styled triple-nave church, with six sets of coffer-vaulting, originally had 16 stained-glass windows, but these were removed as early as 1658 to let more light in. The Zuiderkerk ceased to be a church in 1929 and its art treasures were then stored elsewhere. Its most tragic use was in 1944/45, when it served as a temporary mortuary for the many victims of the "Winter of Starvation" (memorial tablet on the churchyard wall). Since 1950 the Zuiderkerk has been used for various exhibitions, particularly by city planners.

Tower

The tower of the Zuiderkerk, which is almost 80m/262ft high (ascent possible), is among the finest in Amsterdam. The lower section, which shows a clear list to the south-west of more than a metre, is made of brick; then comes a section in sandstone, topped finally by a wooden pinnacle covered with lead. The carillon in the octagonal spire is the work of the Hemony brothers. It has been renovated several times and consists of 47 bells, the largest weighing 3300kg/7277lb, ranging over four octaves.

Information
Centre

In 1988, after extensive renovation work, the church aisle was turned into the Ruimtelijke Ordening information centre. The visitor to the centre will gain a good impression of Amsterdam's architectural and planning development from the Middle Ages into the immediate future. New exhibitions show the most current plans for the city's development.

Zuiderkerkhof

There used to be a cemetery around the Zuiderkerk. One of the two elaborately decorated gateways that provided the entrances to the churchyard has been rebuilt and gives access onto the Sint Antoniebreestraat.

Zuiderzee · IJsselmeer   Excursion

Location
north-east of
the city

Originally the Zuiderzee was a bay in the North Sea. After it was enclosed by a dyke in 1932 its name was changed to the IJsselmeer. The plan was to reclaim some of the land for industry and agriculture and for use as residential areas. Some of the polders, as the reclaimed areas are called, are already in use: the Wieringermeer polder, covering 20,000ha/77 sq.miles, was reclaimed in 1930; the Noordoostpolder (1942) covers 48,000ha/185 sq.miles, and the reclamation of the East Flevoland polder (54,000ha/208 sq.miles) and the South Flevoland polder (43,000ha/166 sq.miles) was completed in 1957 and 1968 respectively.

The town of Lelystad in East Flevoland is to become a residential and industrial centre of national importance. In a special exhibition building near Lelystad harbour there is a permanent exhibition giving information about the land reclamation projects. In South Flevoland the towns of Almere and Zeewolde are also in the process of being built. The primary objective of these polders and of the Markerwaard, which has yet to be reclaimed, is to reduce the pressure of population on the surrounding conurbations. They will be residential, employment and recreational areas.

The remaining lakes around the edges are becoming the sites of swimming pools, camp-sites and marinas. Last but not least, the polders enable important lines of communication to be set up – for example, between the provinces of North Holland and Friesland.

Visitors who are interested in life on the Zuiderzee around the turn of the century should visit the Enkhuizen Zuiderzeemuseum (about 65km/40 miles north-east of Amsterdam). It is an open-air museum complex, consisting of 135 buildings with gardens, canals, roads and a harbour with historic sailing ships lying at anchor. A museum houses five permanent exhibitions dealing with traditions and folklore, fishing, whaling expeditions, the struggle against the sea and the building of dykes. The museum is open daily all the year round from 10am–5pm (the open-air museum is open only from April to October).

Zuiderzeemuseum
Enkhuizen

Practical Information

Accommodation

See Camping, Hotels, Youth Hostels

Advance Booking

AUB (Amsterdams Uit Buro)

Stadsschouwburg, corner of Marnixstraat and Leidseplein, tel. 6 21 12 11
Open: Mon.–Sat. 10am–6pm.
  Advance booking for all Amsterdam music, theatre and ballet perform-
ances. Monthly information sheet available free of charge.

VVV

See Information

Air travel

Airport

Amsterdam's Schiphol Airport is situated about 12km/8 miles to the south-
west of the city near the E 10 Amsterdam–The Hague motorway (see
Amsterdam A to Z, Schiphol Airport).
  There is a direct rail connection between the airport and the Centraal
Station (5am–1am, every 15 mins). The KLM bus runs every half hour
between 6.25am and 11.25pm and calls at every four and five star hotel in
Amsterdam. By taxi the journey from the airport to the city centre costs
around 60hfl.

Airlines

Air France
Luchthlven, tel. 4 46 88 00

Air UK
Postbus/P.O. Box 12009
3004 GA Rotterdam, tel. 37 02 22

Australian Airways/Qantas
Stadhouderskade 6, tel. 6 16 98 81

KLM
Metsustraat 2–6, tel. 6 74 77 47
(Bookings also taken for NLM City Hopper and Nether Lines)

SAA/SAL
Hoosddorp, tel. 5 68 54 47

Antiques

Amsterdam is a paradise for lovers of old and precious things. There are
around 180 antique ships, mainly situated on the Elandsgracht, the Rokin
and in the Spiegelkwartier (Nieuwe Spiegelstraat, Spiegelgracht). The
Spiegelkwartier – near the Rijksmuseum – is one of the best centres in the

◀ *Fleamarket on Waterlooplein*

world for antiques. The very best quality goods available here are, however, no cheaper than in other European cities.

Apart from furniture, glassware, porcelain, jewellery, gold and silverware, old prints, engravings and books, it is also possible to buy musical instruments, nautical instruments, weapons and objects from overseas cultures.

Selection of shops

Amsterdam Antiques Gallery
Nieuwe Spiegelstraat 34
Eleven antiques dealers display their treasures under one roof: porcelain, clocks, jewellery, pictures, icons, silver, furniture and art déco objects.

Antiquariat Singel, Singel 348
For music lovers and collectors of lost melodies.

Ben Bijleveld, Nieuwe Spiegelstraat 45a
Nautical instuments, chronometers from the 19th c.

Eduard Kramer, Nieuwe Spiegelstraat 64
Dutch wall-tiles from the 17th c. to the present; also old wine glasses and oil bottles.

N. J. M. Veenman, Weteringstraat 20
Chinese and Japanese art and antiques.

Markets

Antiekmarkt De Looier, Elandsgracht 109
Open: Sat.–Thur. 11am–5pm (Thur. until 9pm)
Lamps, dolls, musical instruments, glassware, coins, etc.

In the summer months markets with objets d'art and antiques are held on Thorbeckeplein, Spui and the Nieuwmarkt (see Markets).

Antique shops in Spiegelkwartier

Auction Houses

The following is a selection of auction houses where antiques, furniture, objets d'arts and books are put on sale:

Antiekbeurs 700, Van Singelandstraat 24
Christie's, Cornelis Schuytstraat 57
De Eland, Elandsgracht 68
Sotheby's Amsterdam, Rokin 102
De Zwaan, Keizersgracht 474

Banks

Mon.–Fri. 9am–4pm.
   Some banks are open till 7pm on late-night shopping Thursdays.
   The Algemene Bank Nederland at Schiphol Airport is open daily from 7am to midnight.

Opening times

Outside normal business hours money can be changed at the following exchange offices:

Central Station: daily 24 hours
Amstel Station: Mon.–Sat. 8am–8pm, Sun. 10am–5pm
Sloterdijk Station: Mon.–Sat. 7.30am–8pm, Sun. 10am–5pm
KLM House, G. Metsustraat 2–6: Mon.–Fri. 8.30am–5.30pm, Sat. 10am–2pm
Schiphol Airport: daily 24 hours

*GWKs
(Grenswissel-
kantoren)*

Damrak 86: daily 8am–11.45pm
Kalverstraat 150: daily 8am–8pm
Leidsestraat 106: daily 8am–midnight

*Change Express
Exchange Office*

Dam 23–25: daily 8.30am–10pm
Leidseplein 31a: daily 8.30am–10pm
Damrak 1–5: daily 8.30am–10pm

*Thomas Cook
Exchange Office*

The charges for changing money vary from exchange office to exchange office (as much as 10% in charges; hence it is advisable to play safe and use one of the above-named banks!). The charge can often be related to the time of the transaction.

With a Eurocheque card and/or other similar cards it is possible, using a PIN number, to draw cash out of most types of dispensing machines in the city centre.

*Automatic
Cash Machines*

Bicycle Hire

There is really no more novel or comfortable way of getting to know Amsterdam than by bike. Indeed the bicycle is the ideal mode of transport in Amsterdam. The layout of the city is such that it is possible to complete most journeys in under a quarter of an hour. Moreover the municipality positively encourages cycling: there are many cycle paths, and in addition there are many one-way streets which can be used by cyclists travelling in the opposite direction. In most bookshops, for about 7hfl, a cycle-map of Amsterdam and its surroundings is available (Fietskaart van Amsterdam) which gives copious information (supervised cycle stands, bicycle hire, cycle paths, etc.).

Conditions
of hire

Many cycle hire firms charge a rate of 7hfl an hour. General hire 10hfl per day and 50hfl per week. It is also always necessary to leave a returnable deposit of between 100 and 200hfl. Rates for a whole day's hire, or for a weekend, are often considerably cheaper, while it can be even more advantageous still to hire a bike for a number of days. There are also price reductions for groups. To hire a cycle it is necessary to be in possession of a valid passport.

Holland Rent A Bike, Damrak 247, tel. 6 22 32 07
Rent A Bike, Jacobsdwarsstraat 11, tel. 64 55 09
Koenders Take A Bike, Stationsplein 33, tel. 6 24 83 91

Fietsdag

The high status that bicycles have in the Netherlands is demonstrated by the national "fietsdag", which takes place every year on the first or second Saturday in May with over 100 rallies taking place to over 100 destinations.

Cycle Theft

Bicycles are frequently stolen by drug-addicts, so, if you have a cycle on hire for several days, it is advisable to place it in one of the supervised cycle stands (there are two at the Centraal Station).

Warning

Many cyclists do not pay much heed to traffic regulations! Therefore proceed with caution when cycling in Amsterdam, and equally, if you are there driving your own car, keep a watchful eye out for the cyclists!

Bookshops

Choice

The renowned linguistic facility of both the Dutch and the many foreigners resident in Amsterdam ensures that most bookshops will stock British and American books in their original English version.

Allert de Lange, Damrak 60/62
Dutch, English, French and German literature.

Arcadia, Runstraat 33
Rare art books and second-hand volumes in Dutch, French, German and Italian.

De Kookboekhandel, Runstraat 26
Recipe books from all over the world in a range of languages.

"De Kan" organises antique book markets several times a year (information: tel. 6 27 57 94). In addition the organisation provides a brochure in which nearly 300 Amsterdam bookshops and second-hand booksellers are listed, available in the book trade or from "De Kan" (Binnenkadijk 237, 1018 ZG Amsterdam).

Book market

See Amsterdam A to Z, Achterburgwal

Cafés

Pubs

Cafés in the Netherlands are the equivalent of English pubs ("cafés" in the wider sense are called "koffiehuis"). They include "praatcafés", where there is a conscious decision not to have any music playing, so that customer can converse undisturbed. In contrast to these there are "muziek-cafés", which have either live music or music played over loudspeakers. Then there are "schaakcafés", especially for chess-players. Perhaps the most characteristic of all is the "bruin café" (brown café) with its walls and ceiling discoloured by cigarette smoke. Just as typical are the "eetcafés", where between 6 and 9pm simple, reasonably priced meals are served.

During the week bars and cafés normally close at 1am, but at the weekends they stay open until 2 or 3 o'clock.

Selection

De Balie, Leidseplein
Meeting-place for artists in the Theater De Balie, once Amsterdam's city gaol

De Engelbewaarder, Kloveniersburgwal 59
Literary café, also literary readings and live music

Frascati, Nes 59
Artists' café with theatre

Karpershoek, Martelaarsgracht 2
People's café (oldest café in Amsterdam)

Papeneiland, Prinsengracht 2
One of the oldest "brown cafés" in the city

De Prins, Prinsengracht 124
"Parlour-style" café

Rejnders, Leidseplein 6
Meeting-place for artist with old-fashioned interior

Scheltema, Nieuwe Zijdsvoorburgwal 242
Meeting-place for journalists

De Twee Prinsen, Prinsenstraat 27
Another traditional "brown café"; 125 years old

Bim Huis, Oude Schans 73

Jazz lovers

Café Alto, Korte Leidsdwarsstraat 111

't Doktertje, Rozeboomsteg 4

2 Klaveren, De Clercqstraat 136

Chess-players

Max Euwe Schaak Centrum
Max Euweplein 30a

Hotel American, Leidseplein
Art nouveau interior

Sophisticated
atmosphere

Calendar of Events

Horecava; international fair for the hotel and catering trade

January

Carnival procession.
February 25th: commemoration of the strike in February 1941 by Dutch workers protesting against the deportation of their Jewish compatriots, laying of flowers at the De Dokwerker monument, Jonas Daniel Meijerplein (see Amsterdam A–Z, Joods Historisch Museum).

February

Hiswa international watersport exhibition
March 15th: Stille omgang (procession through the old centre in memory of the "Miracle of the Hosts" of 1345).

March

Calendar of Events

April

Mid-April to mid-May: World Press Photo Exhibition (in the Nieuwe Kerk).
Floating Amsterdam: music and theatre performances on the Amstel outside the Muziektheater (information: tel. 6 20 91 35).
April 30th: Koninginnedag (the Queen's Birthday). The whole city is in
festive mood with music and bring-and-buy sales, where everyone (children included) tries to offload unwanted things. (April 30th was originally
the birthday of Queen Juliana. The present Queen Beatrix has kept this
day, even though her birthday is on January 31st.) The main centres of
festivities: Dam, Leidsestraat, Rokin, Spui, Vondelpark. There are bands
playing on Prinsengracht, Spui and Rembrandtsplein.

May

May 4th: Commemoration of those who died in the Second World War
(Dodenherdenking). At 8pm, in the presence of the Queen, two minutes'
silence in memory of the dead is observed at the National Monument on
the Dam.
May 5th: Liberation Day (Bevrijdingsdag – May 5th 1945 was the end of the
German Occupation). At 8pm there is an official ceremony in the presence of the Queen at the RAI exhibition centre. There are also local
celebrations in many districts of Amsterdam (centre for music and dance
group events: Vondelpark).
Saturday before Whitsun: Luilak (literally "Lazybones Day"). Children ring
doorbells and make a lot of noise in order to wake up lazybones and
lie-abeds.

June

Beginning of June: Kunst-RAI (art exhibition). Many art galleries have
special presentation of their pictures (information: tel. 6 20 12 60).
Festival of Fools (in even-numbered years).
Holland Festival (June 1st–30th): cultural festival with music, theatre and
dance from home and abroad, at the Stadsschouwburg (national
theatre), the Theater Carré, Muziektheater, Concertgebouw, etc. (information and tickets: Holland Festival Ticket Line, tel. 6 27 65 66).
June–August: Vondelpark Openluchttheater (open-air theatre): open-air
concerts and theatrical presentations (no charge: every Wed.–Sun.; information: Bureau Vondelparkfeesten, tel. 6 73 14 99).
Grachtenlauf (2nd Sunday in June): 5000 participants run 5, 10 and 18km
along the Prinsengracht and Vijzelgracht. Start is at 11am at Leidseplein
(information: tel. 5 85 92 22).
End of June/beginning of July: World Roots Festival in Melkweg cultural
centre (music, dance and workshops with groups from Africa, South
America and Asia; information: tel. 6 24 17 77).
June–August: summer evening concerts at the Concertgebouw.

July

Ballet Festival of the National Ballet.
International Jazz Festival (at various locations; information: tel. 6 27 62
20).
Summer festival: performances in Amsterdam's smaller, more alternative
theatres (information: tel. 6 25 74 44).

August

On the last Friday in August: Prinsengracht concert (classical music) outside the Pulitzer Hotel (information: tel. 6 22 83 33).
Pall Mall jazz festival: free concerts at various open-air sites in the city
centre.
On the last weekend in August: Uitmarkt (presentation of the new cultural
season with theatre and music: information: tel 6 26 26 56).

September

On the 1st Saturday in September: Floral procession from Aalsmeer to
Amsterdam (starting time: 9.30am; arrival at the Dam in Amsterdam:
about 4pm; information: Bloemencorso Aalsmeer foundation,
tel. 0 29 77/2 51 00.
Mid-September: street festival in the Jordaan quarter.
On the 2nd Saturday in September: many historic buildings which are
normally closed to the public throw open their doors (information:
tel. 6 26 39 47).

Pictura Antiquaris: antiques fair. October
Jumping Amsterdam: international riding event.

On the 3rd Saturday in November: entry of Saint Nicholas (Sinterclaas), November
    who arrives by boat from "Spain" with his followers and, riding on a
    white horse, leads his procession through the city to the Dam, where he
    is welcomed by the Lord Mayor.
Europoort Harbour Exhibition.

December 5th (Pakjesavond): Sinterclaas (St Nicholas Day celebrations), December
    public holiday when presents are exchanged. December 31st (Oude-
    jaarsavond): large firework celebrations in city centre.

Camping

Camping Amsterdamse Bos Campsites
Kleine Noorddijk 1, Aalsmeer, tel. 0 20/6 41 68 68
Open: Apr. 1st–Oct. 31st
More expensive than other campsites. A 10 minute bus ride from station.
Many caravans.

Camping Vliegenbos
Meeuwenlaan 138, tel. 0 20/6 36 88 55
Open: Apr. 1st–Sept. 30th
Mainly for young people and the young-at-heart. Caravans not really wel-
comed at this municipal campsite.

Gaasper Camping
Loosdrechtdreef 7, Gaasperdam, tel. 0 20/6 96 73 26
Open: Mar. 1st–Dec. 31st
Noisy because of motorway; separate section for young people.

Canal bikes (grachtenfiets)

See Water transport

Canal trips

See Sightseeing trips

Car Rental

Nassaukade 380, tel. 6 83 60 61 Avis
Schiphol Airport, tel. 6 04 13 01

Overtoom 121, tel. 6 12 60 66 Budget
Schiphol Airport, tel. 6 04 13 49

Overtoom 51–53, tel. 6 83 21 23 Europcar
Schiphol Airport, tel, 6 04 15 66

Overtoom 333, tel. 6 12 24 41 Hertz
Schiphol Airport, tel. 6 01 54 16

Chemists

Mon.–Sat. 9am–5.30pm Opening times

Children

Emergency service

Ring tel. 6 94 87 09 for information on chemists' that are open in the evening, at night and at weekends. This service is, however, provided on an answerphone and is in Dutch only.

An information sheet detailing the emergency service is also available in individual chemists. Chemists' shops which are closed will usually have a note on the door showing the address of the nearest one which is open.

Children

Visits

There are many different things available for parents wishing to amuse small children – depending on the child's age, temperament and desire for knowledge: visit Amsterdam's Artis zoo or go to a museum such as Aviodome (air and space travel museum), the Scheepvaart Museum (seafaring museum) the waxworks or the Tropen Museum (tropical museum) with its children's section for those aged between 6 and 12. Other options include a boat trip through the canals of Amsterdam or climbing the towers of the Westerkerk, Zuiderkerk and Oude Kerk.

Theatre

Youth theatre "De Krakeling"
Nieuwe Passeerdersstraat 1, tel. 6 25 32 84
Theatre for children of all ages

Puppet theatre

Amstelveens Poppentheater
Wolfert van Borsselenweg 85a, tel. 6 45 04 39

Diridas
Hobbemakade 68, tel. 6 62 15 88
Saturdays and Sundays for children aged 5 and over

Pantijn
Dam, tel. 6 27 91 88
In summer regular performances outside the Royal Palace

Cinemas

The following cinemas have a Wednesday afternoon and weekend children's programme:

Cineac
Reguliersbreestraat 31, tel. 6 24 36 39

Kinder Filmtheater
Roetersstraat 170, tel. 6 22 82 06

Rialto
Ceintuurbaan 338, tel. 6 62 34 88

The Movies
Haarlemmerdijk 161, tel. 6 24 57 90

Tuschinski
Reguliersbreestraat 26, tel. 6 26 26 33

Other entertainments

Kinderkookkafé
Oudezijds Achterburgwal 193, tel. 6 25 32 57
Children can make their own meals here at weekends and serve them to the grown-ups. Advance booking necessary.

Elleboog
Passeerdersgracht 32, tel. 6 26 93 70
On two weekends every month children between 6 and 16 have the opportunity to practise being circus artistes. Advance booking necessary.

Events

There is a section entitled "Jeugd" in the "Uitkrant" periodical giving details of events organised specially for children.

Cinemas

Most cinemas are to be found in the vicinity of Leidseplein. All foreign films are shown in the original language with Dutch subtitles. The cinema schedules are given in various daily newspapers such as "De Volkskrant", "Het Parool" and "Telegraaf", as well as in the magazine "Uitkrant". The programmes change on a Thursday, and performances normally start at 2pm, 7pm and 9.30pm. At the weekend there are also late-night showings. Tickets are usually in the region of 12hfl.

Alfa 1, 2, 3, 4
Kleine Gartmanplantsoen 4 (near Leidseplein), tel. 6 27 88 06

Cinemas

Alhambra 1, 2
Weteringschans 134, tel. 6 23 31 92

Bellevue Cinerama
Marnixstraat 400, tel. 6 23 48 76

Calypso 1, 2
Marnixstraat 402, tel. 6 26 62 27

Cineac
Reguliersbreestraat 31, tel. 6 24 36 39

Cinecenter
(Coraline, Filmhuis Jean Vigo, Peppe Nappa, Pierrot)
Lijnbaansgracht 236, tel. 6 23 66 15

Cinema International 2
Aug. Allebéplein 4, tel. 6 15 12 43

City 1, 2, 3, 4, 5, 6, 7
Kleine Gartmanplantsoen 13 (near Leidseplein), tel. 6 23 45 79

Kriterion
Roeterstraat 170, tel. 6 23 17 08

The Movies
Haarlemmerdijk 161, tel. 6 24 57 90

Theater Tuschinski 1, 2, 3, 4, 5, 6
Reguliersbreestraat 26, tel. 6 26 26 33
This art nouveau building is generally considered to be Europe's finest and best-maintained picture house.

De Uitkijk
Prinsengracht 452, tel. 6 23 74 60

Concert Halls

See Theatres, Concert Halls

Crime

High crime rate

Amsterdam has one of the highest crime rates in the country. By far the commonest offences are theft, burglary and drug-dealing. Murder and attempted murder are very much the exception. Tourists are often a prime target for thefts and break-ins, cars with foreign registration plates being particularly vulnerable to the latter offence. It is therefore imperative not to leave any objects of value (including car radios) and items of luggage in the car, either under the seat or in the boot. It is also advisable to leave it in a supervised car-park.

Amsterdam is also full of pickpockets. Consequently one should be particularly vigilant in railway stations, banks and markets, as well as when using public transport. Valuables should be placed in the hotel's safe; and it makes even more sense to leave expensive jewellery and photographic equipment at home. Statistically the riskiest areas of the city are Zeedijk, the red-light district between the Dam and Nieuwmarkt, the Bloemenmarkt, the area around Anne Frank's House and the shopping streets Dam and Damrak. During the hours of darkness it is also advisable to avoid dark streets and alleys (even in the city centre) – at least when you are alone.

In the event of a robbery you should report the matter straight away to a police station (see Police). Though there is little likelihood of recovering the stolen article, it should be borne in mind that most holiday insurance policies require this to be done.

Currency

Unit of currency

The unit of currency is the Dutch guilder (hfl; also f, dfl and NLG) which divides into 100 cents. There are banknotes for 10, 25, 50, 100, 250 and 1000hfl and coins in denominations of 5 (stuiver), 10 (dubbeltje), 25 (kwartje) cents and 1hfl (guilder), 2.50 (rijksdaalder) and 5hfl.

Currency import/
export

There are no restrictions on the import or export of local or foreign currency.

Cheques, credit
cards

Banks, big hotels, restaurants and shops will take Eurocheques, travellers' cheques and most international credit cards.

Changing money

See Banks.

Customs Regulations

Allowances
between EU
countries

In theory there is now no limit to the amount of goods that can be taken from one EU country to another provided they have been purchased tax paid in an EU country, are for personal use and not intended for resale. However, customs authorities have issued guide lines to the maximum amounts considered reasonable for persons over 17 years of age. These are: 10 litres of spirits or strong liqueurs, 20 litres fortified wine (port, sherry, etc.) 90 litres of table wine (of which not more than 60 litres may be sparkling wine), 110 litres of beer, 800 cigarettes or 400 cigarillos or 200 cigars). There is no limit on perfume or toilet water.

Entry from
non-EU countries

For those coming from a country outside the EU or who have arrived from an EU country without having passed through custom control with all their baggage, the allowances for goods obtained anywhere outside the EU for persons over the age of 17 are: 1 litre spirits or 2 litres of fortified wine or 3 litres table wine, plus a further 2 litres table wine; 60cc perfume, 250cc toilet water; 200 cigarettes or 100 cigarillos or 50 cigars

Duty-free
goods

The allowances for goods purchased "duty-free" from airports, on aircraft and ferries are the same as for entry from non-EU countries above.

Diamond Cutters

The five largest diamond cutters in Amsterdam have come together to form the umbrella organisation Diamond Foundation Amsterdam. They organise conducted tours, demonstrations of the cutter's craft, and video and cinema presentations for individual visitors and parties. It is best to apply in advanced when arranging a conducted tour for a group.

Diamond
Foundation
Amsterdam

Amsterdam Diamond Center B.V.
Rokin 1–5, tel. 6 24 57 87
Trams: 4, 9, 14, 16, 24, 25
Open: daily 9.30am–5.30pm (Thur. 9.30am–8.30pm)

Coster Diamonds
Paulus Potterstraat 2–6, tel. 6 76 22 22
Trams: 2, 3, 5, 12. Open: daily 9am–5pm

Gassan Diamonds
Nieuwe Uilenburgerstraat 173–175, tel. 6 22 53 33
Trams: 9, 14. Open: daily 9am–5pm

Stoeltie Diamonds
Wagenstraat 13–17, tel. 6 23 76 01
Trams: 4, 9, 14. Open: daily 9am–5pm

Van Moppes Diamonds
Albert Cuypstraat 2–6, tel. 6 76 12 42
Trams: 16. Open: daily 8.30am–5pm

Diplomatic Representation

Netherlands Embassies

38 Hyde Park Gate, London SW7 5DP
tel. (0171) 5903 200

United Kingdom

4200 Linnean Avenue NW, Washington DC 20008
tel. (202) 244 5300

USA

275 Slater Street (3rd floor)
Ottawa, Ontario K1P 5H9
tel. (613) 237 5030

Canada

Embassies and Consulates in the Netherlands

Embassy:
Lange Voorhout 10, NL-2514 ED Den Haag
tel. (0704) 27 04 27

United Kingdom

Consulate General:
Koningslaan 44, NL-1074 AE Amsterdam
tel. (020) 6 76 43 43

Embassy:
Lange Voorhout 102
Den Haag; tel. (020) 3 10 92 09

USA

Consulate General:
Museumplein 19
Amsterdam; tel. (020) 6 64 56 61 and 79 03 21

Embassy:
Sophialaan 7
Den Haag; tel. (0703) 1 11 60 00

Canada

Disabled Visitors

The Dutch Tourist Board issue an extensive list of telephone numbers and organisations to assist the disabled traveller in Amsterdam. Some are listed here:

Federatie Nederlandse Gehandecaptenraad
(The Dutch Council for the Disabled)
Jabobsstraat 14, Postbus 169, 3500 AD Utrecht.
Tel. 0031 30 2313454, fax. 0031 30 2340247

Stichting Informatievoorziening Gerhandicapten
Zakkendragershof 34–44, Postbus 70, 3500 AB Utrecht.
Tel. 0031 30 2316416, fax. 0031 30 2341483
Database information on all accessible buildings.

Mobility International Nederland
Heidestein 7, 3971 ND Driebergen.
Tel. 0031 343 521795, fax. 0031 343 516776
Accommodation for groups or individuals.

Hiring of wheelchairs in Amsterdam
Tel. 0031 20 6918001 and 0031 20 6157188

Taxi service for wheelchair users in Amsterdam. Tel. 6134134

Budget. Tel. 0031 23 5671333
Rental cars adapted for wheelchairs.

Library for the blind	See Libraries

Doctors

Medical assistance	Anyone requiring help (doctor, dentist, chemist) should dial 6 24 57 93 (day), 5 92 33 55 (24hr). A Central Medical Service: 06 35 03 20 42 is available for doctor or dentist.
Ambulance	Tel. 06 11 or 5 55 55 55
Hospitals	Academisch Medisch Centrum, Meibergdreef 9, tel. 5 66 91 11
	Onze Lieve Vrouwe Gasthuis, 1e Oosterparkstraat 179, tel. 5 99 91 11
	Sint Lucas Ziekenhuis, Jan Tooropstraat 164, tel. 5 10 89 11
	Slotervaartziekenhuis, Louwesweg 6, tel. 5 12 93 33
	Stichting Kruispost, O. Z. Voorburgwal 129, tel. 6 24 90 31
	V. U. Ziekenhuis, Hospitals, de Boelelaan 1117, tel. 5 48 91 11
Treatment	Visitors from abroad and members of their families can claim medical attention according to Dutch medical insurance regulations, providing three conditions are fulfilled: 1. The visitor must come from a country with which the Netherlands has an international agreement in this field.

2. Medical attention must be urgently needed and promptly claimed in the manner customary in the Netherlands.
3. An international medical form (or a photocopy) must be given to the doctor, hospital or chemist.

The account is settled directly between the doctor, hospital or chemist and the ANOZ Medical Insurance Bureau. Visitors are therefore advised to have with them a few copies of the international medical insurance form (in Great Britain the E111) in order to be able to give a copy to the appropriate authority. It will not normally be necessary to settle the account personally.

Settlement of claims

The relevant authority for the international agreement in the Netherlands is the foreign section of the ANOZ Medical Insurance Bureau, Kaap Horndreef 24–28, 3506 GB Utrecht, tel. 030/61 88 81.

Invalid Transport ANOZ

Drugs

Hard drugs are a real problem in Amsterdam. Drug dealing and drug taking are forbidden by law, but there are still some 8000 heroin addicts in the city, who lodge mainly in the red-light area, or Rosse Buurt as it is known, between the Dam, the Centraal Station and the Nieuwmarkt.

The drugs trade goes hand in hand with a rising crime rate. The Amsterdam authorities are doing their best to tackle this problem and in fact the notorious Zeedijk, where dealing has been centred, has been cleaned up thanks to non-stop police patrols. This sort of action is intended to make it clear to addicts who come here from abroad that they are not wanted in Amsterdam.

With regard to soft drugs such as hashish and marihuana, however, the Dutch police take a relatively liberal line. Most coffee shops in Amsterdam do not have a licence to serve alcoholic drinks; as well as milk-shakes and fruit juices they do often sell speciality teas and space-cakes – beware: consuming these can have hallucinatory effects.

IADA (Institute for Alcohol and Drug Prevention)
Tel. 5 70 23 55
Counselling: Mon.–Fri. 9am–5pm

Drug counselling

GG & GD (Municipal Health Service)
Tel. 5 55 57 45 and 5 55 58 50
Counselling: Mon.–Fri. 9am–5pm
Help and advice concerning drugs-related health problems.

Emergency Services

Police: tel. 06 11
Doctors, dentists: tel. 06 35 03 20 42
Fire brigade: tel. 06 11
Ambulance: tel. 06 11

Food and Drink

The eating habits of the Dutch are in general similar to those of other northern European countries.

In restaurants and hotels a continental breakfast (*ontbijt*) is served: coffee or tea, bread, rolls, jam, sausage or cold meats, cheese and boiled eggs. Lunch is not a very important meal and will generally consist of a snack such as sandwiches, or a light hot meal such as scrambled eggs or

Baedeker Special

"Kaasland" –
Holland, the Land of Cheese

Traditional "cheese-heads" obviously have many uses, not just as shapes into which cheese can be pressed. In the Middle Ages, so it is said, the peasants in the province of North Holland used these wooden cheese shapes as battle helmets, so that the enemy was faced with a whole army of "cheese-heads".

The tradition of cheese-making in the Low Countries, however, goes even further back. Pots and vessels have been found in Friesland which suggest that cheese-making formed part of the local economy as long ago as 200 B.C. The Frisians were descended from people who had migrated from Jutland to the marshes and heathland close to the North Sea coast around 200 B.C. Emperor Charles the Great (768–814) had shown a predilection for their cheese and as a result the Frisians were appointed to supply the imperial court. From the Middle Ages onwards cheese was an important component of the Dutch economy. Around 1100, in Koblenz on the Rhine, Dutch shipowners used to use cheese to pay the tolls imposed on them. The first recorded evidence of Dutch cheese exports dates from the year 1184, when cheese was exported to France. A few towns in Friesland and North Holland soon developed into major trading centres for cheese and butter. In 1266 Haarlem became the first Dutch town to be accorded the right to hold a cheese market. Leiden followed in 1303, Oudewater in 1326 and Alkmaar, the most important trading-place for the spherical Edam cheese, in 1365. In 1270 the town of Amsterdam was given the right to weigh goods and, linked to that, scales for the public weighing of cheese. The cheese was exported to the Baltic lands, France, Italy and, most importantly, to the German-speaking countries. Not only did the Dutch export cheese to other countries, but also their cheese-making skills. For instance, Tilsit cheese came about as the result of Mennonites migrating from the Netherlands to West Prussia in the 16th c. and passing on their cheese-making knowledge.

Until the second half of the 19th c. cheese and butter were produced entirely by hand and, moreover, on the very farms where the milk was collected. With the

rissoles. Among the best-known of such snack-type meals is the "Uitsmijter" ("bouncer", i.e. a sandwich with cold meat and a fried egg on top).

The main meal of the day is taken in the evening. It generally consists of meat, potatoes and other vegetables. As starter there is often soup, and dessert might be yogurt with sugar or baked custard with fruit and cream. After eating the Dutch enjoy a cup of coffee or a liqueur.

The people of Amsterdam enjoy eating out. Besides restaurants with typical Dutch dishes (Nederlands Dis) there are a large number of restaurants with specialities from all corners of the globe. Asiatic cuisine is particularly well represented (see Restaurants).

Mealtimes

Breakfast is served until about 10am in most hotels and restaurants. Lunch is between noon and 2pm. In most restaurants food is served in the evening from 5 to 10pm. Nevertheless, anyone wishing to eat after 10pm will find snacks and simple meals being served in night-time restaurants, pubs and bars.

Dutch cuisine

Traditional Dutch cooking is filling without being heavy. Specialities include simple, substantial hotpots made from potatoes and greens, such as

Baedeker Special

discovery of the centrifuge in 1879, Dutch dairy farms were drawn into the industrial revolution. Production shifted from the farm to the dairy, where the milk could be processed more quickly and efficiently using mechanisation. Today there are over 100 cheese factories which to a large extent have specialised in the production of one type of cheese.

The Netherlands can lay claim to being the largest cheese-exporting country in the world. Its main customers are the other states of the EU. 40% of Dutch cheese exports go to Germany, supplying one quarter of all German cheese consumption. Gouda is the most popular, followed by Maasdam with its large holes and red Edam.

Besides the large cheese factories, the market is supplied with "boerenkaas" (farmhouse cheese) by some 600 individual farms with cheese dairies. Factory cheese production differs from that on the farms in two respects: on the farm the cheese is produced entirely by hand, while in the factories the process is completely mechan-

Cheese specialities of Holland

ised. Secondly the farms used raw untreated full-cream milk, while in the factories the milk is pasteurised and – depending on the type of cheese – skimmed to reduce its fat content. Farmhouse Gouda is therefore a stronger, more full-tasting cheese than factory Gouda and inevitably costs somewhat more.

There are about 70 different types of Dutch cheese. The most well-known are Gouda, Edam and Maasdam. The majority of cheeses are produced from cow's milk, but goat's cheese and, at a more modest level, sheep's cheese are also increasingly finding acceptance.

endives and green or pickled cabbage, with diced bacon and tasty chunks of meat. The "Hutspot" is a popular variation, made up of equal proportions of potatoes, onions and carrots. Thick green pea soup (*erwtensoep*) is a staple national dish in the winter months. Pancakes (*pannekoeken*) can be eaten all the year round – both sweet and savoury with every conceivable variation.

Amsterdamers set great store by snacks between meals. All over the city the visitor will find very reasonably priced snack bars, also known as cafeterias. They usually open at midday and stay open until 1am. Popular dishes include French fries with mayonnaise (*patatje-met*), sausages with ketchup or mayonnaise (*fricadelen*) and meat-balls (*gehaktbal*). Most bakeries sell "saucijzebroodjes", which are tiny sausages enclosed in puff pastry, while in sandwich bars rolls or French sticks with sausage, cheese, fish and salad are available. In addition everywhere there are "febo-automatiek", vending machines from which to buy hot meat snacks. Herring (*haring*) is still a popular choice; this can be bought from fishmongers' or consumed on the spot at one of the many herring stalls (fresh *matjes* is only available from the end of May to the end of June).

Galleries

Sweets

Liquorice fans will be delighted by the many different kinds of "drop", the Dutch liquorice, to suit every taste from sweet to salty. Those who like old-fashioned sweets such as sticks of rock, jelly babies and candy will find plenty to choose from in the sweetshops. Another sweet delicacy is the "Amsterdammertje", a cake filled with marzipan.

At "poffertjes" stands one can buy these small round pancakes, which are cooked in cast-iron pans and served with powder sugar and a knob of butter.

Drinks

Amsterdamers generally prefer to drink beer with meals. As well as the lager types of beer (Pils, e.g. Edel-Pils from Limburg, Hengeloer Pilsener, trappist beer) there is "Oud Bruin", a dark sweet beer, which in the Netherlands is known as "lager". The Dutch also have a special liking for "Grolsch", a light, clean-tasting, particularly delicate beer, which is brewed at the national Grolsche brewery. The heavier Belgian beers, such as Antwerpener Koninck and Palm, and the wheat-beer known as "witt'bier" also enjoy steadily growing popularity.

The other typically Dutch drink is "genever" or "jenever" (gin). An "oude jenever" is a double-strength schnapps made from juniper berries, while a "jonge jenever" is a double-strength spirit made from corn. Small tots of gin (*borreltjes*) are also served with ice or as long drinks with cola or tonic water. There exist old "vintages" of gin which can boast the same distinction as an old cognac but these tend to be drunk only in the special taster bars (see entry) or "proeflokalen". These also stock a large choice of the sweet liqueurs and herbal liqueurs which are so popular in Amsterdam.

Anyone wishing to have a glass of the very best wine should also head for a "proeflokal" or wine-bar. The Netherlands is not a great wine-drinking country and the wines which are served in the average bar or restaurant are hardly likely to satisfy the taste-buds of the discerning wine connoisseur.

Restaurants

See entry.

Galleries

Amsterdam has a great many galleries, so those that follow are just a selection. Most galleries are to be found in the canal area around Leidsestraat and in the museum district. It is also possible to find smaller exhibitions in the Jordaan. Information about current exhibitions can be found in the magazines "Alert" and "Uitkrant".

Selection

Amazone, Singel 72
Open: Tues.–Fri. 10am–4pm, Sat. 1–4pm
Contemporary art, also performances, workshops and literature soirées in the cafeteria.

Canon Image Centre, Leidsestraat 79
Open: Tues.–Fri. noon–6pm, Sat. 11am–5pm
Modern photography, also international photography bookshop, courses and workshops.

Cricri, A. Boerstraat 4
Open: Tues.–Sat. noon–5pm
Works of younger artists exhibiting for the first time.

D'Eendt, Spuistraat 270–272
Open: Wed.–Sat. noon–6pm, Sun. 2–6pm
Contemporary art from all over the world.

The Living Room, Laurierstraat 70
Open: Tues.–Sat. 2–6pm
Contemporary Dutch artists.

Montevideo, Singel 137
Open: Tues.–Sat. 1–6pm
Newest trends in video art.

Stichting de Appel, Prinseneiland 7
Open: Tues.–Sat. 1–5pm
Art from films, photographs and electronic media.

Fons Welters, Bloemstraat 140
Open: Wed.–Sat. 1–6pm
Modern sculpture.

De Vitte Voet, Kerkstraat 149
Open: Tues.–Sat. noon–5pm
Modern ceramics.

Getting to Amsterdam

With good European road connections, getting to Amsterdam is very straightforward. As regards the sea crossing from Great Britain there are various ferry operators offering services and it is best to enquire from a travel agent which is the most suitable. The most widely used crossings from Great Britain to the Netherlands are Stena Sealink's from Harwich to Hoek van Holland and North Sea Ferries' from Hull to Rotterdam.

By car

Amsterdam is a popular destination for coach tours of European cities. There are many such tours available as well as regular coach services to Amsterdam from London and certain other towns and cities in Britain. Check with your local travel agent.

By coach

The main rail service is via the Stena Sealink ferry between Harwich and Hoek van Holland. Further details and reservations are available:

By rail

British Rail International Travel Centre
Hudson Place, Victoria Station, London SW1V 1JY
Tel. (0990) 848848, fax. (0171) 8391189

Holland Rail
Chase House, Gilbert Street, Ropley, SO24 0BY
Tel. (01962) 773646, fax. (01962) 773625

Netherlands Railways
NS Klanten Service, Postbus 2025, 3500 HA Utrecht.
Tel. (302) 354603

British International Rail
Auroa Gebouw, Stadthouderskade 2, 1054 ES, Amsterdam
Tel. 685 05 72, fax. 685 20 30

There are connections between Amsterdam's main airport, Schiphol, and all major U.S. and European airports. A direct service links the airport to the Centraal Station by rail.

By air

Hospitals

See Doctors

Hotels

There are about 270 hotels in Amsterdam with over 22,000 beds. The best known are situated along the canals, in the city centre and in the museum quarter.

Reservations

The VVV (Tourist Information Centres; see Information) can reserve hotel accommodation for personal callers. They also provide a free hotel guide and can help with hotels in places outside Amsterdam. For visits at peak holiday times, such as Easter or Whitsun, hotels should be booked well in advance, either with the hotel direct or through the National Reserverings Centrum (Postbox 404, 2260 AK Leidschendam, tel. 0031 70/320 26 11.

Categories

There are officially five categories of hotels ranging from luxury (5 star) and very comfortable (3 star) to modest hotels with 1 star.

The following list is drawn up according to these categories and gives the hotel address and telephone number together with the number of beds (b.).

Prices

The following prices, in Dutch guilders (hfl), are the average for one night including breakfast, service and tax. Out of season, particularly in winter, it is possible to get rates that are considerably lower.

Hotel categories	single room	double room
★★★★★	350–800hfl	450–850hfl
★★★★	200–400hfl	250–600hfl
★★★	80–250hfl	120–300hfl
★★	50–180hfl	100–250hfl
★	40–150hfl	80–200hfl

★★★★★

Amstel Inter Continental Amsterdam (85 b.)
Prof. Tulpplein 1, NL-1018 GX Amsterdam
Tel. (0031/20) 6 22 60 60, fax (0031/20) 6 22 58 08
This hotel is over 125 years old and was renovated in 1992. It lies on the banks of the Amstel. All the rooms are very well appointed. It has a health centre with a whirlpool, sauna, fitness centre, etc., and an excellent restaurant.

Hotel de l'Europe (183 b.)
Nieuwe Doelenstraat 2–8, NL-1012 CP Amsterdam
Tel. (0031/20) 6 23 48 36, fax (0031/20) 6 24 29 62
The Hotel de l'Europe is regarded by many as the finest in Amsterdam. Built in 1896, it was completely renovated in 1992. The rooms are furnished in the Empire style and offer the ultimate in modern standards of comfort. Its facilities include a swimming pool, sauna, solarium, fitness centre, massage room, its own limousines and mooring for private boats.

Golden Tulip Barbizon Palace (434 b.)
Prins Hendrikkade 59–72, NL-1012 AD Amsterdam
Tel. (0031/20) 5 56 45 64, fax (0031/20) 6 24 33 53
This hotel is located in the very core of the city opposite Centraal Station. The luxurious rooms – some are in the modern new building, others in 17th c. houses along the canal – are individually appointed. A good tip – the hotel's own gourmet Vermeer restaurant.

Holiday Inn Amsterdam (525 b.)
De Boelelaan 2, NL-1083 HJ Amsterdam
Tel. (0031/20) 6 46 23 00, fax (0031/20) 6 46 47 90
This hotel by the Amstelpark can easily be reached by public transport. It can boast superb cuisine and friendly service. Because of its proximity to the RAI Exhibition and Congress Centre it is popular with businessmen.

Hotel Amstel

Grand Hotel Krasnapolsky on the Dam

Hotels

Hotel de l'Europe . . .   *. . . and Hotel Doelen: overlooking the river*

Grand Hotel Krasnapolsky (812 b.)
Dam 9, NL-1012 JS Amsterdam
Tel. (0031/20) 5 54 91 11, fax (0031/20) 6 22 86 07
Built in 1886, this luxury hotel stands opposite the Royal Palace. Several restaurants, some of which are housed within the hotel complex, belong to the hotel. There is a direct KLM shuttle service to Schiphol Airport.

Hotel Pulitzer (417 b.)
Prinsengracht 315–331, NL-1016 HX Amsterdam
Tel. (0031/20) 5 23 52 35, fax (0031/20) 6 27 67 53
Made up of no less than 24 canal houses, this hotel has a rather special Amsterdam "flair". Behind the historic façade lie individually appointed rooms, some finer than others. There is a choice between a view of the inner garden or of Prinsengracht/Keizersgracht.

Amsterdam Schiphol Airport Hilton (383 b.)
Herbergierstraat 1, NL-1118 CA Schiphol-Centrum
Tel. (0031/20) 6 03 45 67, fax 6 48 09 17
This hotel is located on the airport site, but is only 15 minutes by car or rail from the city centre. The comfortably furnished rooms are all sound-proofed.

★★★★   American Hotel (332 b.)
Leidsekade 97, NL-1017 PN Amsterdam
Tel. (0031/20) 6 24 53 22, fax (0031/20) 6 25 32 36
Located near the Leidseplein, the hotel has 188 luxurious rooms and suites furnished in Art Deco style. Directly in front of the hotel is a landing stage from which tours of the canals may be taken. For many years the hotel's own restaurant, the Café Américain, has been a favourite haunt of artists, writers, politicians, etc.

Hotel Amsterdam (145 b.)
Damrak 93–94, NL-1012 LP Amsterdam
Tel. (0031/20) 5 55 06 66, fax (0031/20) 6 20 47 16
Just round the corner from this hotel, which is centrally located in the shopping and commercial quarter, is the Royal Palace. The hotel restaurant offers typical Dutch cuisine.

AMS Hotel Beethoven (110 b.)
Beethovenstraat 43, NL-1077 HN Amsterdam
Tel. (0031/20) 6 64 48 16, fax (0031/20) 6 62 12 40
Many businessmen number among the clientele of this comfortable hotel which lies on one of the main shopping streets in Amsterdam, near the World Trade Center (WTC) and the RAI Congress Centre.

Hotel Estheréa (150 b.)
Singel 303–309, NL-1012 WJ Amsterdam
Tel. (0031/20) 6 24 51 46, fax (0031/20) 6 23 90 01
Family-owned for more than 50 years, this hotel is located in the city centre on one of the most beautiful and quiet canals, behind a 17th c. façade. All the rooms were recently renovated.

Hotel Mercure Amsterdam aan de Amstel (356 b.)
Joan Muyskenweg 10, NL-1096 CJ Amsterdam
Tel. (0031/20) 6 65 81 81, fax (0031/20) 6 94 87 35
As the name suggests, it lies on the Amstel, on the A10 motorway ring-road (exit S110). The 178 rooms, inclusive of two suites and 16 club-rooms, are stylishly appointed. Bed and breakfast is free of charge for children up to 16 years of age; three floors are reserved for non-smokers.

Hotel Sofitel Amsterdam (218 b.)
Nieuwzids Voorburgwal 67, NL-1012 RE Amsterdam
Tel. (0031/20) 6 27 59 00, fax (0031/20) 6 23 89 32
The hotel is in a massive complex with houses dating from the 17th c. The 148 tastefully furnished rooms include one adapted for the disabled and some lounges for non-smokers.

Ambassade Hotel (114 b.) ★★★
Herengracht 335–353, NL-1016 AZ Amsterdam
Tel. (0031/20) 6 26 23 33, fax (0031/20) 6 24 53 21
The hotel rooms are distributed over ten 17th c. canal houses. In spite of its central location the hotel is very quiet. A restaurant is independent of the hotel.

Eden Hotel Amsterdam (454 b.)
Amstel 144, NL-1017 AE Amsterdam
Tel. (0031/20) 6 26 62 43, fax (0031/20) 6 23 32 67
Recently extended, this hotel is located very near to Rembrandtsplein and the floating flower-market. The rooms are well furnished and the service very friendly. However, visitor's cars have to use the public car park opposite.

Amsterdam Toro Hotel (40 b.)
Konigslaan 64, NL-1075 AG Amsterdam
Tel. (0031/20) 6 73 72 23, fax (0031/20) 6 75 00 31
Housed in two stylish buildings dating from 1900, this hotel enjoys an attractive and quiet location on the edge of Amsterdam's largest and most beautiful park, the Vondelpark. From its own garden and terraces there are fine views of the lake in the park. Joggers will be in their element!

Amstel Botel (352 b.)
Oosterdokskade 2–4, NL-1011 AE Amsterdam
Tel. (0031/20) 6 26 42 47, fax (0031/20) 6 39 19 52
How about a three-star hotel-boat? The 176 luxuriously appointed cabins all command a magnificent view of the river.

Hotels

Hotel Marianne (24 b.)
Nicolaas Maesstraat 107, NL-1071 PV Amsterdam
Tel. (0031/20) 6 79 79 72, fax (0031/20) 6 71 21 44
A small hotel in a quiet street near to the centre with purpose-built rooms
and a pleasant lounge.

★★ Amsterdam Wiechmann Hotel (77 b.)
Prinsengracht 328–332, NL-1016 HX Amsterdam
Tel. (0031/20) 6 26 33 21, fax (0031/20) 6 26 89 62
Under family management since it opened in 1947, this is one of the most
beautiful canal-house hotels in Amsterdam.
   Some of the 40 rooms are furnished in modern style, some in antique.
Old Amsterdam lies just around the corner.

Park Lake Hotel Amsterdam (416 b.)
Provincialeweg 38, NL-1108 AB Amsterdam
Tel. (0031/20) 6 91 12 29, fax (0031/20) 6 91 60 90
This relatively new hotel – opened in 1992 – lies in the green centre of
Amsterdam by the little river Gaasp. Golf course and a tennis court.

AMS Hotel Trianon (100 b.)
J. W. Brouwersstraat 3, NL-1071 LH Amsterdam
Tel. (0031/20) 6 73 20 73, fax (0031/20) 6 73 88 68
Peace and quiet can also be enjoyed in this hotel located near the Con-
certgebouw. The rooms are nicely furnished.

★ Atlanta Hotel (60 b.)
Rembrandtplein 8–10, NL-1017 CV Amsterdam
Tel. (0031/20) 6 25 35 85, fax (0031/20) 6 24 91 41
This hotel lies in the centre of Amsterdam, with a fine view of Rembrandt-
plein. It is family-run and has a very pleasant atmosphere.

Hotel Muzeumzicht (27 b.)
Jan Luykenstraat 22, NL-1071 CN Amsterdam
Tel. (0031/20) 6 71 29 54, fax (0031/20) 6 71 35 97
A small, moderately-priced hotel in the museum quarter.

King Hotel (65 b.)
Leidsekade 86, NL-1017 PN Amsterdam
Tel. (0031/20) 6 24 96 03, fax (0031/20) 6 20 72 77
Housed in a 17th c. canal house; good value for money.

Youth hotels Amsterdam International Student Centre (75 b.)
Keizengracht 15–17, NL-1015 CC Amsterdam
Tel. (0031/20) 6 25 13 64, fax (0031/20) 6 20 73 47
A choice of single to four-bedded rooms, all with shower. Special rates for
group bookings and/or for longer stays.

Arena Budget Hotel (600 b.)
's Gravesandestraat 51, NL-1092 AA Amsterdam
Tel. (0031/20) 6 94 74 44, fax (0031/20) 6 63 26 49
All the two, three, four, six and eight-person rooms are fitted with a shower
and W.C.

Hans Brinker (500 b.)
Kerkstraat 136, NL-1017 CR Amsterdam
Tel. (0031/20) 6 22 06 87, fax (0031/20) 6 38 20 60
Value-for-money single and double rooms.

Information

Netherlands National Tourist Office

25 Adelaide Street East, Suite 710
Toronto, Ontario M5C 1YC
Tel. 0 (416) 363 1577

Canada

9, Rue Seribe, 75009 Paris
Tel. 1 43 12 34 20

Paris

NK Shinwa Building
5F5–1 Kojimachi Thiyoda-Ku
Tokyo 102. Tel. 33 22 21 112

Tokyo

Netherlands Board of Tourism
P.O. Box 523, London SW1E 6TN
Tel. (0891) 717777, fax 171 828 7941

United Kingdom

355 Lexington Avenue (21st floor), New York NY 10017
Tel. 0 (212) 370 7367

United States
of America

225 N Michigan Avenue
Suite 1845, IL 60601 Chicago
Tel. 800 953 8824

VVV is the most important organisation for tourists and offers the following
services:

In Amsterdam

Hotel reservation (for the whole of the Netherlands; theatre and concert
bookings; information about all cultural events; bookings for excursions,
canal trips and car rental.

VVV – Tourist Information Centre
Leidseplein 1
Open from Easter to June and in September: Mon.–Sat. 9am–10.30pm,
Sun. 9am–9pm; July and August: daily 9am–10.30pm; from October until
Easter: Mon.–Fri. 10.30am–5.30pm, Sat. 10.30am–9pm.

VVV – Tourist Information Centre
Stationsplein 10
NL-1012 AB Amsterdam
(Postal address: Postbus 3901, NL-1001 AS Amsterdam)
Tel. 06/34 03 40 66, fax. (020) 6 25 28 69
(Telephone information Mon.–Sat. 9am–5pm).
Open from Easter to June and in September: Mon.–Sat. 9am–11pm, Sun.
9am–9pm; July and August: daily 9am–11pm; from October until Easter:
Mon.–Fri. 9am–6pm, Sat. 9am–5pm, Sun. 10am–1pm and 2–5pm

VVV – Tourist Information Centre
Stadionplein/Van Tuyll van Serooskerkeenweg 125
Open: daily 8am–8pm

Alkmaar: Waagplein 3, tel. 0725/11 42 84, fax 072/5 11 75 13

Information
offices in the
vicinity of
Amsterdam

Delft: Markt 85, tel. 0152/12 61 00, fax 015/2 15 86 95

Edam: Damplein 1, tel. 029 93/37 17 27, fax 02 99/37 42 36

Gouda: Markt 27, tel. 01 82/51 36 66, fax 01 82/58 32 01

Haarlem: Stationsplein 1, tel. 023/5 31 90 59, fax 023/5 34 00 93

Hoorn: Nieuwstraat 23, tel. 06/34 03 10 55, fax 02 99/21 50 23

Leiden: Stationsplein 210, tel. 071/5 14 68 46, fax 071/5 12 53 18

Monnickendam (also information office for Marken):
De Zarken 2, tel. 02 99/65 19 98

Volendam: tel. 02 99/36 37 47, fax 02 99/36 84 84

Zandvoort: Schoolplein 1, tel. 023/5 71 79 47, fax 023/5 71 70 03

Language

Dutch
The official language of the Netherlands, and the ordinary spoken and written language, is Dutch. Dutch is also spoken in northern Belgium, under the name of Flemish. There are various dialects of the language, but these are not written except in specifically dialect literature.

Frisian
A related Germanic language, Frisian, is spoken in the northern province of Friesland. It is used in many schools and is increasingly being used in local administration.

English
Visitors without any knowledge of Dutch will have no difficulty in finding their way about in the Netherlands, since English is widely spoken and understood.

The Dutch Language

Dutch is a West Germanic language closely related to the Low German dialects of northern Germany. As early as the 12th century there was a written language (Middle Dutch), which later – particularly after the struggle for independence in the 17th century – developed into modern Dutch. This was the period when political and economic power moved to the northern part of what is now the Netherlands, and the modern literary language is strongly influenced by northern (Amsterdam) usage.

Dutch is strongly Germanic in vocabulary, though there are some borrowings from French.

Pronunciation
Vowels: All vowels are pronounced in the "continental" fashion, without the diphthongisation found in English. The vowels a, e, i and o may be either short or long; the corresponding vowels aa, ee, ie and oo are long; long u or uu is pronounced like the vowel in French "lune", short u something like the vowel in French "peur"; oe is pronounced oo.

Diphthongs: The diphthongs au and ou have the sound of the diphthong in English "cow"; ei and ij (sometimes spelt y) are similar to the diphthong in English "by"; ui is pronounced like the short Dutch u followed by an i or y sound; uw is like a long Dutch u followed by a short oo sound; the combinations aai, ooi and oei are like the Dutch vowels aa, oo and oe followed by a short i; and ieuw and eeuw are like long i and e followed by a short oo sound.

Consonants: The consonants p, t and k are pronounced as in English, though without the slight puff of breath which follows them in English; similarly with b and d, which are unvoiced (i.e. pronounced like p and t) at the end of a word; w is pronounced something like English v; ch as in Scottish "loch"; g a guttural gh, or at the end of a word like ch; j like consonantal *y; r* is always trilled; *sj* is pronounced *sh*. In the combination *sch* the *ch* sound must be pronounced separately from the *s*, not combined (as in German) to make *sh*; in the combination *schr* the three consonants (*s/ch/r*) should similarly be pronounced separately, though the *ch* is frequently omitted, simplifying the pronunciation to *sr*.

There are two forms of the definite article: *de* (common gender and in plural) and *het* (neuter singular). The singular indefinite article is *een*.

Articles

When addressing strangers the formal *U* should be used for "you" rather than the familiar *jij* or *je*. *U*, derived from a term meaning "your honour", is used with the third person singular of the verb. A man is addressed as *mijnheer*, pronounced *meneer*, a married woman as *mevrouw*, an unmarried woman as *juffrouw*. Waitresses, etc., are addressed as *juffrouw* even if they are married.

Forms of address

English		**Dutch**	Cardinal numbers
0	zero	nul	
1	one	een	
2	two	twee	
3	three	drie	
4	four	vier	
5	five	vijf	
6	six	zes	
7	seven	zeven	
8	eight	acht	
9	nine	negen	
10	ten	tien	
11	eleven	elf	
12	twelve	twaalf	
13	thirteen	dertien	
14	fourteen	veertien	
15	fifteen	vijftien	
16	sixteen	zestien	
17	seventeen	zeventien	
18	eighteen	achttien	
19	nineteen	negentien	
20	twenty	twintig	
21	twenty-one	eenentwintig	
22	twenty-two	tweëntwintig	
30	thirty	dertig	
31	thirty-one	eenendertig	
40	forty	veertig	
50	fifty	vijftig	
60	sixty	zestig	
70	seventy	zeventig	
80	eighty	tachtig	
90	ninety	negentig	
91	ninety-one	eenenhegentig	
100	one hundred	honderd	
101	one hundred and one	honderd een	
200	two hundred	tweehonderd	
1000	one thousand	duizend	

1st	first	eerste	Ordinal numbers
2nd	second	tweede	
3rd	third	derde	

½	a half	een half	Fractions
⅓	a third	een derde	
¼	a quarter	een kwart	

Language

	English	**Dutch**
Common expressions	America	Amerika
	American	Amerikaan
	Britain	Groot-Brittannië
	British	Brits
	England	Engeland
	English	Engels
	Scotland	Schotland
	Scottish	Schots
	Wales	Wales
	Welsh	van Wales
	Ireland	Ierland
	Irish	Iers
	Netherlands	Nederland
	Dutch	Nederlands
	Do you speak...?	Spreekt U...?
	I do not understand	Ik versta niet
	Yes	Ja
	No	Neen
	Please	Alstublieft
	Thank you (very much)	Dank U (zeer)
	Excuse me; I beg your pardon	Pardon
	Good morning	Goedemorgen
	Good afternoon	Goedendag
	Good evening	Goedenavond
	Goodnight	Goedenacht
	Goodbye	Tot ziens
	Where is . . .?	Waar is . . .?
	. . . Street	De . . . straat
	. . . Square	De . . . plaats, het plein
	A travel agency	Een reisbureau
	The church	De kerk
	The museum	Het museum
	When?	Wanneer?
	When is . . . open?	Wanneer is . . . open?
	The Town Hall	Het Stadhuis
	A bank	Een bank
	The station	Het station
	A hotel	Een hotel
	Have you a room free?	Heeft U een kamer voor mij?
	Single room	Met een bed
	Double room	Met twee bedden
	With bath	Met een badkamer
	The key	De sleutel
	The lavatory	Het toilet
	A doctor	Een arts, een dokter
	Right	Rechts
	Left	Links
	Straight ahead	Rechtuit
	Above	Boven
	Below	Beneden
	Old	Oud
	New	Nieuw
	What does . . . cost?	Hoeveel kost . . .?, wat kost . . .?
	Expensive	Duur
	Restaurant	Restaurant

English	**Dutch**	
Breakfast	Ontbijt	
Lunch	Middagmaal	
Dinner	Avondeten	
Eat	Eten	
Drink	Drinken	
Much, many	Veel	
Little, few	Weinig	
Bill	Rekening	
Pay	Betalen	
At once	Dadelijk	
Stop	Halt	Traffic signs and warnings
Customs	Tol	
Caution	Pas op	
	Opgelet	
	Waarschuwing	
Slow	Langzaam rijden	
Danger	Levensgevaar	
One-way street	Straat met eenrichtings- verkeer	
No through road	Afgesloten rijweg	
Road works	Bestratingswerkzaam- heden	
Dangerous curve	Gevaarlijke bocht	
Accelerator	Gaspedaal	Car terms
Air	Lucht	
Axle	As	
Battery	Accu	
Bolt	Schroef	
Brake	Rem	
Breakdown	Defect (motor)	
Car	Auto	
Carburettor	Carburateur	
Clutch	Koppeling	
Cylinder	Cilinder	
Direction indicator	Richtingsaanwijzer	
Driving licence	Rijbewijs	
Exhaust	Uitlatpijp	
Fuse	Sekering	
Garage	Garage	
Gasket	Pakking	
Gear	Versnelling	
Grease	Smeerolie	
Headlight	Koplamp	
Horn	Claxon	
Ignition	Ontsteking	
Jack	Crick	
Key	Sleutel	
Motorcycle	Motorijwiel	
Nut	Moer	
Oil	Olie	
Oil change	Olie verversen	
Parking place	Parkeerplaats	
Petrol	Benzine	
Petrol station	Tankstation	
Petrol tank	Benzinetank	
Piston	Zuiger	
Radiator	Radiator	

Language

	English	Dutch
	Repair garage	Reparatie-inrichting
	Spanner	Moersleutel
	Spare part	Onderdeel
	Sparking plug	Bougle
	Speedometer	Snelheidsmeter
	Spring	Veer
	Tyre	Band
	Valve	Ventiel
	Wash	Wassen
	Wheel	Wiel
	Windscreen	Voorruit
	Windscreen wiper	Ruitewisser
Months	January	Januari
	February	Februari
	March	Maart
	April	April
	May	Mei
	June	Juni
	July	Juli
	August	Augustus
	September	September
	October	Oktober
	November	November
	December	December
Days of week	Sunday	Zondag
	Monday	Maandag
	Tuesday	Dinsdag
	Wednesday	Woensdag
	Thursday	Donderdag
	Friday	Vrijdag
	Saturday	Zaterdag
	Day	Dag
	Holiday	Feestdag, rustdag
Public holidays	New Year	Nieuwjaar
	Easter	Pasen
	Ascension	Hemelvaart
	Whitsun	Pinksteren
	Corpus Christi	Sacramentsdag
	Assumption	Maria-ten-Hemelopneming
	All Saints	Allerheiligen
	Christmas	Kerstmis
	New Year's Eve	Oudejaarsavond
At the post office	Post office	Postkantoor
	Head post office	Hoofdpostkantoor
	Stamp	Postzegel
	Letter	Brief
	Postcard	Briefkaart
	Postman	Postbode
	Registered	Aangetekend
	Printed paper	Drukwerk
	Express	Expres
	Air mail	Luchtpost
	Telegram	Telegram
	Telephone	Telefoon

Libraries

Many museums have a comprehensive library on their specialist subject.
There are also many institutes and foundations with their own libraries.

Central Library   Selection
Prinsengracht 587. Tel. 6 26 07 74
Open: Mon. 1–9pm, Tues.–Thur. 10am–9pm, Fri. Sat. 10am–5pm

British Council Library
Keizersgracht 343, tel. 22 36 44

University Library
Singel 425. Tel. 6 25 23 01
Open: Mon.–Fri. 9.30am–5pm and 7–10pm

Library for the blind
Molenpad 1. Tel. 6 26 64 65

Gemeentearchief Amsterdam
Amsteldijk 67. Tel 6 64 69 16
Open: Mon.–Fri. 8.45am–4.45pm, Sat. 9am–12.15pm
City archive; temporary exhibitions

Instituut voor Sociale Geschiedenis
Cruquiusweg 31. Tel. 6 68 58 66
Open: Mon.–Fri. 9.30am–5pm, Sat. 9.30am–1pm
Social history of the western world; its collection includes the writings of
Karl Marx and Friedrich Engels.

Lost Property

Police Lost Property
Steffersonstraat 11, open: Mon.–Fri. noon–3.30pm, tel. 5 59 30 05

Anything which has been lost on the station concourse or in the immediate   Centraal
vicinity should be enquired after at the Lost Property Office (buro gevonden   Station
voorwerpen), open: Mon.–Fri. 7am–11pm, tel. 5 57 85 44.

Articles lost and found on the buses, trams and metro are dealt with at:
"GVB", Prins Hendrikkade 108–114, open: Mon.–Fri. 9am–4pm,
tel. 5 51 44 08

Mastenbroek   Bicycles
Leidsegracht 76, tel. 6 23 23 12

Markets

Amsterdam has 40 markets, most of which are held daily (except Sundays)
between 9am and 5pm.

See Antiques   Antiques

Oudemanhuispoort   Books
between Oudezijdsburgwal and Kloveniersburgwal near the Spui
Market time: Mon.–Sat. 1–4pm
Trams: 1, 2, 5
Postage stamps for exchange and sale, also coins.

Flower market on the Amstelveld

The Albert Cuypmarkt: almost anything for sale

Vlooienmarkt
Waterlooplein
Market hours: Mon.–Sat. 10am–5pm
Trams: 9, 14
The most famous market for bric-à-brac in the Netherlands. Used and new items of clothing (including leather jackets), furniture, books, records, postcards (see Amsterdam A to Z, Jodenbuurt).

Flea market

Rommelmarkt
Looiersgracht 38
Market hours: Mon.–Thur., Sat., Sun. 11am–5pm
Trams: 7, 10
Covered market in the Jordaan. New bargains every day: postage stamps, postcards, records, books, clothing and linen, antiques and much else besides.

Albert Cuypmarkt
Albert Cuypstraat (between Ferdinand Bolstraat and van Woustraat)
Market hours: Mon.–Sat. 9am–5pm
Trams: 4, 16, 24, 25
The Albert Cuypmarkt has roughly 400 stalls and sells almost everything needed in the kitchen or home: butter, eggs, cheese, fish, poultry, local and exotic fruits and vegetables, spices, tea, cakes, biscuits, fabrics, wool, haberdashery, pots and pans and cutlery, clothes (new and second-hand), and thousands of odds and ends, some useful, some not.

Food, clothing
and materials

Between van Woustraat and Ferdinand Bolstraat you can stroll at your leisure (although it gets rather crowded on Saturday mornings) and savour the smells of fresh fruit and fish, watch the people around you, listen to the cries of the stall-holders, test the quality of the goods on offer, simply look around or even pick up a bargain.

Dappermarkt
Dapperstraat in the Amsterdam-Oost district (behind the Tropical Museum)
Market hours: Mon.–Sat. 9am–5pm
Tram: 3

Ten-Katemarkt, near Kinkerstraat
Market hours: Mon.–Sat. 9am–5pm
Trams: 7, 17

Noordermarkt (Boerenmarkt), by the Noorderkerk
Market hours: 10am–3pm
Bus: 39
Organically-grown fruit and vegetables.

Thorbeckeplein
Sun. 11am–6pm (April–October)
Trams: 4, 9, 14

Antiques and
objets d'art

Spui
Sun. 10am–6pm (April–December)
Trams: 1, 2, 5

Nieuwmarkt
Sun. 10am–6pm (April–October)
Metro: Nieuwmarkt

On April 30th (Queen's Day) and May 6th (Liberation Day) anyone is entitled to sell whatever they like without official permission. The city centre is full of vendors with their stalls on those days.

Free market

Motoring Assistance

Automobile Club	ANWB Museumplein 5, tel. 6 73 08 44 Open: Mon.–Fri. 9am–4.45pm, Sat. 9am–noon
Breakdown service	In the event of a breakdown you can ring the ANWB's road patrol, the "wegenwacht", tel. 06 08 88 (nationwide). This service is free of charge if the owner of the vehicle can produce an "international letter of credit" from his or her automobile club. Anyone who is not a member of a motoring organisation affiliated to the AIT (Alliance Internationale de Tourisme) can avail themselves of this service if they take out temporary membership of the ANWB for a month.
State of the road reports	Round-the-clock road reports on weather, traffic condition, etc. can be obtained by calling the ANWB in the Hague on 070/3 31 31 31.

Museums

Admission prices, museums card	The cost of museum admission for adults is between 5hfl and 15hfl. If you plan to do a lot of sightseeing it is worth buying a museums card. These cost 45hfl for an adult (valid for one year) and can be obtained at one of the museums or from VVV tourist information centres (see Information). This card gives free admission to many museums in Amsterdam and the rest of the Netherlands.
Amsterdam Pass	Free or cheaper entry to many of the city's museums is also available with the Amsterdam Pass. This can be purchased at tourist information centres and in some hotels for 30hfl. It allows free entry to, for example, the Rijksmuseum, the Van Gogh Museum, Amsterdams Historisch Museum, the Stedelijk Museum and the Museum Willet-Holthuysen. Price reductions are also granted for various places of interest, excursions (free tours of the canals from certain boat companies), on public transport and in restaurants.
Museum boat	Many of Amsterdam's museums are located on the canals or quite close to them. There is a special boat service, the "museum boat", which makes seven stops (including the Centraal Station and the Rijksmuseum) and enables the visitor to reach some 20 museums and many other places of interest. The boat operates daily between 10am and 6pm at half-hourly intervals.
Museums	Allard Pierson Museum Oude Turfmarkt 127 Trams: 4, 9, 16, 24, 25 Open: Tues.–Fri, 10am–5pm; Sat., Sun. 1–5pm The archaeological collection of Amsterdam University is one of the biggest university museums of this kind in the world. Ancient Egypt is represented by mummies, sarcophagi, figures of gods and animals, plus collections from the Near East, Mesopotamia, Cyprus and Iran. Ancient Greece and Rome are also well represented. Amstelkring Museum See Amsterdam A to Z, Museum Amstelkring Amsterdams Historisch Museum See Amsterdam A to Z, Amsterdams Historisch Museum Anne Frank Huis See Amsterdam A to Z, Anne Frank Huis

Museum boat outside the Anne Frank House

Aviodome (National Aeronautical and Space Travel Museum)
Schiphol Airport
Access by rail from Centraal Station
Open: Apr.–Sept., daily 10am–5pm; Oct.–Mar., Tues.–Fri. 10am–5pm, Sat., Sun. noon–5pm
The development of air and space travel is illustrated with 35 original aeroplanes and various satellites.

Bijbels Museum (Bible Museum). See Amsterdam A to Z, Herengracht

Bilderdijk Museum
de Boelelaan 1105 (in the main building of the Free University)
Bus: 5
Open: only by prior arrangement (tel. 6 45 43 68)
A collection of drawings, engravings and curios illustrating the life of the Dutch poet Willem Bilderdijk (1756–1831), known for his translations of the classics and patriotic poems and plays.

Bosmuseum. See Amsterdam A to Z, Amsterdamse Bos

Electrische Museum Tramlijn
Haarlemmermeerstation, Amstelveenseweg 264
Tram: 16
Open: Apr.–Oct. Sun. 10.30am–5.30pm; July, Aug. also Tues.–Sat.
Trips on old trams from Haarlemmermeer Station which, until 1950, was the point of departure for the steam engine to Amstelveen, Aalsmeer and Uithoorn. The old rails were adapted to take trams, and today the museum tram takes visitors into the Amsterdamse Bos and as far as Amstelveen, a stretch of about 6km/4 miles, making regular use of 15 of the collection of 60 trams, built between 1910 and 1950 in the Netherlands, Germany and Austria. This is a trip particularly enjoyed by children.

Filmmuseum, Vondelpark 3
Tram: 5
Open: daily 10am–10pm (film showings: daily 7pm, 9.30pm; Sun. children's matinees in the afternoon)
This museum is housed in a magnificent building on the edge of the Vondelpark and uses models to recount the history of film-making, supplemented by special exhibitions drawn from foreign film museums. Movie buffs can enjoy screenings of films on particular themes, etc. There is also an extensive reference library.

Geels & Co Koffie- en Theemuseum (coffee and tea museum)
Warmoesstraat 67
Trams: 4, 9, 16, 24, 25. Open: Fri., Sat. 2–5pm
Housed in a beautiful canal house, this museum displays old coffee-roasters, tea machines, coffee-mills, etc. There is also a tasting room and an old shop.

Geelvinck-Hinlopen Huis. See Amsterdam A to Z, Herengracht

Geological Museum. See Amsterdam A to Z, Artis

Historische Verzameling van de Universiteit van Amsterdam
(Universiteitsmuseum De Agnietenkapel)
Oudezijds Voorburgwal 231
Trams: 4, 9, 16, 24, 25
Open: Mon.–Fri. 9am–5pm
The Historic Collection of posters, books, documents, paintings, etc. illustrates the history of the university since 1632. The Agnieten Chapel, in which it is housed, has been part of the university since 1470 and was restored in 1921.

Holland Experience
Waterlooplein/Jodenbreestraat 8–10
Metro: Waterlooplein
Open: daily 9am–10pm
Thanks to modern technology, the visitor can experience at close hand such subjects as "Land of Waterways", "Agriculture and Horticulture" or "Art and Culture".

Informatie-Centrum Ruimtelijke Ordening
(Town Planning Service information centre)
See Amsterdam A to Z, Zuiderkerk

Joods Historisch Museum
(Jewish Historical Museum)
See Amsterdam A to Z, Joods Historisch Museum

Kattenkabinet (Cat Museum)
See Amsterdam A to Z, Herengracht

Kindermuseum TM Junior
See Amsterdam A to Z, Tropenmuseum

Madame Tussaud's Scenerama
See Amsterdam A to Z, Madame Tussaud's Scenerama

Martelwerktuigenmuseum
(Museum of Instruments of Torture)
Leidsestraat 27
Trams: 1, 2, 5
Open: daily 11am–7pm
Medieval instruments of torture.

Multatuli Museum
Korsjespoortsteeg 20
Trams: 1, 2, 5, 13, 17
Open: Tues. 10am–5pm (and by arrangement; tel. 6 38 19 38)
Exhibition commemorating the Dutch writer Multatuli, whose real name
was Eduard Douwes Dekker (1820–87), and who in his free-thinking,
humanitarian novels (including "Max Havelaar or The Dutch on Java"),
sharply attacked the Dutch colonial system.

Museum Amstelkring
See Amsterdam A to Z, Museum Amstelkring

Museum Fodor. See Amsterdam A to Z, Keizersgracht

Museum Overholland
Museumplein 4
Trams: 2, 3, 5, 12, 16
Open: Tues.–Sun. 11am–5pm
This collection, dating from 1987, consists of drawings, watercolours, col-
lages and prints by contemporary, mainly Dutch artists.

Museum Van Loon
See Amsterdam A to Z, Keizersgracht

Museum Willet Holthuysen
See Amsterdam A to Z, Museum Willet Holthuysen

NINT (Dutch Institute for Industry and Technology)
Tolstraat 129
Tram: 4
Open: Mon.–Fri. 10am–5pm; Sat., Sun. noon–5pm
The exhibition is designed to familiarise the visitor with various aspects of
modern technology (energy, photography, communications, etc.).

Persmuseum (Press Museum)
Cruquiusweg 31
Bus: 28
Open: Mon.–Fri. 9.30am–5pm, Sat. 9.30am–1pm
The press museum has a collection of newspapers, magazines, posters,
pamphlets and cartoons dating back to the early 17th c.

Peter Stuyvesant Stichting
Drentestraat 21
Tram: 4
Open: Mon.–Fri. 9am–noon and 1–4pm
Viewing of modern painting and sculpture intended for business and pub-
lic art uses (including Appel, Corneille, Tajiti and Vasarely).

Planetarium. See Amsterdam A to Z, Artis

Rembrandthuis. See Amsterdam A to Z, Rembrandthuis

Rijksmuseum. See Amsterdam A to Z, Rijksmuseum

Scheepvaart Museum (Maritime Museum)
See Amsterdam A to Z, Scheepvaart Museum

Stedelijk Museum. See Amsterdam A to Z, Stedelijk Museum

Theatermuseum. See Amsterdam A to Z, Herengracht

Tropenmuseum. See Amsterdam A to Z, Tropenmuseum

Vakbondsmuseum (Trade Union Museum)
Henri Polaklaan 9
Tram: 9
Open: Tues.–Fri. 11am–5pm, Sun. 1–5pm

Van Gogh Museum. See Amsterdam A to Z, Van Gogh Museum

Vereniging Museumhaven Amsterdam
East side of the IJtunnelkade, opposite Prins Hendrikkade 189.
Permanently open
Examples of historic vessels used in domestic merchant shipping.

Verzetsmuseum Amsterdam (Museum of the Resistance)
Lekstraat 63
Trams: 4, 25
Open: Tues.–Fri. 10am–5pm, Sat., Sun. 1–5pm
This museum, which is housed in a former Jewish synagogue, uses objects, photos, pictures and sound material to provide information about the Dutch resistance movement during the German Occupation (1940–45). Temporary exhibitions are held on the upper floor.

Werft 't Kromhout (shipyard museum)
Hoogte Kadijk 147
Buses: 22, 28
Open: Mon.–Fri. 10am–4pm
Permanent exhibition of shipyard machinery, models and shipwrights' tools, plus some old ships at their moorings.

Zoological Museum (Zoo). See Amsterdam A to Z, Artis

Nightlife

Amsterdam's nightlife centres on three areas. The oldest is around the port, in Nieuwendijk and Zeedijk (see Amsterdam A to Z, Walletjes). The nearby Rembrandtsplein and Thorbeckeplein are full of clubs – the Thorbeckeplein has a bar, nightclub or cabaret in virtually every one of its buildings. Here the floorshows are mostly striptease acts. The third and newest centre for nightlife is in and around the Leidseplein, where there are quite a few discothèques as well. Hotel bars are also a favourite haunt for real nightowls.

Bars

Apollo (Apollo Hotel), Apollolaan 2
Churchill's Corner, Scheldestraat 23
Continental Bodega, Lijkbaansgracht 246
Halfmoon Bar (Amsterdam Hilton), Apollolaan 138
Library Bar (Mariott Hotel), Stadhouderskade 19–21
Mulligans's, Amstel 100
Nasty, Thorbeckeplein 6
Palmbar (Hotel Krasnapolsky), Dam 9
Patiobar (Amsterdam Renaissance Hotel), Kattengat 1
De Stadhouder (Parkhotel), Stadhouderskade 25
Tabarin, Willemsparkweg 223

Bars with
live music

Alto, Korte Leidsedwarsstraat 115
Amstel Hotel Bar, Prof. Tulpplein 1
Bamboo Bar, Lange Leidsedwarsstraat 64
Clock Bar (Crest Hotel), De Boelelaan 2
Joseph Lam Jazzclub, v. Diemenstraat 8
Planobar Le Maxim, Leidsekruisstraat 35
The String, Nes 98

Casino on the Leidseplein

Boston Club (Sonesta Hotel), Kattengat 1
Cash Discothek, Leidseplein 12
Dansen bij Jansen, Handboogstraat 11 (students' discothèque)
Hollywood Star, Singel 447
Honolulu, Kerkstraat 23
Jantjes Verjaardag, Amstelstraat 9
Juliana's, Apollolaan 138–140
Mazzo, Rozengracht 114

Discothèques

Topless bars, striptease and sex shows are to be found around the Rembrandtsplein and Leidseplein, or in the Walletjes, the red-light district.

Sex Shows

Holland Casino Amsterdam
Max Euweplein 64 (near Leidseplein)
Open: daily 2pm–3am
French and American roulette; card-games such as Black Jack and Punto Banco; jackpot machines; also a restaurant, party centre, night club and brasserie.

Casino

Opening Times

Mon.–Fri. 9am–4pm
(outside these hours, see Banks)

Banks

Most bars and clubs close at 1 or 2am, though some nightclubs stay open until 5am.

Bars, Night-clubs

Mon.–Sat. 8am–5.30pm
(emergency service, see Chemists)

Chemists

Parks

Churches	Many churches are only open for services. At other times the verger should be contacted.
Post Offices	Mon.–Fri. 9am–5pm
Restaurants	Restaurants generally close at 11pm and therefore it is best to have placed one's order by 10pm.
Shops	Shops are open as a rule from Monday to Friday 9am–6pm and on Saturdays until 5pm. Most shops also stay open on Thursdays until 9pm. The majority also close over lunch. In addition it is common for shops to close for one morning or afternoon a week, sometimes for a whole day. Department stores generally do not open until 1pm on a Monday, but at lunchtime, of course, they remain open.

Parks

Selection	Amsterdamse Bos See Amsterdam, A to Z
	Beatrixpark next to the RAI congress centre
	Erasmuspark on the Jan van Galenstraat
	Hortus Botanicus UvA (Botanic Garden of Amsterdam University) See Amsterdam A to Z, Hortus Botanicus
	Hortus Botanicus VU (Botanic Garden of the Free University) van der Boechorststraat Open: Mon.–Fri. 8am–4.15pm
	Juliana Park Prins Bernhardplein
	Oosterpark near the Singelgracht
	Rembrandtspark on the Einsteinweg (A 10)
	Vondelpark. See Amsterdam A to Z, Vondelpark
	Zoological Garden (Zoo). See Amsterdam A to Z, Artis

Police

Police headquarters	Elandsgracht 117, tel. 5 59 91 11
District stations	Bureau IJtunnel, IJtunnel 2, tel. 5 59 24 12 Bureau Lijnbaansgracht, Lijnbaansgracht 219, tel. 5 59 23 12 Bureau Raampoort, Marnixstraat 148, tel. 5 59 28 12 Bureau Warmoesstraat, Warmoesstraat 44, tel. 5 59 22 12
Emergency number	The police can be reached 24 hours a day on tel. 6 22 22 22; alternatively use the general emergency number 06 11.

Post

Main post office
Singel 250–256, tel. 5 56 33 11
Open: Mon.–Fri. 9am–6pm, Sat. 9am–1pm

Post offices

Parcel post
Post office at Oosterdokskade 5
Open: Mon.–Fri. 8.30am–9pm, Sat. 9am–noon

Other post offices in Amsterdam are open Mon.–Fri. 9am–5pm.

Postcards sent to any destination within the EU require a 1.00hfl stamp, letters 1.00hfl.

Postal rates

Programmes of events

This is a Dutch-language monthly periodical with details of all cultural events (theatre, cinema, music, dance, etc.), exhibitions, galleries, museums. It is available at the VVV, in the Uitburo (Leidseplein 26), in cultural centres and museums. Free of charge.

Uitkrant

Appears fortnightly in English. It contains an overview of the daily concerts and theatrical perfomances, an address list of bars, museums, restaurants and shops, and also background information about the most important cultural events. Available at the VVV, in the Uitburo and in many hotels. Price 3.50hfl.

What's on

A monthly periodical in Dutch and English giving information about films, music and theatre. Available in shops and restaurants. Free of charge.

Agenda

Appears fortnightly in various languages. It contains advertisements and addresses. Available in restaurants and shops. Free of charge.

City

An English-language publication containing insider reports, information and addresses. Available at newsvendors.

City Life

A cultural supplement to the Dutch daily newspaper.

Het Parool

Public Holidays

New Year's Day, Good Friday (many shops stay open), Easter, the Queen's Birthday (April 30th), Ascension Day, Whitsun, Christmas.

Public Holidays

May 4th (for the victims of the Second World War, not a public holiday), May 5th (Liberation Day; most shops stay open).

Commemorations

Public Transport

Amsterdam is served by a very good public transport network. Most people travel by bus or tram. The construction of the underground system, the Metro, was halted by massive public protest because of its feared environmental impact, but it does have two lines and 20 stations. The buses, trams and Metro run until midnight when night-buses take over.

Bus, Tram, Metro

Co-ordinated city transport	All public transport fares and timetables are co-ordinated by the City of Amsterdam, through its municipal public transport subsidiary, the GVB (Gemeentevervoerbedrijf). The city is divided up into zones with separate tariffs. The fare depends on whether the journey passes through one, two, three or four zones. The distribution of the zones is shown at the various public transport stops.
Strip tickets	There are no single tickets, only strip tickets (strippenkaart). Once you have worked out from the zone plan which zone your destination is in, the strip ticket needs to be appropriately cancelled by the conductor or in the automatic ticket machine. The smallest "strippenkaart" is valid for two trips within the centre by bus, tram or Metro, or one trip through two zones. There are also tickets with 3, 8 or 15 "strippen". The ticket can be used for more than one person if it has enough "strippen".
Day tickets	For visitors it is much easier to buy an all-day ticket. This entitles the holder to a whole day and night's travel on all tram, bus and Metro lines. When staying longer it pays to buy a special 2-day, 3-day or longer period ticket.
60-minute ticket	There are also 60-minute tickets available from conductors on buses and trams.
National strip-ticket	Since the public transport throughout the whole of the Netherlands is divided into zones and all transport operators charge the same tariff per zone, for longer excursions it makes sense to buy the "nationale strippenkaart", which can be used on all Dutch bus, tram and metro lines. The 15-strip ticket must be bought in advance and is obtainable from stations, post offices, VVV offices and transport operators.
Ticket sales	Day and strip tickets can be obtained from all tram and bus drivers and the Metro stations have automatic strip ticket dispensers. These, as well as the multi-day tickets, can also be bought at the GVB information and sales point in front of the Centraal Station.
Information	Detailed information on all aspects of public transport can be obtained at the GVB information and sales point in front of the Centraal Station (open: Mon.–Fri. 7am–7pm; Sat., Sun. 8am–7pm) and at the GVB headquarters at Prins Hendrikkade 108 (open: Mon.–Fri. 8.30am–4.30pm). Information by phone: 06 92 92 (daily 8am–11pm). A free "welcome" leaflet with useful information on public transport and a city plan is available in hotels or at the GVB information points mentioned above and at the GVB counter at the Amstel Station.

Radio and Television

Radio	The Netherlands has five radio channels which can be received over the whole country, some on both FM and medium wave, others on one or the other. Radio 3 broadcasts mainly pop music, Radio 4 mainly classical music.
Television	There are three channels on Dutch television: Nederland 1, 2 and 3. Practically all Dutch households are connected to cable television, so they are also able to receive foreign channels. Satellite television is also now available.

Restaurants

Amsterdam restaurants can offer dishes and specialities from all over the world, and at the full range of prices. Restaurants with the sign "Neerlands

Dis" specialise in Dutch cuisine. In general, clients at restaurants will not be given a free choice of table, but must wait until they are directed to one. Service and VAT are included in the prices, but a 5–10% tip is usual. Most restaurants open at 5 or 6pm and close between 10 and 11pm. After that it is usually possible to get a meal at one of the "night restaurants".

Using the lowest price for a set meal as a criterion, Amsterdam restaurants can be roughly divided into the following categories:

Price categories

Top price category (over 60hfl) = 1st c.
Medium price category (30–60hfl) = 2nd c.
Bottom price category (20–30hfl) = 3rd c.

In the following selection of restaurants their categories are given in brackets as an indication of the likely cost of a meal.

Dorius
Nieuwezids Voorburgwal 5, tel. 4 20 22 24
Traditional Dutch cooking to a high standard (1st c.)

Dutch cooking

Excelsior
Nieuwe Doelenstraat 2–8, tel. 6 23 48 36
Creative cooking, classically elegant décor; the restaurant is owned by the elegant Hotel de l'Europe (1st c.).

Haesje Claes
Spuistraat 273, tel. 6 24 99 98
Cosy surroundings: seats 250; tourist menu recommended (3rd c.).

Hollands Glorie
Kerkstraat 222, tel. 6 24 47 64
Large helpings of good substantial food (2nd c.).

Port van Cleve
Nieuwezijds Voorburgwal 178, tel. 6 24 00 47
Traditional Dutch dishes and steaks (3rd c.).

De Roode Leeuw
Damrak 93, tel. 5 55 06 66
Glazed terrace (2nd c.).

De Trechter
Hobbemakade 63, tel. 6 71 12 63
Small restaurant for gourmets with a fondness for the unexpected (1st c.).

D'Vijff Vlieghen
Spuistraat 294, tel. 5 55 60 15
Occupies five interlinking historic canal houses; very popular with foreigners and locals alike who enjoy the new Dutch cuisine (1st c.).

Restaurants with the sign "Tourist Menu" offer a three-course meal for a set price, at the time of writing 25 hfl.

Tourist Menu

De Gerstekorrel (in the hotel of the same name)
Damstraat 22–24, tel. 6 24 97 71
Good Dutch cooking, various reasonably priced menus (3rd c.)

Oud Holland
Nieuwezijds Voorburgwal 105, tel. 6 24 68 48
Traditional cooking, regularly changing menus.

Lucius
Spuistraat 247, tel. 6 24 18 31
One of the best fish restaurants; advance booking advisable (1st c.).

Fish restaurants

Restaurants

Le Pecheur
Reguliersdwarsstraat 32, tel. 6 24 31 21
Elegant restaurant with garden; foreign fish dishes (1st c.).

Sluizer
Utrechtsestraat 45, tel. 6 26 35 57
Friendly, fairly inexpensive restaurant with a large choice of dishes (2nd c.).

Vegetarian cooking

De Bolhoed
Prinsengracht 60–62, tel. 6 26 18 03
Large menu (3rd c.).

De Vliegende Schotel
Nieuwe Leliestraat 162, tel. 6 25 20 41
Very reasonably priced, with a large selection of dishes (3rd c.).

Chinese cooking

Treasure
Nieuwizds Voorburgwal 115, tel. 6 23 40 61
Top class Chinese restaurant; the dim-sum dishes are particularly delicious (1st c.).

Hoi King
1e Jan Steenstraat 85, tel. 6 62 97 18
Friendly atmosphere; one of the best and most reasonably priced Chinese-Thai restaurants (3rd c.).

French cooking

Christophe
Leliegracht 46, tel. 6 25 08 07
Light food in unpretentious surroundings (1st c.).

Le Garage
Ruysdealstraat 54–56, tel. 6 79 71 76
Friendly atmosphere, advance booking necessary (1st c.).

Gauguin
Leidsekade 110, tel. 6 22 15 26
Unconventional colourful décor; as well as French dishes, Eastern recipes are included in the menu. The choice of desserts is especially creative; a terrace by the canal is particularly inviting in summer (1st c.)

De Groene Lateerne
Haarlemmerstraat 43, tel. 6 24 19 52
The smallest restaurant in the world and one of the oldest inns in Amsterdam.

De Kersentuin
Dijsselhofplantsoen 7, tel. 6 64 21 21
Décor rather heavy; Mediterranean specialities (1st c.).

Le Reflet d'Or
Dam 9, tel. 5 54 91 11
In the Hotel Krasnaplosky, Belle Epoque style, classic French cooking (1st c.).

Greek cooking

El Greco
Lange Leidsedwarsstraat 71, tel. 6 24 85 91
Friendly, in the middle of the red-light district (3rd c.).

Indonesian cooking

Kantijl en de Tijger
Spuistraat 291–293, tel. 6 20 09 94
Friendly service, wholesome food (1st c.).

Speciaal
Nieuwe Leliestraat 142, tel. 6 24 97 06
Relaxed atmosphere, reasonably priced dishes (2nd c.).

Toscanini   Italian
Lindengracht 75, tel. 6 23 28 13   cooking
Modern-classical interior (1st c.).

Yamazoto   Japanese
Ferdinand Bolstraat 333, tel. 6 78 71 11   cooking
In the Okura Hotel, Japanese haute cuisine (1st c.).

Marrakesch   Moroccan
Nieuwezijds Voorburgwal 134, tel. 6 23 50 03   cooking
Attractively furnished, friendly service (3rd c.).

De Kooning van Siam   Thai cooking
Oudezids Voorburgwal 42, tel. 6 23 72 93
Friendly service, delicious food. Grilled egg with curry is a speciality
(2nd c.).

Hollywood   Night
Singel 447, tel. 6 26 30 76   restaurants
Open for meals until 3am, Sat. and Sun. until 4am (2nd c.).

Bojo
Lange Leidsedwarsstraat 51, tel. 6 22 74 34
Inexpensive Indonesian cooking; open until 2am, Fri. and Sat. until 5.30am
(3rd c.).

Shopping

The most famous shopping streets are Kalverstraat, Leidsestraat, Nieuwe-
dijk, Damrak and Rokin in the historic old centre with their large department
stores and exclusive boutiques. Kalverstraat, for example, is particularly
well served by shoe shops.

Other high-quality shops – international fashion houses, high-class shoe
shops, exclusive boutiques – are also located in P. C. Hooftstraat, Van
Baerlestraat and Beethovenstraat. Here the atmosphere is somewhat
quieter and less hectic than in the city centre.

Anyone who enjoys roaming around second-hand shops and other shops
selling curios and bric-à-brac will be in their element in the Jordaan, an old
working-class quarter with its own very individual character. Both here and
in the narrow streets and alleys situated between the canals there are many
small shops which have specialised in one particular item. Near the Rijksmuseum, in and around the Spiegelgracht, there is a concentration of art
and antique shops, as well as numerous galleries.

Amsterdam's 28 markets (see entry) are also an important tourist attraction. The most famous are the Albert Cuypmarkt, the largest and most
comprehensive in the country, the flea market on the Waterlooplein and the
flower market on the Singel.

Shops are usually open from 9am to 6pm, with most staying open until   Opening times
9pm on Thursdays and closing at 5pm on Saturdays. On Mondays the
majority do not open until lunch-time. The smaller food shops do not open
late on Thursday but instead tend to be open on Monday morning. Bakers
open earlier at 7.30am and close at 5pm. There are also shops staying open

De Bijenkorf: the oldest department store in Amsterdam

until midnight (avondwinkels) throughout most of the city. There are shops selling food and everyday goods such as toiletries, as well as delicatessen items – albeit at somewhat higher prices.

Antiques	See separate entry
Ballet and theatrical accessories	Le Papillon Rokin 104
Books	See Bookshops
Camping equipment	Gaasper Camping, Loosdrechtsedreef 7 Neef Sport, Raadhuisstraat 32
Cheese	Alida Hoeve, Zeddeweg 1 De Simonehoeve, Wagenweg 3
Chemists'	Drogimarkt, Rijnstraat 9 B. Heinhuis, Spuistraat 58 Marjo, Zeedijk 68 Speyer, Maasstraat 77
Clogs (klompen)	't Klompenhuisje, Nieuwe Hoogstraat 9a De Klompenboer, N. Z. Voorburgwal 20 Ratterman Woodenshoes, Noorddammerlaan 22 Wooden Shoe Factory, Nieuwezijds Voorburgwal 20
Coffee roasters	Geels en Vo., Warmoesstraat 67
Cosmetics	Duffels, International Cosmetics, Buitenveldertselaan 36

162

Bonaparte, Linnaeusstraat 10 Exclusive, Hoofdweg 478 Focke & Meltzer, P. C. Hooftstraat 65–67 Het Kristalhuis, Overtoom 424 Het Sousterain, Keizersgracht 347 Porcella, Hugo de Vrieslaan 45 Rosenthal Studio Haus, Heiligeweg 49–51	Delft porcelain, glassware and chinoiserie
Dikker & Thijs, Leidsestraat 82	Delicatessen and fine foods
Schaap en Citroen, Kalverstraat 1 and Rokin 12 Bernard Schippen, Kalverstraat 36–38 Elka Watch, Kalverstraat 206 Smit Ouwerkerk, Singel 320 Hans Appenzeller, Grimburgwal 1	Jewellers'
Amstel Diamonds, Amstel 208 Diamonds Direct Herman Shipper B. V., Heiligeweg 3 The Mill Diamonds, Rokin 123 Willem van Pampus Diamond Center, Damrak 97	Jewellers' with diamond cutters
Metz & Co., Keizersgracht 455	Kitchen equipment
Het Kantenhuis, Kalverstraat 124	Linen
André Coppenhagen, Bloemgracht 38	Pearls
See separate entry	Souvenirs
P. C. G. Hajenius, Rokin 92 (purveyor to the court) J. van Beek, Damrak 10 J. Naarden, Damstraat 2a	Tobacco goods
Witte Tandenwinkel, Runstraat 5	Toothbrushes (exclusively)
Heuft Night Shop, Rynstraat 62 La Noche, Linnaeusstraat 24 Nightshop, Stadionweg 316 Overtoom, Overtoom 478	Foodshops open at night
De Bijenkorf, Dam 1 Large range of quality goods.	Department stores

Hema, Nieuwendijk 174
Reguliersbreestraat 10
Chain of stores with cut-price goods.

Magna Plaza, Nieuwezijds Voorburgwal 182
Luxury shopping centre with numerous shops (in a restored Neo-Gothic historic building, formerly a post office). Open since early 1992.

Maison de Bonneterie, Rokin 140
High-class store with piped classical music.

Metz & Co., Keizersgracht 455
Exclusive store for decorating materials and furnishings.

Shopping in sumptuous surroundings: Magna Plaza

Vroom & Dreesmann
Kalverstraat 201
Bilderdijkstraat 37–51
Bos en Lommerweg 357–359
Chain of stores in the medium-price range.

Sightseeing trips

Canal trips

Nearly everyone goes on a canal trip when they are in Amsterdam – there are over 65 glass-topped boats taking visitors through the canals and out onto the Amstel and round the harbour.

It is also quite an experience to do the tour at night, especially the candlelit version, on a boat lit by candles with wine and cheese included in the price.

The tours depart every hour during the summer, and at longer intervals in winter. They last between an hour and half a day, and the commentary is in four languages.

Tours can be booked in the Amsterdam VVV tourist information centres, or with the operators direct. Reduced price tickets are obtainable in youth hostels.

Tour operators

Reederei Lovers B. V., Prins Hendrikkade 25–27
opposite the Centraal Station, tel. 6 22 21 81 and 6 25 93 23

Holland International
opposite the Centraal Station, tel. 6 22 77 88

Reederei Noord-Zuid, Stadhouderskade 25, tel. 6 79 13 70

Reederei Kooij, Rokin on the Spui, tel. 6 23 38 10 and 6 23 41 86

Reederei Plas, Damrak by the station, tel. 6 24 54 06 and 6 22 60 96

Trips in and around Amsterdam can be booked with the following operators (or in the VVV tourist information centres):

Bus tours

Holland International Travel Group, Rokin 54, tel. 5 51 28 12
Key Tours, Dam 19, tel. 6 24 73 10
Lindbergh Travel Bureau, Damrak 26, tel. 6 22 27 66

Excursions outside Amsterdam include trips to the fishing villages of Marken and Volendam, the cheese market at Alkmaar, the tulip fields of the Keukenhof, The Hague, Delft, and the Zuiderzee.

KLM, the Dutch airline (tel. 6 74 77 47) operates flights over Amsterdam on Saturdays from April to October.

Sightseeing from the air

Sightseeing Programmes

The following sightseeing programmes are intended for anyone who only has a short time to spend in Amsterdam. They pick out the highlights to enable visitors to get the most out of their stay. Places described in the A to Z section are given in **bold**.

To get a general impression of the city's highlights, and some kind of feel for that special Amsterdam atmosphere, the first thing to do is to go for a walk round the city centre, starting from the central station (**Centraal Spoorweg Station**). Go south down the busy Damrak to the **Dam**, with the national monument, the **Koninklijk Paleis** and the **Nieuwe Kerk**. Get swept up in the hustle and bustle of the **Kalverstraat**, before pausing for a while in the **Amsterdams Historisch Museum** and the **Begijnhof**. Make for the southern end of Kalverstraat and the Munt tower (see **Muntplein**), then close by, you have the flower market on the **Singel**. Turn eastward along the Reguliersbreestraat to the **Rembrandtsplein** and from there via Amstelstraat and the Blawbrug (view of the **Magere Brug**) cross to the Waterlooplein (see **Jodenbuurt**), where Amsterdam's famous flea market, the Vlooienmarkt is held. Here you can see the new opera house, "Het Muziektheater" (see **Stopera**), the **Mozes en Aaronkerk**, and the **Rembrandthuis**. Turning north along the Sint Antoniesbreestraat you pass the **Zuiderkerk** before reaching the **Waaggebouw** on the **Nieuwmarkt**. Passing through the middle of the **Walletjes**, Amsterdam's red-light district, taking a turn along the **Achterburgwal** and perhaps detouring to the **Oude Kerk**, you arrive back at the Centraal Station again.

One day

If you don't devote the whole day to walking round the centre or spend a long while at individual places, a museum visit can be fitted into the afternoon. Whether it is to the **Rijksmuseum**, **Stedelijk Museum** or **Van Gogh Museum** depends on your particular taste, but since all three museums are quite close together on the south-western edge of the city canal district, it is possible to combine visits to more than one museum.

Undoubtedly the grand finale to a visit to Amsterdam is a boat trip on the canals (see above, Sightseeing), which also takes in the port (see **Haven**). If time is short this can be postponed to the evening when the bridges and the magnificent houses along the canals are illuminated, an experience that will serve to confirm that the best way to get to know Amsterdam is from the peace and quiet of her waterways.

If two days are available to spend in Amsterdam the one-day itinerary can be used but with more time spent on getting to know some places better. In

Two days

the morning, for example, you could visit one of the art museums, the Jewish Historical Museum (see **Joods Historisch Museum**) or the **Anne Frank Huis**. If you opt for the latter this could be combined with a visit to the nearby **Westerkerk** and a stroll along the **Herengracht** in the western part of the old city.

In the afternoon a visit to a diamond cutting centre is highly recommended (see above, Diamond Cutting). A trip on a canal bike (see below, Water transport) is another way of getting to know Amsterdam from the water, this time under your own steam.

Three days

Besides letting you get to know the city better a longer stay also gives you time to take trips to some of the places worth visiting not far from Amsterdam. If the tulips are in bloom a visit to the **Keukenhof** should not be missed. At other times of year, however, it is worth going via **Monnickendam** and **Marken** to **Edam** and **Volendam**, which like Marken is famous for its traditional costumes, and perhaps carry on to **Hoorn**, with its picturesque old buildings. Other options are a day-trip via **Aalsmeer**, where the daily flower auctions are held, and the ancient university town of **Leiden**, to **Delft**, with its old town ringed by canals, or perhaps a visit to the open-air museum of **Zaanse Schans**.

Souvenirs

Typical souvenirs from Amsterdam and the Netherlands include hand-carved clogs (klompen), hand-painted Delft tiles, bulbs, tobacco goods (such as Sumatra cigars), cheese (will last several weeks if stored correctly), a bottle of gin (see Food and Drink) and antiques of all kinds.

As a rule it is best to avoid the overtly commercialised souvenir shops as they are liable to stock clogs and tiles which are not hand-made but come from a factory. The genuine article, on the other hand, is more likely to be found in the "winkels", tiny shops hidden away in side-streets, which not only contribute in no small degree to the charm of Amsterdam, but also make shopping there such a delightful experience. As well as these smaller shops, which have often taken to specialising in particular goods, such as cookery books, artistic greeting cards, valuable clocks or toothbrushes (!), the shopper will find plenty to choose from in any of the large department stores, specialist shops (see Shopping) or many markets (see Markets).

Souvenir shops

Duivis, Nieuwendijk 148
J. Kaaks, Hooftstraat 32
Studio 54, Kalverstraat 54
Tendenz, Singel 540

Sport

In Amsterdam all sporting interests, both active and passive, are exceptionally well catered for.

Bowling

Bowling Centre Knijn, Scheldeplein 3, tel. 6 64 22 11
Open: 10am–1am

Fitness

Garden Gym, Jodenbreestraat 158, tel. 6 26 87 72
Open: Mon., Wed., Fri. 9am–11pm, Tues., Thur. noon–11pm, Sun. 10am–8pm

Splash Renaissance, Kattengat 1, tel. 6 27 10 44
Open: Mon.–Fri. 10am–10pm, Sat., Sun. noon–6pm

Sporting Club Leidseplein, Korte Leidsedwarsstraaat 18, tel. 6 20 66 31

Ajax Stadion, Middenweg 401 Olympia Stadion, Stadionplein 20	Football stadium
Sportpark de Weeren, Volendammerweg 316, tel. 6 32 55 58 Sportpark Overamstel, Oudekerkerdijk 148, tel. 6 65 18 63 Amsterdamse Golf Club, Zwarte Laantje 4, tel. 6 94 36 50	Golf
Amsterdamse Bos and the Vondelpark are excellent places for jogging.	Jogging
There are minigolf courses in the Amstelpark, Amsterdamse Bos and the Sloterpark.	Minigolf
Amsterdamse Manege (Amsterdamse Bos), Nieuwe Kalfjeslaan 25, tel. 6 43 13 42	Riding
Jachthaven Waterlust (Amsterdamse Bos), Boeierspad, tel. 6 44 51 82	Sailing
Watersport Twellegea (near IJsselmeer), Nieuwendammerdijk 284, tel. 6 32 48 77	
Frans Otten Stadion, Stadionstraat 10, tel. 6 62 87 67 Open: Mon.–Fri. 9am–11pm, Sat., Sun. 9am–6pm	Squash
Squash City, Ketelmakerstraat 6, tel. 6 26 78 83 Open: Mon.–Fri. 9am–1am, Sat., Sun. 9am–11pm	
Squash World, Oranje Vrijsaatkade 9, tel. 6 63 09 03 Open: daily 9am–midnight	
See entry	Swimming
De Tennis Pool, Kollenbergweg 2, tel. 6 91 16 07 Open: Mon.–Fri. 8.30am–5pm	Tennis
Frans Otten Stadion, see above under Squash	

Stations

Amsterdam's Centraal Station (see Amsterdam A to Z, Centraal Spoorweg Station) is the hub of the local and long-distance transport network. Information and reservations: Mon.–Fri. 8am–8pm, Sat., Sun. 9am–5pm.	Centraal Station
Amstel Station, Julianaplein Mulderport Station, Oosterpoortplein Amsterdam RAI, Europaboulevard Amsterdam Zuid, World Trade Center	Other stations
National: tel. 06 92 92 International: tel. 6 20 22 66 Mon.–Fri. 8am–10pm, Sat., Sun. 9am–10pm	Train information

Swimming

Bedius, Spaarndammerdijk Flevopark, Zeeburgerdijk 230 Florapark, Sneeuwbalstraat 5 Jan van Galen, Jan van Galenstraat 315 Mirandabad, De Mirandalaan 9 Sloterparkbad, Slotermeerlaan 2	Open-air pools

Taster Bars

Indoor pools	Florapark, Sneeuwbalstraat 5
	Marnixbad, Marnixplein 5
	Mirandabad (incl. wave machine), De Mirandalaan 9
	Sloterparkbad, Slotermeerlaan 2
Bath-houses	Andreas Bonnstraat 28
	Marnixplein 9
	Da Costakade 200
	Le Sweenlinckstraat 10

Taster bars

Proeflokale

Taster bars, or "proeflokale", where the main drinks served are brandy and liqueurs, are an Amsterdam speciality. In some what you get is often not a ready-made tipple but a concoction mixed to that particular bar's own recipe. The glass will be filled so full that you have to get down and bend right over it to take the first sip. Otherwise you run the risk, however steady your hand, of spilling some of that precious liquid!

Belgique, Gravenstraat 2, tel. 6 25 19 74
De Admiral, Herengracht 319, tel. 6 25 43 34
De Drie Fleschjes, Gravenstraat 18, tel. 6 24 84 43
Hooghoudt, Reguliersgracht 11, tel. 6 25 50 30
In de Wildeman, Kolksteeg 3, tel. 6 38 23 48

Taxis

Getting a taxi

Dial 6 77 77 77 to order a taxi. Certain taxi ranks can be contacted directly:

Centraal Station, tel. 5 70 42 00
Dam, tel. 5 70 42 01
Nieuwmarkt, tel. 5 70 42 05
Westermarkt, tel. 5 70 42 08

Fares

The fare is made up of a basic rate plus the rate for the distance covered, plus any supplement for night-time. The fare includes the tip, but the driver will certainly not object if it is rounded up to the nearest guilder.

Water taxis

See entry

Telephone

International
direct dialling

International calls from the Netherlands can be made from public phone kiosks, post offices and the telecenters listed below. To call internationally direct from a public phone kiosk you need to put in at least 25 cents, wait for the dialling tone, then dial the international code 00, and again wait for the dialling tone. As soon as you hear this, go ahead and dial the code for the country immediately followed by the area code (minus the first 0) and then the subscriber's number. A minute's call within Europe costs 1.20hfl. Note that at most kiosks it is possible to use a "telecard" (available in units of NLG 10, 25 or 50 at post offices, stations, Vroom en Dreesmann department stores, Primafoon – the Dutch Telecom outlet, Tourist Offices and all tobacconists) as well as coins.

Telecenter

Telehouse, Raadhuisstraat 48–50. Open: daily 6am–1am
International telephone, fax and telegram service.

Tele Talk Center, Leidsestraat 101
Open: daily 10am–midnight
International telephone, fax and telegram service.

From the Netherlands:	Australia	61	Country codes
	Canada	1	for direct
	South Africa	27	dialling
	United Kingdom	44	
	United States	1	
To the Netherlands:		31	
Area code for Amsterdam:		20	

Theatres and concert halls

In Amsterdam there are some 40 theatres, with an emphasis on the avant-garde and experimental. Without any knowledge of Dutch, however, theatrical performances are not really accessible, though during the summer months certain plays are staged specially for foreign tourists. (Information: Theater Instituut, Herengracht 168, Tues.–Sun. 11am–5pm, tel. 6 23 51 04.)

Theatre, dance, ballet, opera

Bellevue, Leidsekade 90, tel. 6 24 72 48
Experimental theatre.

De Brakke Grond, Nes 53–55, tel. 6 24 03 94
Modern Flemish drama.

De Engelenbak, Nes 71, tel. 6 24 03 94
Every Tuesday amateur actors can put their credentials to the test.

Frascati, Nes 63, tel. 6 23 57 24
Small, experimental theatre; Dutch productions.

Koninklijk Theater Carré, Amstel 115–125, tel. 6 22 52 25
The former circus (completed in 1887) is today Amsterdam's largest theatre for plays, cabaret, musicals, dance, revues, stage-shows and circus performances (see Amsterdam A to Z, Theater Carré).

Kleine Komedie, Amstel 56–58, tel. 6 24 05 34
Mainly English-language performances, cabaret presentations.

Marionettentheater, Nieuwe Jonkerstraat 8, tel. 6 20 80 27
For adults.

Mickery, Rozengracht 117, tel. 6 23 67 77
Experimental theatre with foreign troupe.

Muziektheater (Opera)
Waterlooplein 22, tel. 6 25 54 55
Opera and ballet performances. The "Stopera", as the opera house is called, is home to the Netherlands Opera, the National Ballet and the Netherlands Ballet Orchestra and also plays host to visiting foreign companies (see Amsterdam A to Z, Stopera).

Nieuwe de la Mar, Marnixstraat 404, tel. 6 23 34 62
Small theatre for comedies and farces.

Shaffy, Kelzersgracht 324, tel. 6 23 31 11
Experimental theatre, dance and drama.

Theatres and concert halls

Theater Carré on the Amstel

Stadsschouwburg, Leidseplein 26, tel. 6 24 23 11
Amsterdam's most beautiful theatre; mainly used for plays, but also for opera and ballet performances.

De Stalhouderij
1e Bloemdwarsstraat 4, tel. 6 26 22 82
Smallest theatre in the city (seats 40); English-language performances.

Children's theatre

See Children

Classical music concerts

Amsterdam has two famous symphony orchestras: the Royal Concertgebouw Orchestra, which customarily performs, as its name suggests, in the Concertgebouw, and the Netherlands Philharmonic Orchestra, whose permanent home is the Beurs van Berlage (Koopmansbeurs). In addition many international soloists and orchestra regularly visit Amsterdam. The normal time for a concert to start is 8.15pm.

Beurs van Berlage, Damrak 243, tel. 6 27 04 66
This is where the Netherlands Philharmonic, the Netherlands Opera Orchestra and the Netherlands Chamber Orchestra regularly perform. Both concert halls in the Beurs van Berlage, the AGA Hall and the Wang Hall, boast superb acoustics (see Amsterdam A to Z, Koopmansbeurs).

Concertgebouw, Concertgebouwplein 2–6, tel. 6 71 83 45
This is the home of the Koninklijk Concertgebouw Orchestra. The hall has a wonderful acoustic. Every Wednesday between September and May there is a free lunchtime concert at 12.30pm (see Amsterdam A to Z, Concertgebouw).

Ijsbreker, Weesperzijde 23, tel. 6 68 18 05
Experimental music by contemporary composers.

There are many churches where classical music is performed (organ music, choral music, Baroque chamber music, but also jazz).

Engelske Kerk. Begijnhof 48, tel. 6 24 96 65

Koepelzaal (former Lutheran church)
Kattengat 1, tel. 6 23 98 96

Nieuwe Kerk, Dam, tel. 6 26 81 68

Oude Kerk, Oudekerkplein 23, tel. 6 25 82 84

Waalse Kerk, Oudezijds Achterburgwal 157, tel. 6 23 20 74

BIM-huis. Oude Schans 73 –77, tel. 6 23 13 61   Jazz, pop, rock
Modern and experimental jazz on Thursdays, Fridays and Saturdays.

Paradiso, Weteringschans 6, tel. 6 26 45 21
In a former church. Besides pop, reggae, African and Latin American music, modern classical compositions are also performed.

Melkweg, Lijnbaansgracht 234, tel. 6 24 17 77
Multi-media cultural centre. Theatre, video, music festivals and concerts (rock, folk, jazz) with artistes from all over the world.

See entry   Programme of events

See entry   Advance booking

Time

Central European Time (one hour ahead of Greenwich Mean Time) is the normal time in force in the Netherlands, but during the summer months (the end of March to the end of September) clocks are advanced 1 hour.

Tipping

In the Netherlands tipping (15%) is usually for special service only, but it has become common practice in restaurants, cafés, hotels and taxis to round up payment to the nearest whole guilder for a small bill and the nearest 5 guilder for the larger ones. Attendants in ladies' toilets usually receive one or two kwartjes, i.e. 25 or 50 cents.

Traffic regulations

The speed limits are 50kph/31mph in built-up areas, 80kph/50mph outside   Speed limits
built-up areas and 120kph/75mph on motorways (80kph/50mph for cars with trailers).
    In traffic-calmed areas – indicated by a sign showing a white house on a blue background – the speed should be no more than walking pace.

In Amsterdam traffic from the right should always be assumed to have   Right of way
priority. This applies even to the smallest side-street, and drivers would be well advised to watch out for every junction, even when on wide main roads.

Water transport

Lighting	Main beam or dipped headlights must be used from half an hour after sunset until one hour before sunrise. During daylight hours lights must be used if weather conditions make this necessary. Main beams may not be used in built-up areas if there is sufficient street lighting, or outside built-up areas when facing oncoming traffic or following close behind another vehicle, or if there is street lighting at regular intervals.
Drinking and driving	The legal limit in the Netherlands for alcohol in the blood is 0.5 parts per thousand.
Seat belts	Seat belts are compulsory.
Bicycles in traffic	Amsterdam has at least as many cyclists as motorists. The Dutch treat cyclists with great care and consideration, and they are usually allowed a much bigger safety margin than in other countries. Watch out for junctions with cycle tracks where cyclists often have the right of way!
Parking	The Amsterdam police will tow away cars which are parked on pavements or any other place where parking is clearly forbidden. Vehicles which have been towed away can be reclaimed from the "Parkeerbeheer" at Cruquiuskade 25, tel. 5 55 98 30 on payment of between 200 hfl and 300 hfl. Given the number of foreign cars which are broken into, it is best to park on the edge of the city, in a hotel car park or in a multi-storey car park. In any case – apart from multi-storeys – parking spaces in the city centre are notoriously difficult to find. These usually only exist where there is a parking meter and normally it is not permitted to park for any longer than an hour. This can cost 4hfl. If the time on the meter has been exceeded, the police are likely to clamp the car. The owner will then have to report to the appropriate police station (address, opening times and telephone number are indicated on the yellow ticket which will have been left under the windscreen wipers) and pay both the parking charges and a fine (120hfl). In the event of wanting a car to be unclamped at night, application must be made to the "Parkeerbeheer" at Cruquiuskade (see above). Those not wishing to risk getting a parking ticket can buy a voucher allowing all-day parking from the "Parkeerbeheer" costing 24hfl: the department concerned is at Korte Leidsedwartstraat 2 and is open Mon.–Sat. 7.30am–11pm.
Multi-storey car parks	A'dam City, Waterlooplein 22 Bijenkorf (dept. store), on the Leidseplein Byzantinum, Tesselschadestraat 1 Europarking, Marnixstraat 250 Falcon Parking, Valkenburgerstraat 74 Muziektheater, Waterlooplein Parking Plus, Prins Hendrikkade 20 Prinsengracht, Prinsengracht 542 Victoria Parking, Centraal Station
	Parking charges normally range from 2 hfl for half an hour and 10 hfl for a whole day.

Water transport

Apart from the canal sightseeing boats (see Sightseeing trips) there are various other methods of transport in Amsterdam which involve the water.

Grachtenbus (canal bus)	The grachtenbus (canal bus) runs at half-hourly intervals and follows the following route: Centraal Station – Westermarkt – Leidsestraat – Leidseplein – Rijksmuseum. The journey lasts about an hour. A day ticket costs 12.50hfl.

An alternative to the traditional taxi is provided by the water taxis, which can be booked on tel. 6 22 21 81. The boats are fitted with electronic meters, and one hour costs about £30. For this price, however, up to eight passengers can be conveyed.

See Museums

Ferries to North Amsterdam (no charge) leave every 10 minutes between 6.30am and 9pm from behind the Centraal Station.

Grachtenfiets (canal bikes) are two or four-seater pedalos which enable visitors to explore Amsterdam's canal routes for themselves. A brochure is provided for everyone hiring a boat which describes four possible routes and sets out the "rules" – basically other boats on the canals have priority!
   Landing stages (boats can be returned at the jetty of one's choice) are as follows: Leidseplein (between Marriott and American Hotels), Stadhouderskade (between the Rijksmuseum and the Heineken Brouwerij), Prinsengracht (by the Westerkerk) and Keizersgracht (corner of Leidsestraat).

Canal Bike, Weteringschans 24. Tel. (20) 6 26 55 74
Watersportbedrijf, Mauritskade 1. Tel. (20) 6 92 91 24

Water taxi

Museum boat

Ferry

Grachtenfiets

When to go

Amsterdam is worth a visit at any time of year, but is especially attractive in the spring when the parks and bulb-fields are in full bloom. In the autumn the city and indeed the whole country is bathed in the same clear light that suffuses the works of the Dutch Old Masters.
   It is worth stating that those willing to travel in the winter, and out of season, should get an excellent deal in terms of hotel accommodation.

Climatic table	Temperature in °C		Hours of sunshine	No. of days of rainfall	Precipitation in mm
Months	Average maximum	Average minimum			
January	4.6	0.5	1.8	14	73
February	5.2	0.6	2.5	11	53
March	8.7	2.7	3.6	9	46
April	12.6	5.9	5.5	9	48
May	17.1	9.3	6.9	9	50
June	20.1	12.4	7.2	9	53
July	21.6	14.5	6.3	11	80
August	21.5	14.5	5.9	11	90
September	18.9	12.3	4.8	12	83
October	13.9	8.4	3.2	12	86
November	9.0	4.9	1.8	14	82
December	6.0	2.1	1.3	13	70
Annual	13.3	7.3	4.2 (1549)	134	814

Youth Hostels

Stadsdoelen, Kloveniersburgwal 97, tel. 6 24 68 32
184 beds. Open: Mar.–Oct.

Vondelpark. Zandpad 5, tel. 6 83 17 44, 315 beds. Open: all the year round

Index

Principal Sights of Tourist Interest

Imprint

75 colour photographs, 13 ground plans, 6 town plans, 2 general plans, I elevation, 1 special plan, 1 large map

German text: Birgit Borowski, Achim Bourmer, Karin Reitzig, Reinhard Strüber
Editorial work: Baedeker-Redaktion (Birgit Borowski)
General direction: Dr Peter H. Baumgarten, Baedeker Stuttgart

Cartography: Franz Huber, München; Hallwag AG, Bern (large city map)

Source of Photographs: Birgit Borowski (56), Herman Brinks (2), Diamond Centre (1), Fotogentur Helga Lade (3), Frau Antjes Feinschmecker-Studio, Aachen (1), Historia-Photo (3), IFA-Bilderteam (1), IZB (1), Niederländisches Büro für Tourismus (1), Otto (4), Reinhard Strüber (4)

English text: Crispin Warren

Revised text: David Cocking

Editorial work: Margaret Court

6th English edition 1997

© Karl Baedeker GmbH, Ostfildern (Kemnat)
Original German edition 1996

© 1997 Jarrold and Sons Limited
English language edition worldwide

© 1997 The Automobile Association
United Kingdom and Ireland

Published in the United States by:
Macmillan Travel
A Simon & Schuster Macmillan Company
1633 Broadway
New York, NY 10019–6785

Macmillan is a registered trademark of Macmillan, Inc.

Distributed in the United Kingdom by the Publishing Division of the Automobile Association, Fanum House, Basingstoke, Hampshire RG21 2EA

A CIP catalogue record of this book is available from the British Library

Licensed user:
Mairs Geographischer Verlag GmbH & Co.,
Ostfildern-Kemnat bei Stuttgart

Printed in Italy by G. Canale & C.S.p.A – Borgaro T.se –Turin

ISBN 0 7495 1691 7 UK